Something in These Hills

Something in These Hills

The Culture of Family Land in Southern Appalachia

John M. Coggeshall

The University of North Carolina Press CHAPEL HILL

This book was published with the assistance of the Fred W. Morrison Fund of the University of North Carolina Press.

Set in Merope Basic by Westchester Publishing Services
Manufactured in the United States of America

Library of Congress Cataloging-in-Publication Data

Names: Coggeshall, John M., author.
Title: Something in these hills : the culture of family land in southern
    Appalachia / John M. Coggeshall.
Description: Chapel Hill : The University of North Carolina Press, 2022. |
    Includes bibliographical references and index.
Identifiers: LCCN 2022015996 | ISBN 9781469670249 (cloth ; alk. paper) |
    ISBN 9781469670256 (paperback ; alk. paper) | ISBN 9781469670263 (ebook)
Subjects: LCSH: Appalachians (People)—Land tenure—Social aspects. |
    Land tenure—Social aspects—Appalachian Region, Southern. |
    Appalachians (People) —Ethnic identity. | Appalachian Region, Southern—
    Civilization. | LCGFT: Ethnographies.
Classification: LCC F210 .C64 2022 | DDC 975.6/9—dc23/eng/20220420
LC record available at https://lccn.loc.gov/2022015996

Cover illustration: Rocky Bottom Baptist Church, Pickens County. Photo by the author.

To my parents, John H. and Myra Coggeshall.
Above all else, you gave me two things: roots and wings.

Contents

A gallery of figures follows page 108

Acknowledgments

In many ways, this book has reminded me of what I love most about being an anthropologist: the opportunity to help give voice to those whose voices may have been ignored or overlooked and to restore dignity and respect to those lives.

To the best of my recollection, this research project began with a request sometime in the late summer of 2006 by Tom Swayngham and Greg Lucas, both with the South Carolina Department of Natural Resources (DNR), to document the lives and stories of the old-timers who had lived in the Jocassee and upper Keowee Valleys of Pickens and Oconee Counties, South Carolina. Tom and Greg also provided me with an initial list of contacts and invited a retired DNR biologist, Sam Stokes, to help me meet these folks. Sam and I enjoyed many trips together in my first year of research, and he introduced me to some amazing people. Unfortunately, Sam passed away on June 24, 2019.

Both Tom and Greg have demonstrated incredible patience as their initial hopes for a collection of stories from the old-timers has morphed into two prequels: *Liberia, South Carolina* (University of North Carolina Press, 2018), about an enclave of descendants of formerly enslaved African Americans in upper Pickens County, and then this book. While it took me several years to realize it, many people in the mountain counties talked about their family land in ways that differed from that of general American culture. That difference then inspired me to present their perspectives in this book before I offer a collection of mountain stories in a future work.

Fieldwork formally began in the early fall of 2006, with the bulk of my interviews taking place in 2008 and 2009 but continuing into 2012. I would like to thank the eighty-eight men and women of Greenville, Pickens, and Oconee Counties who volunteered their time and memories for the interviews that have enhanced this study. While all of you may not be quoted in this book, I sincerely enjoyed having the opportunity to meet you and listen to your perspectives.

Since the beginning of fieldwork, twenty-one individuals have passed away. I would like to remember and thank Sam and Leecie Baker, Bill Batson,

Brown Bowie, Lloyd Cannon, Lester Chapman, Dock and Alice Crowe, Blanche Burgess Hannah, Gerald Holcombe, Jefferson "J. D." McGowens, Oliver "Hub" Orr, Albert "A. C." Owens, Grover Owens, Robert Perry, Frank Porter, Ann Poulos, Charles Powell, Edgar Smith, Sara Snow, and Pauline Thrift. It was a great pleasure to have had the opportunity to sit and talk with you.

The Harry Hampton Memorial Wildlife Fund, partnered with the South Carolina DNR, provided $9,500, and the Clemson University Research Investment Fund Program added another $6,000 to support the Jocassee Gorges Cultural History Project, under which I interviewed the mountain residents. Almost all of this money paid the Clemson University graduate and undergraduate students who transcribed the interview tapes, and I am grateful for the professionalism and patience shown by all of them. During the course of ten years, forty-six students helped to transcribe the interviews. With apologies to Rudyard Kipling, "while I've likely overworked you, and severely underpaid you, I sincerely, deeply thank you, undergrads."

Friends and colleagues have read various drafts of chapters, the entire manuscript, or both, and I am grateful for the thoughtful and helpful suggestions from Wes Cooler, Karen Hall, Greg Lucas, Cathy Robison, Cindy Roper, Tom Swayngham, Randy Tindall, and Melinda Wagner. I also appreciate the comments from the two anonymous reviewers for this manuscript who helped me to extend its theoretical direction, rethink some details about its organization, and add some concepts.

One of these reviewers described the manuscript as "readable, and, with photographs, it would be stunning." I had hoped to pay for a professional photographer by submitting an internal Clemson grant, but unfortunately the pandemic prevented that possibility. Instead, most of the photographs appearing in the book are my own. I obtained a better "Oconee Bells" photo from a friend, Sue Watts, and received permission from Bob Spalding to use his photo of "Bob's Place" before the fire. I sincerely appreciate the help of these individuals. But to improve my own photos, a good friend from my graduate school days, Randy Tindall, offered his professional photo-editing advice free of charge. Randy rejected or approved the photos I sent him and offered editing advice on cropping and shading. If the book truly has transformed from "readable" to "stunning," it is thanks to Randy Tindall.

Thanks to Lucas Church, acquisitions editor at the University of North Carolina Press, for encouraging me to submit the original manuscript and to usher it through the revisions process. Thanks also to Erin Granville, managing editor, for guiding me through the final edits and page proofing stages. I also appreciate the technical editing contributions of Michelle Witkowski and Yvonne Ramsey at Westchester Publishing Services. Thanks also to Allison Daniel and Hannah Taylor, both with Professional Editing at Pearce (Pearce Center for Professional Communication, Clemson University), for compiling the index. I also sincerely appreciate the proofreading assistance from Clemson undergrads Darby Alvarenga, Jupiter Chastain, Alyssa Ciccone, Abby Cram, and Rose M. Keller.

Finally, I want to thank my wife, Cathy Robison, for giving me the time, space, and love to see this book through to completion.

Something in These Hills

CHAPTER ONE

Opening the Black Box of Landscape
Examining Southern Mountain Concepts of Place

Introduction

"Where the Blue Ridge yawns its greatness" is the opening line of Clemson University's alma mater song, generating images of the majestic southern Appalachian Mountains within an hour's drive of the campus located in upper South Carolina. But in contrast, the slow, ominous opening notes from a dueling banjo and guitar produce entirely different images of these same mountains. Both tunes describe the same granitic cliffs, deep valleys, and tumbling rivers of South Carolina's Blue Ridge, in the northwesternmost part of the state. Perhaps there is "something in these hills," as Clemson alumnus Joe Sherman[1] penned in the university's most iconic and resonant phrase. But what is this "something" that generates feelings of both beauty and danger from the same geophysical features? Translating these deeply felt emotions into words and concepts that outsiders can comprehend is the subject of this book.

To explicate the essence of this "something," the book explores two themes; they are presented in the order in which I as an outsider to the region came to recognize them.[2] The first theme examines the apparent contradiction between a menacing and a majestic landscape, explored in chapters 3 (the outsider recognition of the contrast) and chapter 4 (the insider recognition of that same contrast). As an outsider myself I began the research with this theme already in mind, anticipating an obvious contrast between the outsider negative stereotypes of the region (represented by the "Dueling Banjos" theme from the film *Deliverance*) as well as the positive perceptions of the same spaces that almost any visitor and resident can recognize. In other words, most Americans already have stereotypes of "hillbillies" and the potential dangers arising from characters and scenes from popular media such as *Deliverance*, and yet visitors flock to the southern Appalachian region for myriad recreational and residential opportunities. Simultaneously, insiders also recognize a contrast between the majesty of the place (represented by the lines from Clemson's alma mater song) and the comforting familiarity of their home alongside the region's natural and social dangers, sometimes from their own neighbors. My initial research question was how is this oppositional contrast culturally possible?

If one views this area as "liminal" or "contested," the duality becomes more understandable. Liminality, an idea explained by anthropologist Victor Turner,[3] is the "in-between" times of a ritual transformation, where initiates are molded and re-created during the ritual process. They are in between one social state and the next (e.g., child and adult). The ritual process transforms them into the new state. Adapting Turner's concept, contested or liminal spaces may be seen as those in between two opposing entities. Contestation by neighboring entities might take multiple forms—environmentally (beautiful and dangerous), socially (land disputes between families), historically (Native American and colonist, capitalist developer and local landowner), economically (naive hillbillies and disingenuous companies), residentially (visitor canoeist and local fisherman), and symbolically ("pure Americans" or "yesterday's people"). Thus, the menace or majesty theme stems from the alternating directions from which one views the contrast: either menacing or majestic, depending on multiple variables and multiple perspectives; those living in this contested space may be viewed as in between various entities as well.

A second major theme explored in this book is the cultural significance of land for many Appalachian residents. How do many residents become so emotionally attached to their family land that losing it (to development, say) hurts almost like the loss of a relative, while retaining it becomes a lifetime's goal? I explore this theme in detail in chapters 5 and 6, reflecting my more gradual recognition of the idea. I also critique this theme in the context of current theorizing about Appalachia because I will argue for a somewhat different explanation of the cause of this emotional connection to land.

"From the plantation paradigm to [Wilbur J.] Cash's version of [Frederick] Turner's frontier thesis, the sense of place has been a prominent part of the historical and social reality in the South, and the discussion of its role has demonstrated the dialectic of Southern mythology," rhetorician Stephen Smith observed.[4] That same emphasis of a sense of place occurs, more specifically, in the mountains of upper South Carolina.[5] As in many other cultures, for this area's long-term residents landscape is "an anonymous sculptural form" fashioned by human agency and continually being reshaped and reexperienced, archaeologist Christopher Tilley noted.[6] More specifically, for mountain people in the Appalachians, including those in the South Carolina mountains, land is not only culturally sculpted, reformed, and reexperienced but also merges with family and becomes culturally animated, anthropomorphized into another member of one's family.

How does this process occur? Families place the names of their ancestors upon the land. Homes may be built from materials on (or in) the land or by the hands of the owners themselves. People use the land for multiple resources in addition to farming and timbering. Families continue to own the same land through multiple generations, and they continue to occupy that same family land century after century. Because of this deep-time occupancy, remembrances of that land accumulate, placing layers of memories on the same landscape. In family cemeteries on family land, individuals are literally embedded in their family land so that through time land and families merge. Because of this synthesis, family land anthropomorphizes, adopting a spiritual and human essence. Unfortunately, at times family land may be lost (for a variety of reasons), and thus the loss triggers an emotional response similar to the loss of a flesh and blood relative. To maintain a connection despite this loss, objects from family land are retained as if they were relics from a deceased loved one. This cultural process resembles attitudes found throughout Appalachia; they are documented here for South Carolina's mountain residents as well.

This second theme took me several years to comprehend. In fact, I was embarrassed that I had not recognized it earlier in the research process. What is this intimacy with the landscape like? Imagine hiking on a trail through the mountains for the first time. Everything is new—the rocks on the hillsides, the curves of the hills, and the sounds of birds and of falling water. The hiker is aware of the beauty of the place but also alert to potential dangers—tree roots to circumvent, poison ivy to avoid, and trail markers to heed. This was like my awareness of the first theme. Then imagine hiking this same trail every week. The hiker then would notice seasonal appearances of wildflowers, recently fallen trees, the changing depth of water in creeks, and the secretive signs of animals—in other words, hikers would notice much greater detail of the landscape. This was similar to my discovery of the second theme of the book. In the same way as hikers learn to appreciate the subtle and sublime beauty of a familiar trail, it is my hope that by the end of this book readers will have transformed their views of the southern Appalachians from the superficiality of an enigmatic frontier occupied by peculiar hillbillies to a more profound understanding of an anthropomorphic landscape entwined with family by means of memory and possession. By hiking numerous times over the trails of ethnographic information, I took this same intellectual journey in my own process of discovery, and it will be the intellectual journey of my readers in the chapters that follow.

Every scholarly book must situate the author's argument within related ideas. While I contextualize the general direction of the book's themes in the following sections of this chapter, I reserve some supportive scholarly references for later chapters. This is done for two reasons. First, I prefer to present the less obvious informant perspectives on cultural ideas such as family and land in later chapters, reflecting my own gradual recognition of these ideas. More important, though, is that by reserving some citations for later chapters, I can present informant thoughts and comments in appropriate cultural context and then demonstrate by means of scholarly citations that these ideas are not unique to specific individuals or to the mountains of South Carolina but instead are characteristic of other regions and (perhaps) other cultures too.

Perceiving Appalachia

While researchers of Appalachia agree on several general cultural values shared by long-term residents in the region, including the critical importance of family and land,[7] the relationship between Appalachia (and its residents) and the rest of the United States has been viewed in multiple ways, and many views have contributed to the liminality of the place as well as to its contrastive menacing or majestic symbolic images. Several of these perspectives on Appalachia's relationship with the larger United States are reviewed below.

But first, how is the region defined? Moreover, what entity is meant by the term "Appalachia"—a geological region, a geographical one, a cultural area, or a political division? Most researchers agree that there is an entity, distinct from other U.S. areas, designated as "Appalachia," but the term certainly varies in boundaries.[8] Within Appalachia there are multiple subdivisions, again potentially differentiated geologically ("Blue Ridge"), culturally ("southern Appalachia"), economically ("coal country"), or politically ("upper South Carolina"). This book focuses on a part of southern Appalachia, specifically that part of southern Appalachia consisting of the three uppermost counties in South Carolina (Oconee, Pickens, and Greenville); Rabun County, Georgia (contiguous with Oconee across the Chattooga/Tugaloo Rivers); and Jackson, Transylvania, and Henderson Counties in North Carolina (generally contiguous with Pickens and Greenville Counties). To avoid repetition, I will use several terms to describe this area: the mountains (of South Carolina), southern Appalachia, and Blue Ridge. All indicate the same region within the covers of this book. Geophysically, the area contains the South Carolina Blue Ridge escarpment along with the adjacent states' river drainage areas into or through this space and the immediate downslopes of the area's rivers through the South Carolina upper piedmont toward the Atlantic. Culturally, the study area shares many elements with traits found in the entity described by other authors as "Appalachia." In fact, that is the point: the values toward land described in the area are not unique (as other Appalachian authors will attest); rather, they are characteristic of the Appalachian cultural region but are examined here in greater and more critical detail.

A Frontier with Contemporary Ancestors

One very common view of Appalachia is that the region has served and continues to serve as a frontier in American settlement. Journalist Wilbur J. Cash promoted the idea that the history of the entire South (not just of Appalachia) before the American Civil War "is mainly the history of the roll of frontier upon frontier—and on to the frontier beyond." In the "vast backcountry" of the Atlantic colonies, Cash continued, "there lived unchanged the pioneer breed," the Scots-Irish, Moravians, Lutheran peasants, and Scots Highlanders. Historian Harry Caudill described these early settlers as "a raggle-taggle of humanity"—orphans, petty criminals, debtors, and draft dodgers—who exhibited traits such as "sturdy self-reliance" and "fierce independence" and were "wholly undisciplined and untamed." But, Bryon Giemza proclaimed, the Scots-Irish immigrants, "a wily and untamable people, proved equal to the task of taming a frontier."[9]

By the nineteenth century, Cash explained, life had barely progressed past "Indian fighting" and was still largely the business of "coon-hunting, of 'painter' [panther] tales and hard drinking." To the eve of the Civil War, Cash believed, the entire South, including Appalachia, was just "a few steps removed from the frontier stage." Furthermore, the devastation to the South after the Civil War created a new southern frontier, serving to benefit the North at the South's expense. Howard Odum and Rupert Vance, two prominent southern historians, later elaborated on Cash's "frontier" idea.[10]

An alternate view, that of David Fischer, argued that the Appalachian area was not really a "frontier," since the term applied to the region during the late eighteenth and early nineteenth centuries was "the backcountry," suggesting "which way the colonists were facing in that era." In other words, "frontier" implied that the settlers faced westward, while "backcountry" implied that they faced eastward, toward the English settlements along the

Carolina coast. Regardless of which way the settlers metaphorically faced, Fischer traced the major cultural characteristics of Appalachian residents back to cultural traits from northern Ireland and especially from the border-lands in between England and Scotland. The borderlands, Fischer observed, constituted an outlaw region, ruled by "feud violence and blood money," whose emigrants imported to the Appalachians a "double-distilled selection of some of the most disorderly inhabitants of a deeply disordered land."[11] Whether facing the Appalachians or the Atlantic, the first settlers occupied an ambiguous borderland.

"To the first settlers" of the Appalachians, Fischer continued,

> the American backcountry was a dangerous environment, just as the British borderlands had been. Much of the southern highlands were "debatable lands" in the border sense of a contested territory without established government or the rule of law. The borderers were more at home than others in this anarchic environment, which was well suited to their family system, their warrior ethic, their farming and herding economy, their attitudes toward land and wealth and their ideas of work and power. . . . The ethos of the North British borders came to dominate this "dark and bloody ground," partly by force of numbers, but mainly because it was a means of survival in a raw and dangerous world.[12]

According to the folk description of their descendants, these Scots-Irish immigrants "appeared as storm troopers of civilization and embodied the ideals that made America the exceptional place that most assumed it was."[13]

As a side but critically important note, in much of the literature Appalachia has been "whitewashed" as mainly a European American descendant space, especially after having genocidally eliminated most of the Native Americans from their traditional homelands. But a growing body of scholarship has documented the presence of African Americans (enslaved and free) living alongside their white neighbors, especially in the larger river valleys or those within tillable floodplains. For numerous political and social reasons, these people are often overlooked or erased from histories and from the landscape, often deliberately.[14] At the same time, Native Americans of various groups, along with mixed-race individuals, continued to reside alongside the Scots-Irish and other European American groups. As the following explanations unfold, notice what a difference it makes to the discourse when viewing the southern Appalachians as a multicolored quilt rather than a monochromatic white blanket.

Logically, those who live on the frontier or borderlands and embody the ideals of American exceptionalism must still be "our contemporary ancestors," somehow frozen in time and mysteriously preserving cultural traditions and behaviors from a legendary, "authentic" past. Educator John C. Campbell described the Southern Highlander as "the true American, . . . the early pioneer type. . . . In his veins there still runs strong the blood of those indomitable forebears who dared to leave the limitations of the known and fare forth into the unknown spaces of a free land." According to folklorist David Whisnant, this process of glorifying the "purity" of mountain residents began in the late nineteenth century in order to mute folk protest over the actual political and economic forces overtaking the area at that time. "In the recesses of the Appalachian Mountains these fundamental elements of the American character are found today in stark simplicity," Berea College (Kentucky) English professor James Raine wrote, "uncontaminated by the rush of business or the greed of money. . . . This rich deposit of true Americanism is a priceless possession, the unspoiled heritage of the American people." As summer visitors ventured into the mountains, historian Henry Shapiro argued, contemporary writers noted that the "primitive conditions of pioneer days . . . seemed only to heighten the contrast between Appalachia and America." By the early twentieth century, with their cultural value of individualism contrasted with the general American value of cooperation, Highlanders had become what Campbell described as "a people strange and peculiar and somewhat dangerous."[15]

Popularizing this idea was William Frost, then the president of Berea College in southeastern Kentucky. In 1899 Frost published in the *Atlantic Monthly* an essay titled "Our Contemporary Ancestors in the Southern Mountains." A journey into eastern Kentucky, Frost observed, "brings us into the eighteenth century." Many writers romanticized this idea, shifting the time frame back even further. James Raine, another Berea professor, thought he found himself "still among Shakespeare's people. This is the real Forest of Arden. From the old log house where I live . . . we can ride [by horse] in four hours into the seventeenth century." Writer Charles Wilson, strolling through the same forests of Arden, described "a land of Elizabethan ways—a country of Spencerian speech, Shakespearean people, and of cavaliers and curtsies. . . . Elizabethan English, as well as Elizabethan England, appears to have survived magnificently in these isolated Southern uplands." Of course, by portraying the area as "English and Scotch-Irish,"[16] this picture whitewashed the area and delegitimated any African American (or other ethnicity's) presence.

According to Charles Wilson, the area's "first settlers brought with them Elizabethan ways of living, and these ways have lasted in a country of magnificent isolation, one little touched by the ways of a modern world." Berea's President Frost extolled this "contemporary survival of that pioneer life which has been such a striking feature in American history." Journalist W. J. Cash described the "Southern mountaineer" as "the forgotten man of the land." "Mured up in his Appalachian fastness, with no roads to the outside world save giddy red gullies, untouched by the railroad until the twentieth century was already in the offing, this mountaineer had almost literally stood still for more than a hundred years." "No other such individualist was left in America—or on earth," Cash concluded.[17]

One of the beneficial consequences of a long history of a "frontier-like existence," writer John Opie opined, is that Appalachian residents have a specific characteristic "almost removed from mass society—a profoundly fundamental human need to have a 'habitat' and know it intimately. The mountaineer might be called a 'living fossil' because he seems to remind an urban society of the world it left behind. The Appalachian mountaineer stands as a reminder of a personal quality of life that has become rare in contemporary American society. He knows he belongs." In part because of the Elizabethan cultural heritage and in part "modified by the physical environment," the Appalachian mountaineer reflects a "harmonious relationship that exists between him and the natural setting he occupies," Edgar Bingham concluded.[18]

On the other hand, social worker Jack Weller viewed this geographical and social isolation in more negative terms, describing his Appalachian neighbors in the early 1960s as "a people apart, molded by the peculiar forces of the terrain, the pressure of economics, and the lack of contact with outsiders." In their portrayal of upper east Tennessee, historians Michael McDonald and John Muldowny described the residents in the 1930s in much the same way, as "an isolated and static society which generally offered little opportunity for improvement."[19]

"Consider then these forces in synopsis," historian Harry Caudill summarized in 1963: "The illiterate son of illiterate ancestors, cast loose in an immense wilderness without basic mechanical or agricultural skills, without the refining, comforting and disciplining influence of an organized religious order, in a vast land wholly unrestrained by social organization or effective laws, compelled to acquire skills quickly in order to survive, and with a Stone Age savage as his principal teacher. From these forces emerged the mountaineer as he is to an astonishing degree even to this day."[20]

Because of the perception of geographic isolation and cultural stagnation, historian David Hsiung argued, Appalachian residents had been "othered," or assumed to be different from "typical" Americans. Appalachia became "a discrete region, in but not of America." If Appalachia were a separate region, historian Henry Shapiro asked of his readers, who then has benefited from this discrimination? By the 1920s, John C. Campbell noted that outsiders described the region as the backyard of the South, with southerners and Highlanders resenting outsider stereotypes. Historian Harry Caudill supported the "contemporary ancestors" perspective for southern mountaineers, because "an astonishing number of his [the mountaineer's] habits, tastes and outlooks had come down to him little diluted from his pioneer fathers of the eighteenth century, but in the meantime he had acquired serious defects which had not plagued his forebears." Ron Eller described Appalachians as "a Janus-faced 'other'" in American consciousness: a contrast between people "who were at once quaint and romantic and yet a burden to American success." Scholar Robert Higgs elaborated on the image of a romantic "child of Rousseau, . . . at home in the mountains . . . with little or no regard for the niceties of lowland society," contrasted with "the myth of the mountaineer as fundamentalist freak, sexual pervert, and necrophiliac." "It's as though Southern Appalachia is the corner of America that America forgot," journalist Bronwen Dickey wrote, "and the virtues that are generally lauded as defining the American frontier identity—self-reliance, resourcefulness, hard work—are now ripe material for ridicule."[21]

The Evolution of a Stereotype: "Hillbillies"

Embodying and symbolizing this contrastive perspective of the residents of Appalachia, the "hillbilly" emerged as a stereotype of a people not just isolated from or bypassed by civilization but also ignorant, skeptical, scornful, or defiant of it.[22] By the late nineteenth century, American culture perceived hillbillies as apart from civilization but with that separation viewed in two distinct directions: either as superstitious and obstinate (and thus potentially dangerous) or as naive and unadulterated (and thus quaintly antiquated).[23] Subcategories of whites such as hillbillies, anthropologist John Hartigan Jr. argued, preserve the homogeneous appearance and unmarked status of "whiteness" by siphoning off certain negative qualities. On the other hand, writer Jerry Williamson speculated, "my assumption is that the hillbilly mirrors us, and like most mirrors he can flatter, frighten, and humiliate. As a rough-and-ready frontiersman, he can be made to compliment American men. . . . Put him in the same woods, but make him repulsively savage, a monster of nature, and he now mirrors an undeniable possibility in American manhood. In other words, we want to be him and we want to flee him."[24]

ONE DIRECTION IN WHICH Williamson traces the hillbilly stereotype reflects "necessary frontier rudeness that produces the rural fool who up-ends our complacent assumptions about ourselves." This "simplicity" trait might be viewed as either intellectual ignorance or innocent naivety, enhancing "America's strongly ambivalent view of that region." Included in the former perspective would be media stereotypes exemplified by such characters as the residents of Dogpatch, USA (e.g., Li'l Abner), portrayed by creator Al Capp as blissfully unaware of much of American society. The function of such characters, Williamson argues, is to reinforce the self-perceived superiority of the middle class. The latter perspective (innocent naivety) would be reflected by the Clampett family as the Beverly Hillbillies and the Taylors and Pyles of Mayberry, all of whom often outsmarted the "city slickers" while remaining largely unaware of or disinterested in "civilized" society. Like medieval fools, writer Sandra Ballard explains, these characters serve as "mockers, truth-tellers, and mirrors of culture, subversive identities that overlap and intertwine."[25]

On the other hand, the hillbilly stereotype of isolated mountain folks might also imply the "otherness" of unpredictable danger. John Shelton Reed believed that this reputation for violence has a deep history in the South. "In the southern hills," Reed proposed, "great family feuds and the murderous exploits of moonshining outlaws helped to keep the image of Southern violence before the public." Berea College president William Frost traced the institution of feuding to Scots-Irish roots and claimed that feuding had continued because mountain folk "have not yet grasped the decidedly modern notion of the sacredness of life." Historian David Fischer blamed borderland Scots-Irish child-rearing practices for creating "a society of autonomous individuals who were unable to endure external control and incapable of restraining their rage against anyone who stood in their way." Given the fact that the cast and crew of the film *Deliverance* viewed locals as "violent, inbred rednecks," journalist Bronwen Dickey concluded that "the shocking violence of *Deliverance* . . . [just] ratcheted up the stereotype."[26]

"Perhaps no other movie has been as influential as this one [*Deliverance*] in shaping what people think they understand about the southern mountains, and also what they think they understand about themselves and the way they confront such threats as the southern mountains are supposed to be," Jerry Williamson observed. In fact, a still from the movie is the cover photograph for anthropologist John Hartigan Jr.'s book *Odd Tribes*. The "narrative heart" of both the book and movie, environmental writer John Lane argued, is the contrast between the region's "value system rooted in isolation" and rugged individualism against the "more communal life of the city." For decades, outside observers had weighed these characteristics of isolation and individualism on a social scale of benefits and drawbacks, with urbanized outsiders typically concurring with historians McDonald and Muldowny that while isolation drew mountain communities closer together, the people "failed to benefit from the alternatives offered by that broader world of urbanism and modernity."[27]

Consequences of the Hillbilly Stereotype

Traits of isolationism and individualism, tied with those of rebelliousness, antiauthoritarianism, and anti-intellectualism, ultimately stem from the frontier mentality of the early Scots-Irish settlers, social worker Jack Weller argued in his book *Yesterday's People*.[28] These traits have been compounded by economic exploitation, historian Harry Caudill observed:

> The essential element of the [Cumberland] plateau's economic malaise lies in the fact that for a hundred and thirty years it has exported its resources, all of which — timber, coal, and even crops — have had to be wrested violently from the earth. The nation has siphoned off hundreds of millions of dollars' worth of its resources while returning little of lasting value. For all practical purposes the plateau has long constituted a colonial appendage of the industrial East and Middle West, rather than an integral part of the nation generally. The decades of exploitation have in large measure drained the region.[29]

Because of the extraction of capital, schools, libraries, health facilities, and other critical institutions were not built. Public officials were corrupted by the wealth of the large companies.[30]

As the mountain economy worsened due to isolation, Weller continued, the young and ambitious left; those remaining behind included "the unambitious, who could tolerate a subsistence living at home . . . ; the aged, the sickly, and the retarded; and the psychologically immobile, who could not move away from the familiar, protective mountain culture. There are also some families who moved away and came back again, utterly discouraged and beaten. . . . Surely these folk add little to the morale of an already defeated population."[31] This "attachment to place and family" becomes a liability for a modern mobile society, Weller warned, and "this debilitating dependence the mountaineer can no longer afford." Consequently, Weller observed, "the fierce loyalty of mountain people to home is mostly a loyalty to the only culture in which they feel secure and which operates in ways they know and appreciate. . . . From the vantage point of middle or upper class culture, moving is easy. For the mountaineer, moving is a kind of death to his way of life. It cuts him off from his sustaining roots."[32] Eventually, historian Harry Caudill concluded, the residue of ambition in those left behind would "evaporate in the arms of Welfarism and in the face of repeated failures," leaving behind "an agglomeration of misery." Defeatism becomes the "fundamental psychology" of mountaineers, thus explaining their lack of economic betterment, Weller decided. "Company domination and paternalism and two decades of uninspired Welfarism have induced the belief that control of his [mountain residents'] destiny is in other hands," Caudill concluded. Caudill also blamed "inbreeding with its attendant genetic pitfalls" on the erosion of mountaineers' traditional values of self-reliance.[33]

Adopting an updated version of Caudill's and Weller's perspective (and of Oscar Lewis's outdated "culture of poverty" idea in general) is lawyer J. D. Vance's autobiography *Hillbilly Elegy: A Memoir of a Family and Culture in Crisis*. While Vance proudly claimed his Scots-Irish hillbilly ancestry, he also blamed the "Greater Appalachia" culture for a range of traits, from "low social mobility to poverty to divorce and drug addiction," concluding that "my home is a hub of misery." A continual theme of Vance's book is that "there is a lack of agency here," creating the cultural value of "learned helplessness." Despite a superficial acknowledgment that poverty creates sociological and psychological parallels between impoverished rural whites and impoverished urban Blacks (see also Caudill's materialist explanation above), Vance ultimately concluded that the problem of underdevelopment in Appalachia is "about psychology and community and culture and faith." "How much of our lives, good and bad," Vance asked his readers, "should we credit to our personal decisions, and how much is just the inheritance of our culture, our families, and our parents who have failed their children?"[34]

Popular culture portrayals of Appalachian residents as "a culture in crisis" or "contemporary ancestors" may serve larger cultural or economic goals. For example, folklorist Ted Olson argued that in the late nineteenth century, popular views of Appalachian residents as "pure" Americans were created to juxtapose the feared cultural impact of European immigration diluting American society. Viewing Appalachia as virtually pure white further supported the "legitimacy" of the United States as a white-dominated place in general, since "our contemporary ancestors" were exclusively European American. Today's misperception of Appalachian folk as poor whites, scholars Angela Cooke-Jackson and Elizabeth Hansen noted, "permits dominant culture, as represented by the mass media, to justify the marginalization of this subgroup while validating its own status."[35]

Materialist Views of Appalachia's Contested Spaces

In addition to cultural superiority or inferiority when compared to others, the varied portrayals of mountain residents also support exploitative purposes, but these portrayals also varied by the ability of mountaineers to resist their domination or to control their contested space. For example, in 1899 while President Frost of Berea College warned that change was coming to "this Arcadian simplicity," he assumed that the simple folk of the mountains might not be able to resist "the jackals of civilization. . . . The lumber, coal, and mineral wealth of the mountains is to be possessed, and the unprincipled vanguard of commercialism can easily debauch a simple people. The question is whether the mountain people can be enlightened and guided so that they can have a part in the development of their own country, or whether they must give place to foreigners and melt away like so many Indians." Frost hoped that America's intelligentsia would save the mountain folk by importing educational enlightenment, informative publications, improved hygiene, and bloodless conflict resolution.[36]

On the other hand, the cultural manipulation of mountain residents' images as simplistic or backward may have recognized their agency and thus served to defuse or subordinate their resistance. In the nineteenth century, as sociologists Kathleen Blee and Dwight Billings argued, the creation of feud narratives for Appalachian residents established in the national consciousness that the region was "a dark zone of chaos and violence in desperate need of 'civilizing' influences from the outside"; such a label "gave American readers a framework through which to view the profound changes that were taking place at the turn of the century . . . and the spasm of violence that was accompanying its industrialization." Folklorist Ted Olson reasoned that portrayals of Appalachian residents as "backward" then justified their economic exploitation or physical removal in order to favor capitalistic timber and mining interests.[37] In actuality "a politically motivated struggle over economic development," historian Altina Waller explained, "the pejorative term *feud* was used by the dominant culture as a politically useful category to explain the violence of mountain dwellers as well as excuse the violence incurred in their subjection." On the other hand, as folklorist David Whisnant documented, northern capitalists of the late nineteenth century deliberately depicted mountain residents as "quaint" or "other" in order to prevent their self-organizing to resist economic and political exploitation. At the very least, this "othering" of Appalachian residents created their strong sense of "place-identity," sociologist John Stephenson concluded.[38]

Since Appalachian resources such as coal and timber were being extracted from the "uncivilized" hillbilly owners of those lands in order to benefit shareholders of external corporations and with little capital reinvestment in critical social institutions, Appalachia in effect had become a "colonial appendage" to the eastern and midwestern states, as historian Harry Caudill had initially proposed, or an "internal colony" of the nation, as more recent scholars have suggested. As sociologist Helen Lewis explained, "dominant outside industrial interests" have controlled, exploited, and continue to "maintain their domination and subjugation of the region," parallel to the process of colonialism in other parts of the world. Exclusive housing and commercial development also might reflect colonialist exploitation, as outsiders appropriate land through various means and then force the locals out of their homelands and into smaller and less valuable parcels.[39]

Since the extraction of Appalachian resources, especially coal and timber, ultimately feeds not just a national market but also a global one, then logically Appalachia becomes not just an internal colony of the United States but also the periphery of a world system, because outsider forces (both national and international) have more powerful means to take and control resources. "From this perspective," sociologist David Walls observed, "Central Appalachia [the coal region] must be analyzed in the context of advanced capitalism in the United States. In some instances, . . . we may have to expand our horizon to the framework of the world capitalist system." In such a system, Appalachian resources and occupants remain on the periphery of globalized capitalism, with the core of international companies (some headquartered in the United States) exploiting the area by extracting resources for a global market, investing little infrastructural or social support in return, and then marketing expensive finished products (e.g., televisions and drugs) and cultural materials (e.g., popular music and fashions) specifically targeted to the impoverished and backward hillbillies. Like colonized peoples everywhere, Appalachians now find themselves exploited, marginalized, impoverished, and yet cognizant of their peripheral position and increasingly angry about it. As scholars Helen Lewis and Edward Knipe warned, "if colonized peoples always rebel, then we must wait and see what happens in Appalachia."[40]

What forms might colonial rebellion take, specifically within Appalachia? Despite frequently being portrayed as simplistic, backward, or naive and overwhelmed and exploited by the forces of global capitalism, perhaps Appalachian residents remain "marginal" on purpose. Is their "complete self-sufficiency" a drawback or a benefit? Is their social isolation due to an unfortunate bypassing by civilization or a deliberate avoidance of it? In an intriguing look at the history of Southeast Asian hill tribes, political scientist James Scott has argued that these tribes have engaged in an ongoing struggle with surrounding state-level societies for thousands of years. By avoiding incorporation into "civilized" societies and thus by avoiding civilization as much as possible, these independent mountaineers have been viewed by lowlanders as "our living ancestors." Between the lowlands and hills lies the "outlaw corridor," the borderlands between these societies. At times creating alliances with state-level societies and at other times avoiding or attacking them, all in order to benefit themselves, hill tribes successfully have manipulated multiple aspects of their cultures in order to accomplish these goals, Scott concluded. Modes of production (favoring self-sufficiency), economic exchange (valuing sharing), political alliances (between families), raiding, kinship ties (extended families), religious beliefs (emphasizing egalitarianism), language and dialect manipulation (adopting or avoiding standardized forms), and even the manipulation of oral history are all strategies these hill tribes have utilized to optimize the benefits and minimize the risks of dwelling near a state-level society. Remaining in difficult-to-reach higher elevations, mountain peoples have maintained as much autonomy as possible from state-level control through their active agency millennium after millennium. Maintaining values of "egalitarianism and autonomy both at the village and familial level" has created for these mountain peoples "an effective barrier to tyranny and permanent hierarchy."[41]

Scott's ideas fit well with the concepts developed several decades earlier by economic anthropologist Rhoda Halperin. Halperin described the active agency of rural mountain residents in Kentucky who avoided capitalistic exploitation by American society by living "the Kentucky way." First of all, Halperin distinguished between "deep rural," those living almost off the social and economic grid, from "shallow rural," those who are in between the city and "deep rural"; these folks utilize the Kentucky way to reap the benefits of a larger capitalist economy while simultaneously maintaining their social and economic autonomy from that larger economy. To do this, Halperin explained, shallow rural residents utilize "multiple livelihood strategies." These strategies include a rural residence, subsistence gardens, food processing and storage, gathering wild plants, hunting and fishing, growing cash crops, working local wage labor jobs, and exchanging goods and services reciprocally within extended families.[42]

By utilizing Halperin's Kentucky way as an example of the Appalachian hill tribes' utilization of Scott's agency, it is possible to view the residents of the southern Appalachians as deliberately living in the shallow rural (sometimes deep rural) "outlaw corridor" liminal spaces and tactically using the forces of modern capitalism to navigate a successful strategy for existence while maintaining as much economic and political (and perhaps even cultural) independence as possible. As folklorist Michael Ann Williams advised, "one must look beyond reasons of poverty to fully understand" cultural practices and beliefs. From this perspective, land becomes a commodity to hold, trade, or use as part of this strategy. Concentrations of mobile homes clustered in hollows or near the homeplace "may provide a freedom from the heavy indebtedness incurred by the purchase of a house" as well as a physical manifestation of the social ties between close kin utilizing the Kentucky way. This economic concern about maintaining small-scale farms created the powerful "sense of place" recognized by insiders. Then, struggles of land as patrimony (insider view) versus land as commodity (outsider view) create a "class struggle," anthropologist Allen Batteau concluded. With this materialist perspective, negative stereotypes of mountaineers are cultural creations used to justify the removal of "yesterday's people" from valuable land.[43]

Postmodern Views of Contested Spaces

If the South views itself in opposition to the North, then Appalachia more specifically appears to be in opposition to certain qualities as well, such as modernism, urbanism, and perhaps nationalism and capitalism.[44] In fact, sociologist Dwight Billings argued, Appalachia is a separate region because writers see it that way. "Oppositional images of place have, of course, been extremely important in anticolonial nationalist movements," and it is possible to view the Appalachians in opposition to hegemonic control by external forces. Visible evidence of these external forces of control may appear as dams (familiar in the Blue Ridge foothills), for these structures serve as "iconic landmarks of modernization" reflecting a dialectic between nature and urbanization. In this "inseparable dialectic of creation and destruction," geographer Maria Kaika continued, "iconography and discourse play the role of the ideological negotiator between the competing interests that produce contemporary urban and nonurban landscapes." A liminal borderland full of liminal meanings, the Appalachian region requires "more refined analysis" to "comprehend how and why people resist and accommodate" acculturation and domination by outside forces — from whatever directions "inside" and "outside" are portrayed.[45]

While various forms of a materialist or world systems theory might explain the Appalachian value of land and the relationship between mountaineers and outsiders, a postmodernist perspective enhances an understanding of the region as a space contested by multiple forces and groups, multivocalic in meaning and ambivalent in cultural comprehension. Anthropologists Setha Low and Denise Lawrence-Zuniga defined "contested spaces" as "geographic locations where conflicts in the form of opposition, confrontation, subversion, and/or resistance engage actors whose social positions are defined by differential control of resources and access to power."[46]

Using this approach, it is first critical to differentiate space from place. By examining social networks, folklorists Lisa Gabbert and Paul Jordan-Smith explained, researchers can understand more completely "how undifferentiated space may be transformed into identifiable and encoded place."[47] Likewise, geographer Yi-Fu Tuan differentiated "space," a more abstract term, from "place," an entity endowed with value and meaning.[48] In Tuan's thinking, space is open, free, and threatening; place is secure and stable. Citing both Tuan and de Certeau to define the concepts further, anthropologist Angele Smith defined place as having

a physical tangibility . . . because it marks past (and potentially continuing) actions and experiences with and in the landscape. Places in the landscape give meaning and identity to people, who have real emotional attachments rooted to the landscape through their memories and heritage (e.g., of their home or homelands). In contrast, *space* is dialectical and about process, motion, and action; it is not tangible in the same sense as it is always in the process of becoming. . . . Perhaps more useful is to combine or bridge these two concepts in a dialectical relationship. Thus, in order to make sense of the lived experience of people we must link these two concepts of space and place within the landscape. That is, landscape bridges and encapsulates both the action and fluidity of space and the rootedness and memory/history of place.[49]

"When space feels thoroughly familiar to us," Tuan concluded, "it has become place."[50]

Tuan also recognized the continuum and impact of "experience" on space and place: "experience can be direct and intimate, or it can be indirect and conceptual, mediated by symbols. . . . One person may know a place intimately as well as conceptually. He can articulate ideas but he has difficulty expressing what he knows through his senses of touch, taste, smell, hearing, and even vision." Tuan acknowledged that there has not been much work on "how people feel about space and place, to take into account the different modes of experience (sensorimotor, tactile, visual, conceptual), and to interpret space and place as images of complex—often ambivalent—feelings." How might one document these subtle human experiences, Tuan wondered? Artists often have done it, so researchers turn to "works of literature as well as in humanistic psychology, philosophy, anthropology and geography" to record "intricate worlds of human experience."[51]

Adopting Tuan's suggestion has been anthropologist Miles Richardson, who sought to understand the process by which humans "experience place and . . . simultaneously transform that experience into symbols, symbols that then communicate the experiential meaning of the place and, in so doing, bring it into being." Richardson argued that "contextualism" offers "the best hope of explicating how place grows out of experience and how it, in turn, symbolizes that experience." This "socially produced space," archaeologist Christopher Tilley elaborated, "combines the cognitive, the physical and the emotional into something that may be reproduced but is always open to transformation and change. . . . It follows that the meanings of space always involve a subjective dimension and cannot be understood apart from the symbolically constructed lifeworlds of social actors. . . . What space is depends on who is experiencing it and how. . . . Because space is differentially understood and experienced it forms a contradictory and conflict-ridden medium through which individuals act and are acted upon." "Imagine those moments when the hills abandon themselves to a social imaginary," anthropologist Kathleen Stewart proposed, "when the place becomes a phantasmagoric dream space—a wild zone beyond the pale filled with things dangerous, tragic, surprising, spectacular, and eccentric."[52] Perhaps this is a way to view the liminality of the mountains: the Blue Ridge yawns its greatness for Clemson's graduates at the same time a Blue Ridge river, the Chattooga, delivers ominous images.

However, a people may also be created by perceptions of space. As anthropologist Angele Smith explained, "Landscapes are made by the people that engage with them, and in making landscapes, the people themselves are made: their sense of place, belonging, and their social identity is constructed alongside the construction of their social landscape. . . . Landscapes are thus meaningful not only to individuals but also to collective groups that share a commonness of experiences and memories." From this postmodernist perspective, "the places were not preexisting empty stages to be filled with activity; they took on meaning only when activity gave them form. . . . History, biography, memory, and emotion all merged with and settled in the landscape," anthropologist Miriam Kahn observed. Existential space is "replete with social meanings wrapped around buildings, objects and features of the local topography, providing reference points and planes of emotional orientation for human attachment and involvement."[53]

Tuan provides an example. For Australian Aborigines,

> landscape is personal and tribal history made visible. The native's identity—his place in the total scheme of things—is not in doubt, because the myths that support it are as real as the rocks and waterholes he can see and touch. He finds recorded in his land the ancient story of the lives and deeds of the immortal beings from whom he himself is descended, and whom he reveres. The whole countryside is his family tree. . . . Human places become vividly real through dramatization. Identity of place is achieved by dramatizing the aspirations, needs, and functional rhythms of personal and group life.[54]

But "it is not enough to conclude that places are imagined entities," scholars Gregory Ashworth and Brian Graham indicate; "rather, if individuals create place identities, then obviously different people, at different times, for different reasons, create different narratives of belonging. Place images are thus user determined, polysemic and unstable through time." Geographer David Harvey described this multivocality as a "contested terrain of competing definitions." To describe thoroughly the cultural meaning of landscapes, anthropologists must also document "the polyphony of voices they hear and represent ethnographically," Margaret Rodman noted; "by joining multilocality to multivocality," anthropologists can discover how spaces are constructed, how they link to other spaces, how spaces represent people, "and begin to understand how people embody places."[55]

From this perspective, places may be amorphous, their residents ambiguous, and their meanings ambivalent. In contemporary thought, anthropologists Gupta and Ferguson wrote, "actual places and localities" are becoming "ever more blurred and indeterminate." Behavioral scientist Fritz Steele described the relationship between place as object and place as emotional trigger as a "'transactional system,' with each giving and receiving something from the other." Even "wilderness . . . is indeed a social construct whose definition varies from interest group to interest group," environmental sociologist Donald Davis observed. Since "sense of place is not possessed by everyone in similar manner or like configuration," anthropologist Keith Basso declared, "sense of place issues in a stream of symbolically drawn particulars—the visible particulars of local topographies, the personal particulars of biographical associations, and the notional particulars of socially given systems of thought." In other words, "the same locality may be perceived and apprehended in very different ways according to the immediate intentions of those who observe it," Basso concluded.[56]

As an example, writer Jerry Williamson cites Marjorie Nicholson on her description of mountains for the ancient Greeks. According to Nicholson, "the names of Greek mountains had root meanings like 'tempestuous,' 'wild,' 'terrifying,' 'the hunger range.' These names reveal a complicated (that is, ambiguous) feeling of simultaneous 'awe and aversion.' . . . And when actual people went into actual mountains—where anything could happen at any moment, where literal survival was an active question and might be a matter of physical competence—the possibilities of mountains simultaneously thrilled and terrified."[57]

Globalized Capitalism and Perceptions of Place

While a materialist perspective has described the economic and social strategies by which hill dwellers navigate their interaction with external social forces and while a postmodernist perspective has established the ambiguity and multivocality of places such as the Appalachian Mountains, anthropologists Akhil Gupta and James Ferguson ask more recent questions: "How are spatial meanings established? Who has the power to make places of spaces? Who contests this? What is at stake?"[58] Anthropologists must now "pay particular attention to the way spaces and places are made, imagined, contested, and enforced" as "different communities of people try to negotiate different interpretations of the same landscape. Thus landscapes can be dynamic and even volatile places that witness removals and clearances in the attempt to exclude and erase some inhabitants from the land."[59]

Adopting a more fluctuating perception of the flow of global capital and power, contemporary theorists have applied Arjun Appadurai's globalization concepts to the position of Appalachian residents within the world system.[60] Initially developed to describe the areas affected by the removal of Appalachian mountaintops for coal or the cultivation of agricultural products such as tobacco, the model explains how the extraction of such globalized commodities directly impacts individuals along a continuous chain of production and consumption, from a truck driver in Kentucky to a street vendor in New Delhi. In fact, considering the historical extraction from the Appalachian Mountains of global commodities such as beaver pelts and deer hides, labor (from underpaid, enslaved, or indigenous peoples), timber, cotton, corn, alcohol (as moonshine), and "nature" (as a marketable entity for tourism), in addition to coal and tobacco, anthropologist Ann Kingsolver has argued that the Appalachians have been part of the global economy for centuries. As demonstrated by the Kentucky way and other strategies described earlier, "there is agency, certainly, in the ways that people make sense of and manage their engagement with the global," Kingsolver wrote, "but the structural forces at play are so often rendered invisible in popular accounts of rural upland regions." As geographer David Harvey noted, places "are a distinctive product of institutionalized social and political-economic power." Emily Satterwhite described this perspective as "the new critical regionalism."[61]

One of the consequences of this new globalized perspective is the development of what Kingsolver described as "strategic alterity," or the deliberate debasement of local labor and peoples in order to justify their exploitation by global forces. Strategic alterity would explain the various manifestations of the hillbilly stereotype: these would be people who, because of assumed characteristics of backwardness, ignorance, stubbornness, or pugnacity, cannot comprehend, appreciate, or utilize the real market value of their land and its treasures; because of this, external or internal exploiters are in a better position to extract, capitalize, and consume these materials for both the global market and their personal enrichment and enjoyment. It is no coincidence, anthropologist Allen Batteau observed, that "the image of Appalachia as a strange land and peculiar people was elaborated at the very same time that the relationships of external domination and control of the Southern Mountain Region's natural and human resources were being elaborated." As community scholar Gabriel Piser warned, "in the regional legacy of colonialism, turning unruly land and people into well-disciplined and economically productive regions and populations requires the destruction of existing forms of knowledge and ways of life."[62]

As these general ways of life are ridiculed, marginalized, or destroyed by the forces of globalized capitalism, one of the existing forms of local knowledge that transforms is the cultural interpretation of land. First, the external (core) cultural values of rationalism and efficiency redefine land as a commodity rather than as a family legacy. Simultaneously, sociologist Barbara Ellen Smith explained, the forces of development under neoliberal capitalism convert the open spaces of "commons" into private properties or render formerly accessible public lands as now unusable places due to environmental pollution or destruction (such as with mountaintop removal).[63] This privatization process generates the Appalachian emotional connection to place as a reaction in order to resist the appropriation of the commons and to reclaim a legitimate and empowered position in the chain of globalized capitalism. In other words, "a specific 'place' does not acquire meaning through some bounded, internal history, but through the specificity of its relationships with social processes and histories that stretch far beyond a particular locale," Appalachian scholars Barbara Smith and Stephen Fisher concluded.[64]

"Never self-evident, never 'given,'" Smith and Fisher explain, "place is coming alive as a potent force in the hands of those who understand not just its shortcomings but its critical, democratic, and collective potentials and are able to harness its emotive and symbolic powers for progressive political uprising." Consequently, scholars Dwight Billings and Ann Kingsolver continue, "*place*, as much as anything, is *action* more than passive context. It is about what people *do*—in one way or another, in concert, contestation, or consternation—as they try to make sense of and live with the nearby and distant forces in their lives." Especially in "border zones" (such as the liminal space of the Appalachians), anthropologist Ann Kingsolver observed, one can detect how "place-based notions of identity are constructed and contested." Ultimately, since neoliberal globalized capitalism promotes the idea of privatizing public space, sociologist Barbara Ellen Smith argued, this force generates the place attachments in Appalachia that scholars have described for decades. As geographer David Harvey had predicted, given these forces there is a "search for an authentic sense of community and of an authentic relation to nature."[65]

While scholars Barbara Ellen Smith and Stephen Fisher embrace this perspective, they also recognize that deeper sentiments may be engendered as outcomes of globalized capitalism. In discussing mountaintop removal in the central Appalachians, they acknowledge that there are some residents who "view place as constituted through the material and metaphorical homeplace of mountains," and thus mountaintop removal destroys both the physical environment and "the very soul of the place itself" due to a "past of intergenerational continuity on the land." As "the security of places has been threatened" by globalized capitalism, geographer David Harvey noted, "such loss of security promotes a search for alternatives, one of which lies in the creation of both imagined and tangible communities in place." Smith and Fisher conclude that "the tension between a collective investment in place, a shared sense of identity with place, and the private appropriation and even destruction of place forms a crucible of possibility that is just beginning to be realized."[66]

But these "place attachments are inevitably at least in part about the past," sociologist Barbara Ellen Smith cautions, "about defense of a place that activists seek to preserve, and place-based organizing is therefore not only inward-looking in the sense of being localistic, but potentially backward-looking and reactionary," even exclusionary toward outsiders. Given this perspective, then, the defense of place in Appalachia explains the insularity and assumed racial homogeneity of the Appalachian locals. In other words, the reaction to a recently evoked sense of place might be the (re)definition of the threatened space (in this case, Appalachia) as the selective homeland of "our contemporary ancestors," defined by a Scots-Irish heritage to the exclusion of any other ethnicity.[67]

While anthropologist Mary Anglin acknowledges the general stages in the evolution of this potentially exclusionary outcome, she cautions that the thesis relates primarily to the coal fields of central Appalachia, and she would prefer an approach that describes in a more nuanced way the flow of capital back and forth between local and global and the various responses to the vacillating flow along that continuum. As scholars Barbara Smith and Stephen Fisher observe, globalized capitalism occurs across expanses of space, while communities produce responses to these forces locally. Multiple constituent groups might respond in myriad ways to this flow, including international, national, and local beneficiaries. In fact, Fisher and Smith add, researchers should focus on the "internal profiteers" as well as "other internal inequalities, such as race and gender."[68]

"We recognize . . . that space is at once material, social, cognitive, and ideological," anthropologist Angele Smith noted; "in keeping with these explanations, the current understanding of landscapes similarly recognizes that the landscape is inherently connected to social relations, power, meaning, and social identity, and because of those connections it is often a site of contestation." Contested spaces, Gupta and Ferguson argued, are interstitial zones "of displacement and deterritorialization" that shape "the identity of the hybridized subject." While these interstitial zones may create ambiguity in symbolic meaning, Gupta and Ferguson asserted that such places also have become the "'normal' locale of the postmodern subject." Viewed in this way, Gupta and Ferguson observed, physical proximity between diverse groups may be overridden by other factors such as race, class, gender, and power; the wealthy in Bombay and London may have more in common than the wealthy and poor in London suburbs. Where individuals actually reside is "beside the point," scholars Fisher and Smith continue; "the issue is gross inequality in ownership and control of resources that are fundamental to human survival." "Like 'place' and 'space,'" anthropologist Eric Hirsch recognized, "notions of 'inside' and 'outside' are not mutually exclusive and depend upon cultural and historical context."[69]

Beyond Globalism: A New Perception of Place

This more recent postmodern perspective conceives of strategically "othered" Appalachian residents as end nodes on strands of globalized capital, reacting to and controlling as best they can the uneven flow of resources across the globe and responding to neoliberal trends of land privatization, pollution, and destruction with a consequent emotional response to preserve and protect remaining common lands. The manipulation, aggrandizement, or loss of capital across these strands by individuals now are no longer seen as entirely dependent upon place of residence or family history (i.e., insider/outsider) and instead are affected by such factors as gender, class, race, local economy, and subregion of Appalachia. Thus, what becomes critical to an understanding of the sense of place in Appalachia is the process by which individuals and collectives in the mountains come to control, manipulate, or respond to the flow of capital across the globe. And according to current thinking, one of the most typical responses to globalized neoliberal capitalism is for certain groups or individuals to resist these forces by struggling to retain control of land, whether it be commons or family property.

However, I argue that this interpretation needs to be modified. Is the emotional tie to land that scholars long have identified as characteristic of Appalachian residents a *response to* globalized neoliberal capitalism, or is this tie *manifested by* this trend? In other words, is the Appalachian emotional attachment to land a consequence of globalization (as many contemporary theorists contend or perhaps imply), or is this emotional attachment to land already present in the region's cultural system and only emerges consciously under the potential stress of confiscation or destruction of land due to globalization, effectively serving as another tool of agency in the cultural arsenal of defending spaces? I see this as a subtle but critical distinction.

In order to examine critically the influence of globalized neoliberal capitalism on southern Appalachian residents, first we might discuss the degree of influence of the force itself on individuals. Anthropologists Catherine Kingfisher and Jeff Maskovsky argue that neoliberalism should be viewed not as a "thing that acts in the world" but instead as a process among other processes to which humans respond in various ways. Just as culture is "disarticulating and rearticulating, disjunctive and contradictory," so is neoliberalism and the personal responses to this force, the authors conclude.[70] This "disjunction" explains in part why there exists in southern Appalachia a diversity of reactions to the forces of neoliberal capitalism.

Geographer David Harvey outlines a possible strategy to combat the neoliberal constrictions on public lands, replaced instead by "a comprehensive project for the collective management of the commons and the dissolution of autocratic and despotic state powers into democratic and collective management structures."[71] Perhaps the emphasis by locals to maintain family-owned lands, jointly (if sometimes contentiously) managed by extended families, reflects an example of active resistance to neoliberal forces as hypothesized by Harvey.

I propose that a second critique of the impact of neoliberal capitalism on individuals in the study area is the ambiguity of the implied dichotomy between "public" and "private" space. Under neoliberalism, formerly public space becomes delimited and restricted by access to all but a select few, often exacerbating class differences. Thus, formerly public lands in the southern Appalachians become fenced off behind gates, causing or exacerbating a cultural desire to retain family lands.

But in the confines of the study area, the assumed dichotomy between public and private space is more nuanced. For most of the twentieth century, large portions of land were held privately by timber companies (see chapter 2), but the companies allowed public access for local extraction of non-timber resources (e.g., hunting and herb collecting). Today, large portions of that same land are now publicly owned as state parks or conservation lands but ironically with greater restrictions (e.g., seasonal licensed hunting and federal environmental protections). In contrast, in the past private land may have been accessible to others for various activities (with landowners' permissions) or may not have been accessible; today gated communities and suburban developments restrict more lands than in the past, but more acreage is also available through protected state parks and recreation areas. The assumed dichotomy between public and private manifests in reality as "disjunctive and contradictory," with the region having much more liminal spaces with liminal residents.

Anthropologist Ilana Gershon introduces a third critique of the impact of neoliberalism on cultural values toward land. Gershon contrasts a "sociological imagination" with an "anthropological" one. For the former, researchers "differentiate themselves from their interlocutors by juxtaposing different understandings of how levels of scale interconnect." For the latter, researchers explore "how practiced epistemologies shape and are shaped by the structures of relationships." From this anthropological perspective, Gershon continues, "people continually struggle to make neoliberal principles livable given their other understandings of how one is social." David Harvey predicted a "spirit of revolt" in which "values of truth and beauty replace the cold calculus" of capitalistic alienation. In ethnographic reality, then, the cultural value toward land may or may not be directly caused by neoliberalism; what is important, however, is the fact that many residents must mitigate the impact, perhaps relying on values of "truth and beauty" in their "toolkit" of "practiced epistemologies." From this perspective, Gershon concludes, "the ethnographer can begin the work of explanation that differentiates perspectives" by doing what we do best and "heed[ing] our interlocutors."[72]

Taking Gershon's suggestion to "heed our interlocutors," let us review the responses from the central Appalachian informants cited by sociologist Barbara Ellen Smith, who argued that these responses emphasize "use values and the direct consumption of nature by women as well as men rather than commodification of natural resources and the economic development that can presumably occur as a result of masculine employment" primarily in mountaintop removal coal extraction. However, in the actual interviews conducted by writers Silas House and Jason Howard, the extensive comments by the women also cited by Smith parallel almost exactly the sentiments expressed by my own informants in the chapters that follow. For example, Judy Bonds, the tenth generation residing on her family land in West Virginia, remembered "'the smell of the rich, beautiful black earth. That's how it is in Appalachia—you are the mountain and the mountain is you.'" Sisters Anne Shelby and Jessie Lynn Keltner, picking blackberries on their homeplace in eastern Kentucky, described the land to House and Howard as "a *part* of their family," and they moved over the land "the way someone might run their thumb over the knuckles of their mother in her old age." Furthermore, the authors summarized the sisters' perspective on their family land as "holy ground."[73]

Then, as the sisters reflected on what might happen were they to lose their family land, Anne Shelby commented that "'people from the mountains often try to explain—in songs and poems—why we feel this way about the mountains. But it's hard in a way because it's inexplicable, really, why we feel so much better with hills around us.'" Later in the interview her sister Lynne added, "'You don't necessarily have a consciousness of something so much until there's the threat that you might lose it. . . . As long as we had it, we didn't have to think so much about it.'"[74] As the women explained, both of them felt that their emotional connection to their land had been subconscious until brought to the level of consciousness by the potential threat of destruction or loss of family land.

But this subconscious sentiment toward family land is not only found in the central Appalachian coal fields. Over 200 miles to the east in southwestern Virginia, anthropologist Melinda Wagner and her student team documented the same emotional ties to family land with the same difficulty by informants in articulating that tie consciously. Then about 150 miles farther south, local organizers Nina Gregg and Doug Gamble, in writing about preventing development near the Great Smoky Mountains in eastern Tennessee, noted that while members of local organizations may "have deep personal connections to place, these connections do not often rise to organizational consciousness, discourse, or strategy."[75] As subsequent chapters of this book will reveal, this is precisely the same sentiment expressed, often with the same degree of difficulty, by my informants.

I believe that this deep emotional attachment to family land explains why many residents struggle to verbalize an emotion they cannot easily articulate but only feel on a more profound, subconscious level, because most locals never had to express that sentiment consciously until specifically asked about it. It is as if locals wonder doesn't everyone feel this way about family land? What other way is there to feel about family land? Why wouldn't a person want to retain family land? Until presented with other ways of thinking about family land, whether challenged by potential loss or questioned by curious researchers, many locals perceived only *their* way of thinking about land as culturally normal. In other words, the default cultural value is "family land is critically important" and only rises to the level of conscious expression when presented with an alternative value or a potential threat.[76]

Further evidence that this deep emotional tie to land is not a relatively recent response to relatively recent neoliberal land loss but is instead an entrenched cultural value stems from the fact that many locals perceive family land with such emotion, sincerity, and profundity that this cultural value cannot be recent. While it is true that new cultural values might arise within a generation, I believe that this emotional tie to land has multigenerational roots. For individuals to describe family land as symbolically a part of their own bodies or to become physically ill at the thought of having to sell family land requires a multigenerational sentiment that could not have such significant an impact on human psychology over a relatively brief period of existence. In order for this sentiment to be such a visceral part of Appalachian culture and to be on such a profoundly subconscious level, the emotional connection to family land must be a fundamental cultural attribute and not a recent consequence of globalism.

Moreover, for most of the families whose members speak in the chapters that follow, their own family land is not immediately threatened by development, nor have they lost family land to recent transformations, and yet their emotional commitment to family land remains indominable. For example, the Nelson, Valentine, Abney/Daniels, and Edison families still own, occupy, and use their family land; lakes, subdivisions, and gates do not pose an imminent threat to their lands. After the deaths of Joshua and Anne Flowers, their homeplace sits empty and overgrown yet undeveloped, unsold, and preserved. While it is true that family heads very frequently ponder the ultimate disposition of family lands in generations to come, they all hope and expect to continue owning their current property into the unknown future. At the same time, as readers will hear in the following chapters, these families express deep emotional love for their family lands. This sentiment, then, can and does exist in mountain families even without the potential threat of loss due to globalized capitalism.

From my perspective, then, long-term residents certainly could recognize the impact of neoliberal globalized capitalism on their own decisions but also still possess this sentiment toward family land as a cultural component. When faced with the potential of neoliberal land loss, locals consciously give voice and action to a cultural value that had remained dormant until then. I believe that the ethnographic evidence demonstrates that the deep emotional tie to land expressed by many Appalachian residents is not generated by the forces of neoliberal capitalism but is instead a preexisting cultural value that is given conscious expression by these forces.

Discarding the "Outsiders and Insiders" Dichotomy

Given the current postmodern perspective about the complex impact of the flow of globalized capital on local residents and also given the enhanced awareness by scholars of the influences of class, ethnicity, race, education, gender, and urban/rural residency on the accumulation and manipulation of this globalized capital, many contemporary researchers have argued that it no longer makes sense to separate "insiders" from "outsiders" in a simplistic dichotomy. Instead, as anthropologist Ann Kingsolver observed, individuals may be "placed" into a variety of identities, depending on social context or their location in the global economy.[77]

My fieldwork has found that many year-round residents of upscale retirement communities view themselves as "locals," for they shop locally, vote locally, pay local property taxes, and often volunteer in local schools and community organizations. Yet at the same time, long-term residents easily recognize these same individuals as "recent" arrivals, with no family ties to the lands they now occupy and frequently having much greater socioeconomic status and social capital (e.g., retired corporate leaders) than their "hillbilly" neighbors. Environmental psychologists differentiate between "place attachment" (the affective bond between people and their favored place) and "place identity" (a component of personal identity). Thus, recent arrivals might have a strong sense of place attachment, but natives have a stronger sense of place identity. While gated community residents may love their new region, they would have more in common with gated community residents in Sun City, Arizona, than with their Eastatoee Valley neighbors five miles away.[78]

For example, Benjamin and Denise Craig described a time when the Eastatoee community held its biannual potluck meeting and had invited as speaker a prominent national ecologist affiliated with a nearby university. Several women from the Cliffs (gated) communities attended, but they never returned for additional meetings. "I don't believe we were that back-woodsy," Mrs. Craig joked, "but no one ever came back. . . . When they came to the meeting the ladies looked nice and everything, but they really didn't talk to us. . . . I don't think they stayed to eat" afterward either. "Well, they didn't bring anything," her husband explained, "and I guess they didn't feel like they should stay and eat." "They didn't have to bring any 'cause we had plenty of food," Denise Craig countered, "but you know, next time maybe they should bring some!"

On the other hand, as scholars have noted, local residency by itself does not necessarily differentiate insiders from outsiders either. For example, by definition, individuals such as Debbie Fletcher and Cash Godbold (see chapter 2) should be considered outsiders because they did not reside year-round in Jocassee Valley but only summered there as teenagers, the former visiting relatives and the latter working at his aunts' summer camp. However, Fletcher considered herself a local because of her family's generational ties to Jocassee Valley, while Godbold (by his writings) would remain a non-local, lacking those generational ties.

Temporal longevity in the area likewise does not by itself define an insider. For example, Jeffrey Donnelly was born in upper Pickens County and has deep generational roots. However, for most of his adult life he lived in a different region of the United States, only recently having returned to the area and retiring on family land. On the other hand, Amy Driver has lived in upper Oconee County for over forty years, raising her family and working as a guide on the Chattooga River. Yet, since Ms. Driver's family moved here when she was a young adult, locals would consider her to be an outsider, having no multigenerational ties to land.

Compounding the ambiguity of the liminal space of the southern Appalachians are these liminal or postmodern actors moving in and out of the area, residing in and out of the area, confounding attempts to categorize them into a neat dichotomy. Individual or group identities as insiders or outsiders thus vary depending on social context, as scholars had explained earlier. Anthropologist William Schumann describes this process as "place-making," "selectively cultivating some narratives of belonging while erasing other meanings from public discourse." "All place-making in Appalachia," Schumann observed, "operates on the principle of *marking difference* between one reading of human-environmental relations and all others."[79] Thus, upon which principle of marking difference might we divide some from others in order to explore the more profound and subconscious cultural difference toward family land?

As postmodernists recognize, there are many variables, even intersectional compoundings, by which we might categorize people who live in the study area. This book focuses on one critical variable: a deep emotional tie to land. I will label those with this emotional connection "inhabitants." These are individuals who see family land as a metaphorical part of their own family. Consequently, they "inhabit" their lands through a cultural process described in chapters 5 and 6. In contrast to inhabitants are those with the common American attitude that land is a commodity, valued for its utilitarian or recreational characteristics but without a significant sentimental association as profound as that of inhabitants. Geographer David Harvey labeled this perspective as that of "bourgeois political economy."[80] Not all inhabitants dwell in the South Carolina mountains, nor is everyone who resides in the mountains an inhabitant. As one Eastatoee Valley inhabitant observed, residents may live in the same spaces, but they do not *live* in the same spaces; for example, they do not wave to valley inhabitants as they drive through the valley toward their home. As postmodernists have recognized, the inhabitant perspective transects race, class, gender, ethnicity, and all other variables; inhabitants I have interviewed include both women and men, young adults and seniors, those of African and European heritages, and those with varied educational and career backgrounds.

While many scholars utilizing the globalized capitalism explanatory framework have cautioned against privileging one group's perspective over those of other groups, it is precisely the inhabitant attitude toward land that I have found most intriguing. During my years of fieldwork, I gradually came to recognize this perspective as I listened more carefully to what my informants were struggling to explain to me. Furthermore, as discussed earlier, this sentiment is not unique to the southern Appalachians, but it is characteristic of this region. Because this emotional sentiment toward land contrasts markedly with a more materialistic perspective, I choose to investigate this sentiment.

Using this postmodernist perspective and focusing attention on the region's inhabitants, the Appalachian Mountains are more than a frontier or backcountry with dangerous or simplistic contemporary ancestors and more than an enclave of hill tribes escaping or manipulating the forces of globalized neoliberal capitalism. Likewise, as anthropologist Melinda Wagner noted, inhabitants and their ancestors are not a smaller-scale society with a concept of land as sacred space or themselves as part of nature, nor are they equivalent to capitalistic societies viewing land as property with economic or utility value. Instead, Wagner continued, Appalachian residents are between these poles: "land is identified with the people who have lived there; the land is given meaning by the human activities that had happened and are happening on it."[81]

But the mountains are also a contested space, an "interstitial zone" both symbolically and materially, where inhabitants and residents create oppositional views of the same place. Whether majestic or menacing, the mountains symbolically represent beauty and danger simultaneously to both inhabitants and residents. At the same time, the mountains are contested economically as a valuable resource to be owned and consumed (timbering, vacationing) as well as a symbolically important place to be inherited and remembered. Moreover, the ambiguous space is also contested by occupancy: residents who move to the area for its beauty and economic value and inhabitants who resent the clashes with resident values, resident consumerism, and resident usurpation of spaces. There is indeed "something in these hills," but "the black box of landscape requires 'opening' and its contents themselves brought into view."[82]

Methods

Contacted by the South Carolina Department of Natural Resources (DNR) in August 2006, I was invited to collect stories from the older European American residents of the Jocassee Gorges region in upper Oconee and Pickens Counties. Over the next several years as I expanded the research area into upper Greenville County and included African Americans in the interviews, I began to notice that some mountain residents spoke about their family land in a way unfamiliar to me. As discussed above, it was this difference that eventually stimulated my curiosity about this sentiment and transformed the initial research question into the directions taken in this book.

Along with interviews, observations of the area have been conducted since I first began the study, primarily because I continue to live, work, and recreate in the area. During some interviews, informants escorted me around their property or on short hikes into the forest and talked about the significance of places we passed or viewed from a distance. For decades I have attended community festivals such as the July 4 Hillbilly Days in Mountain Rest and the September Apple Festival in Westminster (both in Oconee County) and the spring Azalea Festival in Pickens and the mid-October Pumpkin Festival in Pumpkintown (both in Pickens County), observing crowds, booths, and items for sale (such as T-shirts and bumper stickers). I have attended the monthly Soapstone Baptist Church Fish Fry fundraising event at least eight times annually for several decades, speaking with newcomers and regulars every month. Perhaps the most memorable expedition I took was a field trip with DNR officers by pickup truck into the wilderness area of the Jocassee Gorges to speak informally with groups of bear hunters in the field.

For the research project, I first cleared the plan through the appropriate university review process and then contacted possible contributors, asking to speak with them in a place of their choice, at a time of their choice, and with whomever else they wanted to be present. Friends often suggested other possible contributors. For every interview, I always introduced myself as a professor from Clemson University (a title that carries some prestige in upper South Carolina, known regionally as the Upstate) and then described the research project in a brief and appropriate way. I always left a note for additional contact and sometimes also a business card. I could not disguise my class, ethnicity, and regional midwestern origin (revealed by my accent), nor did I try to do so. Instead, I utilized my resident identity to seek further explanations of the meaning of land to inhabitants, not having been raised in the culture of the region and thus not really understanding their point of view. Inhabitants relished the idea of explaining their perspectives to me; several times, locals enjoyed teasing me with "you're not from around here, are you?" as they tried to explain their favorite foods, common local expressions, or the cultural significance of land. On the other hand, whether consciously or not, residents always acknowledged my accent and "placement" in social context; thus, I believe that they felt more comfortable describing their perspectives of inhabitants to me.

Establishing rapport, or a sense of trust between researcher and informant, required a set of skills ideally shared by all field-workers. While I did not disguise my obvious ethnicity, education, employer, or accent, I tried at all times to express interest and empathy in the presented points of view. Early in my fieldwork, one of my better-educated and more widely traveled informants cautioned me about being honest: "If you want to get yourself in trouble up here, be something you aren't to them, especially if you're doing it for some purpose. . . . Tell them what you got on your mind and they'll respect you for it. They don't have to agree with you, but don't bullshit them. It'll backfire on you every time."

For example, after I introduced myself, my university position, and the project to a local married couple (one spouse with a high school education, the other with a seventh-grade education) living far into the mountains, and after the interview had been under way for some time, the husband told me that I was unlike those Clemson "doctors" because, like "these people that live in the subdivisions, they don't associate with us poor people too much. [But it seems] . . . like you're kind of down home a little bit"; he then touched me on the shoulder, perhaps symbolically including me in the "local" group. In contrast, while interviewing a retired corporate executive and his wife over iced tea in a lakeside restaurant in a gated community, I was surprised by the fact that the couple called me by my familiar name from the beginning of the interview, unlike every local I had interviewed until that time. I interpreted this as another attempt to include me in their group but this time into their upper-middle-class nonsouthern status.

Fieldwork required at least one memorable challenge. Early in the research I had been introduced to Robert Davidson by retired DNR biologist Sam Stokes, and we had been talking about eating groundhogs. Stokes observed that it had been a long time since he had eaten groundhog, whereupon

Davidson replied that he had some in his refrigerator and asked if we wanted some. Having never eaten groundhog before, I courageously said "sure." In a little frying pan Davidson placed some dark meat from the refrigerator; I could see a small vertebral column and a long bone. He placed the warmed meat on paper plates on his small kitchen table, and I tried it—it had been fried, so the meat was stringy. I cleaned my plate, however, except for the tiny groundhog bones.

About seventeen African Americans and about seventy-two European Americans were interviewed for a total of about 144 hours of digital recordings (see the appendix for brief informant biographies). Informants ranged in education from at least one with a doctoral degree to some with perhaps a third-grade education and from retired corporate executives in expensive lakeside mansions in manicured retreats to part-time manual laborers living in mobile homes on unpaved back roads. Interviews ranged from thirty minutes to several hours, and participants may have been asked for follow-up interviews as well. People were always told that they need not answer any question about which they felt uncomfortable, and they had the right to ask that the recorder be turned off at any time. This happened occasionally, especially during discussions about neighbors or known moonshiners, although no one refused to be recorded. Transcripts of every interview were done by paid undergraduates, double-checked against the original interviews by me, and then returned to every participant by mail. In a few instances informants (or their descendants) thanked me for the return of the transcript, and then I asked for and was granted a follow-up interview.

Relatively few actual names of living people appear in this book. All contributors had been promised anonymity during the interview sessions, in keeping with the best practices of anthropological research. Pseudonyms were selected from a random list of first names and then a separate random list of family names, with care to avoid common family names in the region. Pseudonyms were alphabetized in the chronological order I interviewed people, using the alphabet at least three times. If individuals had a chance to read and approve their quoted information, their actual names were used (if they had agreed). If published accounts (such as local histories) provided real names, those real names were included here as well but not matched to my anonymous interviews even if the same person was involved. In all other instances with living individuals, pseudonyms were used. For issues involving deep background or for especially sensitive topics, the level of anonymity was raised to "a resident" or "an older woman." Every word quoted was actually said, but sometimes those speakers remain anonymous for their own security.

Quotations by informants have been edited for length but otherwise have not been corrected for grammar. Sometimes brackets are used to add a word or letter to render the quote more easily understandable. Dialectical (and sometimes obsolete) forms of nouns and verbs such as "chimley" (chimney) and "knowed" are left in the text; other obsolete words are explained in notes. While scholars referenced in secondary sources are distinguished with their professional attributions, informants are merely quoted by name. Most of the information in chapters 3 through 6 are the views of residents and inhabitants rather than my own. I have tried to present the views of my informants throughout the book and to keep my own voice in the background, emerging in chapter 7 for concluding remarks.

Interviews with inhabitants with a deep history to the area were conducted in a variety of settings. Most of the interviews were held in informant homes or (weather permitting) on a back porch or gazebo; one interview was at a camping site at Devil's Fork State Park. For the first several interviews I was accompanied by a locally well-known retired DNR biologist, Sam Stokes, who introduced me and vouched for my credentials. Many interviews were held between childhood friends (now adults) or with both spouses simultaneously, which often made for enjoyable discussions of their lives together. Several times multiple generations contributed: a mother and her young adult son, a father and his adult son and daughter-in-law, a niece and her elderly uncle, another niece and her aunt, and parents and an adult daughter. In one interview I met in the family homeplace with several siblings, a niece, and her own daughter, three generations around a kitchen table in the ancestral home.

I conducted fewer interviews with more recently arrived individuals. A popular local author (and friend) knew several residents in a lakeside gated community, and through her intervention I gained entry and conducted most of these interviews in private homes behind the gates. I met one couple for lunch in a lakeside restaurant inside that same gated community. All these couples were permanent residents of the Upstate, having chosen to retire to the area. At the invitation of one of these residents, I met at their community building with an all-female book club to talk about my research and to solicit additional views on the South Carolina mountains. I also interacted with another group of retirees from a nongated series of lakeside developments during a presentation I gave as part of a county celebration.

The questions after the talk became a focus group of perceptions. I interviewed one resident at her Blue Ridge place of business and several others in their private homes outside of any gates.

Conclusion

"For any sense of place," anthropologist Keith Basso wrote, "the pivotal question is not where it comes from, or even how it gets formed, but what, so to speak, it is made with. Like a good pot of stew or a complex musical chord, the characteristic of the thing emerges from the qualities of its ingredients. And while describing that character may prove troublesome indeed (always, it seems, there is something ineffable about it), the elements that compose it can be selectively sampled and separately assessed."[83] Using Basso's metaphor, the following chapters describe the varied ingredients in the "good pot of stew" that constitute the varied meanings for land in the mountains of South Carolina. Chapter 2 provides the ecological and historical overview of the study area. Chapter 3 examines the contrastive attitudes toward land by residents as both dangerous and beautiful; then, the discussion seeks their understanding of the sense of community, the meaning of land, and an empathetic attempt to understand the perspectives of inhabitants who lost the land that they, the residents, now occupy or enjoy. Chapter 4 presents the inhabitants' perspectives on the contrast between land as both beautiful and dangerous, with more details about the dangers since they know their own area more intimately. Chapter 5 then takes the inhabitants' approach to the meaning of land and analyzes that meaning by means of a "thick description." Chapter 6 uses this inhabitant understanding of land to examine in more detail the process by which the anthropomorphizing of land is completed. Chapter 7 summarizes both resident and inhabitant perspectives on the themes of the book and synthesizes them—or tastes the stew (using Basso's metaphor)—and informs readers of the cultural insights that might be gained from such tasting.

CHAPTER TWO

A Dangerous, Inhospitable Place

Environmental and Historical Background

Environmental Setting

The Jocassee Gorges region of upper South Carolina preserves one of the most beautiful areas in the southeastern United States.[1] At the very edge of the Blue Ridge Mountains, cold mountain rivers and streams carve deep gorges through igneous or metamorphic rock and tumble over cliffs, creating spectacular waterfalls. Boulder-strewn rivers such as the Horsepasture, Whitewater, Toxaway, and Chattooga (much of the setting for the *Deliverance* film) gather together onto the Piedmont and flow toward the Atlantic Ocean. Protruding above the trees are occasional outcrops of granitic rock, with sheer steeply curving sides and romanticized names like Table Rock, Bald Rock, Glassy Mountain, and Caesar's Head.

Ironically, the pastoral scene of the Blue Ridge Mountains belies tremendous mountain-building forces that originally shaped this landscape. As described by geologist Carolyn Murphy, the landmass that eventually became South Carolina began as a continental fragment from an earlier geological time, separated by a narrow sea from an arc of volcanic islands to the east, much like Hawaii today. As the African continental plate collided with the North American plate after about five hundred million years, rocks of the continental fragment and island arc (today the Blue Ridge and upper Piedmont, respectively) were slammed into each other and then pushed farther west, heating and twisting them into metamorphic rocks and creating the characteristic southwest/northeast trends of the southern Appalachians. As the plates collided and overrode each other, the friction and pressure melted some subterranean rocks into magma, which eventually cooled and formed masses of granite deep beneath the surface. Subsequent mountain building and erosion gradually raised and exposed these massive igneous and metamorphic mounds into distinctive peaks and bare rock surfaces, such as Table Rock (figure 1) and Glassy Mountain (figure 2). A second mountain-building event occurred about a hundred million years later as an African plate slammed into the North American plate a second time, further bending and twisting the southern Appalachian rocks.[2]

Because of these tectonic forces, the physiography of the upper part of South Carolina (and farther into North Carolina and Georgia) bears evidence of these collisions. Some rivers, such as the notorious Chattooga and the smaller Saluda and Big Eastatoee, follow their respective southwest/northeast valleys out of the mountains. Other rivers, such as the Horsepasture, Toxaway, Thompson, and Whitewater, slice directly through the escarpment, carving narrow valleys and gorges with high, sharp ridgetops.[3] While these valleys are typically narrow, occasionally they widen out into flatter floodplains such as the cliff-hemmed Horsepasture area or the tillable Jocassee Valley.

Fueling these rivers is a tremendous amount of rainfall. As moisture-laden clouds drift into the U.S. interior from the Gulf of Mexico, the southern Appalachians intercept the clouds and compel them to release moisture before climbing over the mountains. Consequently, the heaviest moisture falls on the southeastern slopes of the highest peaks. Other than the rainforest of the Pacific Northwest, the southeastern Appalachians receive some of the highest rainfall amounts in the continental United States. For example, Transylvania County, North Carolina (the major headwater collecting area for the Jocassee Gorges rivers), "*averages* an astonishing eighty-six inches of rain each year, an amount that nearly classifies it as a rainforest."[4]

A combination of water volume, mountain gradient, and rock hardness creates tremendous whitewater rivers in many valleys. The igneous and metamorphic rocks erode by waterborne material, from boulders to sand grains, slowly scouring out the rocks into beautiful but deadly sculptures. Sometimes massive volumes of water squeeze through yard-wide troughs called "narrows"; other times, millions of years of churning material have carved out potholes, or circular depressions, even tubes, into impervious bedrock. The deadliest river phenomena are hydraulics, where water falls over a ledge, churns backward into the wall or deeper into the bedrock, and creates a circulating vertical whirlpool. A small amount of surface water continues to flow over the hydraulic, creating the impression of innocence. Depending on the force of the tumbling water, swimmers or boaters may become trapped in the whirlpool and drown.

Because of this rainfall, the southern Appalachians support a tremendous amount of biodiversity. Cove forests abound in the cool, moist, rarely frozen valleys on the mountain slopes. Hardwoods include species of oaks, hickory, and (historically) American chestnut trees (*Castanea dentata*), along with species of hemlock (*Tsuga* spp.) and tulip poplar (*Liriodendron tulipifera*). Subcanopy species include mountain laurel (*Kalmia latifolia*, locally called "ivy") and rhododendron (*Rhododendron* spp.). Along the ground grow numerous plant species, including ginseng (*Panax quinquefolius*) and yellowroot (*Xanthorhiza simplicissima*), traditionally prized for medicinal purposes.[5]

Coupled with the unique combination of steep valleys, sharp ridges, and higher elevations, the rainfall creates unique microenvironments harboring rare and exotic flora and fauna. Perhaps the best known of these rare plants is the Oconee Bell (*Shortia galacifolia*), a relative to the more common galax (*Galax urceolata*). The plant grows low to the ground, about the diameter of a small dinner plate, with evergreen leaves about an inch or so in diameter (figure 3). Locally abundant in a narrow band along stream banks forming a thick green blanket, it is found only in steep-sided valleys in a few counties in southwestern North Carolina and in Pickens and Oconee Counties, South Carolina. In mid-March the plant produces delicate fifteen-millimeter (half inch–sized) bell-shaped white blossoms. Because of the unique combination of temperature, moisture, humidity, and elevation necessary for propagation, the rare plant is treasured where found, with protected areas such as that at Devil's Fork State Park near the former Jocassee Valley.

In fields or open areas in the lower elevations, especially along roads, spread green waves of tangled vines—kudzu (*Pueraria montana*), the scourge of the South. Originally imported by the federal government during the Great Depression to help curtail soil erosion in old cotton fields, the plant spread rapidly, filling pastures and overwhelming virtually anything that did not move—junked automobiles, living trees, and abandoned buildings. Susceptible to frost and thus limited to lower elevations, the plant does produce an attractive flower in the spring, more than offset by its capacity to overwhelm all other vegetation and vegetative matter. Because of an extensive root system and woody, tangled branches, the vine is very difficult to eradicate.[6]

Besides plants, the region's abundant rainfall supports a tremendous diversity of wildlife, some rare or endemic or both, some common, and some reintroduced. Fish include native brook trout (*Salvelinus fontinalis*) and nonnative rainbow and brown species in the cool mountain streams and colder lakes, along with largemouth bass (*Micropterus salmoides*) in the warmer waters. Reptiles include venomous snakes such as copperheads (*Agkistrodon contortrix*) and timber rattlers (*Crotalus horridus*); the steep, narrow, moist valleys create dozens of ecological "islands," sheltering a world-renowned number of different salamander species. Relying heavily on the acorn (and historically the chestnut) crops are black bears (*Ursus americanus*), with hunting competition from bobcats, coyotes, and (perhaps) mountain lions (*Puma concolor*). Elk have been reintroduced to the Great Smoky Mountains National

Park and occasionally wander outside park boundaries. Although less common in decades past, deer and turkeys abound and provide plentiful targets for hunters.[7]

Historical Setting

By the early eighteenth century, the Cherokees occupied the northeastern part of today's South Carolina. Large towns were located in the major floodplains, such as those along the Keowee and Big Eastatoee Rivers. As British settlements pushed inland from the coast, the Crown established forts among the Cherokees in order to secure their cooperation in wars against first the French and then the colonists. Although relatively short-lived, Fort Prince George, in the upper Keowee River valley, overlooked the largest Cherokee Lower Town, Keowee. By the end of the American Revolutionary War, however, both had been abandoned.[8]

With the removal of the Cherokees after the 1780s, the area opened for American colonial settlement. Originally large tracts of land went to land speculators, Revolutionary War veterans, and then the European American pioneers; their descendants "became the Appalachian gentry" by the early nineteenth century, anthropologist Allen Batteau wrote. Later came the small farmers, Batteau continued, "for whom acquiring land, however marginal, was a form of upward mobility." Forced to labor on farms in the floodplains and to work light industries such as mills and smithies were enslaved African Americans, always a component of southern Appalachian life. As folklorist Ted Olson noted, the traditional culture that evolved in the Blue Ridge area was a syncretism of several distinctive Old World cultures (from both Europe and Africa) that by necessity were tailored to a New World environment, with additional cultural information about wilderness survival borrowed from the Native Americans. By the early nineteenth century, "a distinctive Blue Ridge culture survived among those who remained behind."[9]

For the first nonnative settlers, "the surrounding forest was much more than board feet on the stump," environmental sociologist Donald Davis observed; "the mountain woodlands were a living matrix of plants, animals, and shared memories—a critical if not vital part of mountain life and culture." The abundance of free-flowing water allowed "small family farms to flourish independently without the aid of any earthly power and encouraged a sense of stubborn autonomy among the farming folk who settled there," historian David Fisher noted. Those who lived outside the major river valleys carved out farms in the remaining floodplains, free-ranged their livestock through the hills, and transformed much of their corn crop into "runs" of moonshine. Besides the distilling process—and the term "run"—these settlers contributed characteristic words to the area's dialect, such as the aspirated "(h)it," "you-uns" (plural for "you"), and the distinctive pronunciations of "chimley" (chimney), "strenth," and "lenth."[10]

Another significant contribution by these mountain residents was the establishment of the region's "dangerous" reputation. As early as the late eighteenth century, explorer John Lederer, one of the first colonists to explore the Virginia Blue Ridge, described the environment as "a dangerous, inhospitable, impenetrable place," with bears, cougars, wolves, and snakes. Researcher Katherine Ledford noted that by the early nineteenth century, the settlers were described with increasingly negative terms. The result, she concluded, is the first step toward the hillbilly stereotype, "a characterization that has, on one level, been used to justify economic exploitation of the mountains and mountaineers for over two hundred years."[11]

After the American Civil War, freed African Americans settled in small pockets throughout the South, including the southern Appalachians and the Upstate, farming and laboring. Existing with whites in an uneasy symbiotic relationship requiring tact and caution, Blacks often worked in the same fields and drank from the same dippers as their white neighbors yet simultaneously lived in fear of physical harassment and in relative poverty of resources. Segregated Black schools received inadequate funding and outdated textbooks into the 1960s. Throughout the Upstate, African Americans recall with vivid terror episodes of white gangs beating Black youths, gunfire aimed at Black houses, lynchings, and arson. Simultaneously, some white neighbors remained supportive or at least indifferent to the presence of Upstate Black residents.[12]

By the early twentieth century, journalist Horace Kephart described the "typical" mountain man: "Among reading people generally, South as well as North, to name him [as a southern mountaineer] is to conjure up a tall, slouching figure in homespun, who carries a rifle as habitually as he does his hat, and who may tilt its muzzle toward a stranger before addressing him, the form of salutation being: 'Stop thar! Whut's you-unses name? Whar's you-uns a-goin' ter?'" Historians McDonald and Muldowny provided an excellent summary of the traditional ways of life in the southern Appalachian Mountains prior to World War II. Claudia Whitmire Hembree offered a more intimate look at life in Jocassee Valley during this same time.[13]

Far from the legal centers of major cities and even relatively distant from county seats, people traditionally relied on neighbors (often also family) for support and settled disputes among themselves. Because of their borderlands cultural background and because they were beyond the reach of significant civil authority, historian David Fischer argued, "backsettlers shared an idea of order as a system of retributive justice. The prevailing principle was *lex talionis*, the rule of retaliation. It held that a good man must seek to do right in the world, but when wrong was done to him he must punish the wrong-doer himself by an act of retribution that restored order and justice in the world." Thus, from the late eighteenth century the idea of blood feuds became established in the mountains. Even into the twentieth century, "guns bulged in pockets, and knives were standard equipment," journalists Mike Hembree and Dot Jackson reported. Hembree and Jackson interviewed one Pickens County resident who explained, "'We had no law back in there [in the Horsepasture], and we needed none.'"[14] Those living within the law knew better than to report on those living just beyond the edge. Eccentricities of all types were tolerated, and "local characters" abounded in every neighborhood.

The most notorious region of the South Carolina mountains was an area called the "Dark Corner" around Glassy Mountain in northern Greenville County, "noted for illegal whiskey making, mountain feuds, numerous killings, and lawless acts." Mann Batson, a local journalist, cited a paper on the life of Amos Owens, specifically describing the residents of northern Greenville County: "'while not always depraved by nature, their peculiar calling forced them to become outlaws, and some of them outside of a deep-seated hatred on the "revenuers" as they were called in the vernacular of the moonshiner, and the deep-seated defiance of the "Government" were good neighbors, and in other respects honest men, the noblest work of God. In their isolated environments they could raise little but corn, and being remote from railroads and commercial centers, their bread and butter problem required that they make all they could of the cereal.'" Local historian Alexia Helsley believed that "the area's remoteness produced a small population of independent, self-reliant individuals with a unique culture. Families were close-knit. Few roads connected the Dark Corner with the outside world. . . . The cultural uniqueness of the Dark Corner persisted into the twentieth century." Helsley concluded: "Clearly, life in the Dark Corner could be dangerous. On moonlit nights, death walked the quiet byways. Law officers, according to some accounts, walked into the Dark Corner but not out."[15]

By the early twentieth century, cotton mills had become significant employers in most of the upper Piedmont towns, offering secure wages and drawing white mountain folk from the hills and valleys into electrified homes on paved streets and better schools. Jobs remained segregated by Jim Crow laws, and the best jobs and wages went to whites, while Blacks were relegated to segregated neighborhoods and menial tasks, such as loading and unloading wagons and trucks, cleaning bathrooms, and sweeping floors. Black cooks and nannies cared for white households, often enabling both white spouses to work.[16]

Through the decades of the twentieth century, as wage-labor capitalism siphoned more folks from self-sufficient farms, mountain valleys transformed into tourist destinations. Writer Edgar Bingham described the process of development for western North Carolina, equating tourism with "the exploiter of coal and timber." Initially, construction jobs would invigorate local labor, but more permanent jobs would be seasonal and lower wage, such as cooks, wait staff, and maintenance. To the tourists, locals may market craft items or garden produce, enhancing household income but transforming "authentic" crafts into trinkets. The ultimate result "is and has been to introduce a job orientation no longer directly associated with the land and to shift the local economy farther away from the self-sustaining pattern of the past," Bingham observed. As a result, Bingham concluded, mountain people become placed "in a position of almost perpetual subordination to the outside dominated financial manipulators, more firmly cementing the status of inferiority imposed upon mountain people by the rest of the nation."[17]

This general pattern reached the Jocassee Valley as well. The Jocassee Camp for Girls, managed prudently by Columbia (SC) sisters Sarah and Lucile ("Miss Ludy") Godbold, brought in outsiders and outsider ideas. Miss Ludy, a former 1922 Olympic track and field champion, was said to be so protective of her female charges that she "could back a bulldog off a plate of country ham," as a local inhabitant joked. Among others, the Godbolds hired their nephew Cash, who worked at the camp as a teenager: "I remember it as one of the best vacation spots I have ever experienced," he wrote; "the Whitewater River sang me to sleep at night and the cool valley was a wonderful alternative to the summer heat in Columbia." Hotels also brought in outsiders with new ideas, and the best known of the hotels was the Attakulla Lodge, named after a legendary Cherokee chief. "Collectively these summer people helped change the valley from a wintertime ghost town to a summertime paradise," a former resident recalled. Eventually, modernization penetrated even the deepest mountain coves, bringing electric lights, refrigerators, radios, televisions, and broadened horizons.[18]

At the same time moonshining persisted, clustered especially in locally known places. Former Jocassee Valley inhabitant Claudia Hembree admitted that "liquor making was a big part of the lifestyle of some of the residents. . . . The valley lent itself well to this activity, and the practice continued until the [Jocassee] dam was built. . . . The valley itself was remote, and it was easy to tuck a still away in a little 'holler' where it would go unnoticed by the outside world." Above Eastatoee Valley, Sugar Likker Road led into Reedy Cove, just below Sassafras Mountain. "'Up any branch up there, I can show you an old still-place, where one has been,'" a local man confessed to journalist Dot Robertson. Eastatoee Valley resident Daniel Hall had been told that "the old moonshiners could look at a stream and tell by what was growing on the stream how good that water was, and whether it would make good liquor." "'But you'll not find better nor more honest people anywhere than these people that have always been here,'" journalist Robertson reported her source adding. Karen Veal, a reporter for the *Athens Daily News*, interviewed in 1988 a retired Internal Revenue Service agent about his career in the late 1950s in northeastern Georgia:

> "Most of the arrests we made were of people who barely made a living making or selling whiskey," he said. "And a lot of times we would come up and take a fellow's still and his wife would cook us a fine meal. These people were good folks who wouldn't lie about what they were doing. They were usually farmers who made a little whiskey on the side. . . . We'd shut them down and then let them get started up pretty good before we shut them down again. We knew they would keep on doing it and they knew we would keep on arresting them," he said.[19]

Traditionally, American chestnut trees were a significant part of the southern Appalachian forests, constituting perhaps 25 percent of the tree species in some areas. In addition to providing food for wildlife, the nuts from the trees also supported the feral hogs of the early settlers and provided a valuable protein source for the settlers themselves. The chestnuts would roll down the mountains into the streams, Patrick O'Connell asserted, "so them hogs lay there where they drink water and eat until all they can do is get up on their front feet. They'd be so big, . . . couldn't get their back feet up. They're too heavy." Moreover, the bark produced tannin (needed for tanning hides); the wood was used for homes, outbuildings, and fences; and chestnuts could be peddled in the more urban areas for additional cash.[20]

Beginning in the Northeast in the early twentieth century, the chestnut blight (a fungus) eventually spread into the southern Appalachians; by the 1940s, all the mature trees had died. The ecological and economic impacts were devastating, so devastating in fact that environmental sociologist Donald Davis argued that the loss of this free forest commodity undermined the ability of Appalachian farmers to remain self-sufficient, driving mountaineers into the mill towns and urban centers and increasing their dependence on an externally controlled capitalist economy. "With the death of the chestnut," Davis concluded, "an entire world did die, eliminating subsistence practices that had been viable in the Appalachian Mountains for more than four centuries."[21]

As the chestnut trees died, timber companies expanded, providing mountaineers with another entry point into the larger capitalist market. Since the late nineteenth century, companies had extended iron rails and land purchases into the high country in an insatiable thirst for lumber. Besides workers, timbering needed logging roads that provided greater access into and out of steep-sided valleys.[22] Over the decades, corporations bought more and more land from private owners. By the early twentieth century, the Singer Sewing Machine Company owned large tracts of land in the Carolina mountains, but according to retired South Carolina Department of Natural Resources biologist Sam Stokes, the company cut only the highest-grade timber for veneers for sewing machine cabinets; once that timber had been cut, the land again went on the market. One principle purchasing company, Crescent Land and Timber, was a fully owned subsidiary of Duke Power (today Duke Energy), a company with an eye for much greater development.

Targeting the Keowee River and its tumbling mountain tributaries, in the early 1960s Crescent Land and Timber (Duke Power) began a major push to buy as much land as possible in order to construct an interconnected series of hydroelectric lakes and a cooling pool for an atomic reactor.[23] When the company "shook that money at them," a local woman reported, local residents were "scared out" by the imposing legal and economic power. "They stole that land from those people," she asserted. Families were divided by support or opposition to relocation. Churches and most identifiable graves were also relocated (in the 1930s, the Tennessee Valley Authority [TVA] faced the same challenges). "When construction on the [Jocassee] dam began in the 1960s," environmental writer John Lane summarized, "the utility cut the timber, moved out whole communities, tore down century-old farmsteads, inundated numerous major archaeological sites [such as the Fort Prince George and Keowee Town Cherokee sites], . . . and relocated summer camps [such as Camp Jocassee for Girls]." Yellow poplars over two hundred years old were felled, some as large as seven feet in diameter and two hundred feet tall.[24]

"So the die was cast," journalists Mike Hembree and Dot Jackson wrote. "Not many who lose a birthplace, a homeplace, a piece of sacred earth to a dam through eminent domain are going to bless the dammer. Certainly many did not bless Duke Power. But the expressions of the unwillingly displaced after 30 years are wistful, sometimes painful, rarely ever bitter." A local woman related that "we watched the water come up" every Sunday from the front porch of the new Mt. Carmel Baptist Church; her neighbors would watch the water cover the houses. It was a "sad feeling," she sighed. "'Miss it?'" one displaced woman told Dot Robertson. "'Oh, Lord yes. It was sort of like putting a wild pig in a pen. But we're used to it here, now'" (the TVA faced similar outcomes and responses in the 1930s).[25]

Regional naturalist Dennis Chastain described a generational difference between those displaced by the lakes and those of later generations. "'I would say the first generation of people who were displaced by the lakes generally don't use the area as a resource because it is a very different type of resource than what they were used to,' he said. 'They are largely hunters and people who just like to get out in the woods. But their children and grandchildren do tend to have boats, and they go up to the lakes and fish, water ski and camp. It's kind of unfair, I guess, that the first generation of people who were displaced didn't get a lot in return.'" Residents remain divided about the superior or inferior deals their ancestors received. While surrendering "a piece of sacred earth" (see chapter 6) proved to be disheartening to all, some reaped economic advantages and obtained more urbanized homes closer to medical and educational institutions.[26] Others, however, recognized the enormous economic difference between a "fair market value" for timberland far up a hillside and the tremendous increase in value when those same timbered hillsides become lakeside shorelines and are further subdivided into multiple units of million-dollar home lots in private gated communities.

During the flooding of the valleys, a movie crew collected footage for an upcoming Hollywood film, *Deliverance*, based on James Dickey's novel by the same name. The fictional story chronicles a horrific weekend float trip by four Atlanta businessmen, led by Lewis Medlock (played by Burt Reynolds), down a river in far northeastern Georgia just before the river is to be dammed for hydroelectric power. Some of the scenes were filmed on the Chattooga River (figure 4), with the climactic scenes on the Tallulah River in Rabun County, Georgia. However, the scenes depicting the moving of a church house, the exhumation of bodies from a cemetery, the bulldozing and dynamiting for dam construction, and the dammed river water inundating standing trees were all filmed at the construction of the Lake Jocassee Dam or the subsequent flooding of Jocassee Valley. With an almost exclusively male cast, the film depicts a rugged sense of masculinity in which all four canoeists are eventually penetrated (by a compound-fractured femur, a bullet, an arrow, and a phallus) and who "penetrate" the wilderness at the same time. "'Don't ever do nothing like this again,'" Sheriff Bullard (played by author James Dickey) ironically advises survivor Ed Gentry (played by Jon Voight). By the end of the movie, every viewer would agree with that command.

James Dickey's son Christopher, then in his early twenties, accompanied his father on location and described the story as "so compelling it became part of American culture." The movie spurred a tremendous increase in regional rafting companies, an explosion in regional tourism, and the declaration of the Chattooga by the federal government as a Wild and Scenic River in 1974, thus protected from development but restricted from former customary usage, such as roads to the riverbanks. At first welcomed by locals as protecting a valuable resource, federal restrictions on access to the river soon evolved into local resentment of external federal control. "Backwoods roughnecks trying to scare off paddlers sometimes fired warning shots from the bank, strung barbed wire across the river to slash up rafts, or even hauled boats right out of the water," writer Bronwen Dickey (the author's daughter) reported. A quarter-mile boundary on both riverbanks excluded road access for automobiles, making traditional river baptisms and family picnics much more difficult.[27] Forbidden by federal restrictions from herding his cattle to the river for water, a cattle rancher (according to a local river guide) jokingly objected that he would find it difficult to obey the restrictions because his cows could not read the "no trespassing" signs!

Inspired by the machismo of the movie's protagonists and supporting the new rafting companies, thousands of tourists (mostly suburban and college-aged males) flooded the Chattooga River valley to challenge the now-famous river even after federal protection. Like the movie's protagonists, most were unprepared for what they found, triggering a host of accidental drownings and expensive emergency rescues in inhospitable terrain. "This irresistible urge . . . to do the river—the 'Deliverance syndrome'—became a topic in the mainstream press, made the network news, and put a severe strain on the thirty-two-man Rabun County [Georgia] rescue squad and the local sheriff's department," writer Jerry Williamson observed.[28]

The new tourism interest also generated a backlash of regional resentment at the portrayal of local residents in the film. "'The movie didn't do Oconee County any good at all,'" a county councilman complained to a local paper in 1975; "'it was very inappropriate for our section and it has brought the river to the attention of a lot of people.'" An Oconee County resident told "under-cover" essayist Bronwen Dickey even a generation after the movie's premier that "'the worst thing that ever happened to this area was'" (and she feared what she expected to follow) "'that *Deliverance.*'" Bronwen Dickey continued:

> I was silently grateful that he didn't know who I was. Half of me wanted to apologize to him for something, and half of me didn't feel there was anything to apologize for. That was a feeling that I walked around with my entire time in Chattooga country: a shadow of guilt about the lasting legacy of *Deliverance* doing battle with the pride of my father's work. I've often wondered what it must be like to have grown up in North Georgia [or northwestern South Carolina] and to see your life, your town, your way of living flattened out for someone else's purposes and eventually turned into a national punch line.[29]

But Dickey could have added, not just a national punch line, but one also saturated with impending horror. "'Squeal like a pig' [an approximation of the line uttered by actor Bill McKinney playing the "Mountain Man" during the male rape scene] long ago entered the demotic vocabulary" of American popular culture, scholar Jerry Williamson noted.[30]

By the 1990s Duke Power (today Duke Energy) began marketing the former hillsides (now lakeshores) to private real estate development companies, which eagerly constructed a series of luxurious and sometimes exclusive communities along the lakeshores and in the mountain coves. Drawing upon his experiences in western North Carolina, Edgar Bingham described the general process: buyers from external major corporations offer land prices that "unsuspecting natives find difficult to refuse," since the prices are more than the value of land based on traditional subsistence. "Many sell" but then discover that local land values generally escalate quickly, leaving them the choices of becoming "menials for the developers" or having to leave the area completely. Those who remain recognize that their land is now too valuable for farming, so they sell to developers or become developers themselves. "When rich folks build million-dollar vacation homes on similarly expensive lots, land values and property taxes for everyone go up, and that happens with more frequency every year," Bronwen Dickey observed. New settlements also have integrated formerly isolated mountain communities into general American society, undermining more traditional ways. "The effect . . . has been to replace the natives with 'new' mountaineers—mountaineers without a real attachment to the land whose demands or expectations have tended to be in conflict with rather than in harmony with the mountain habitat,"

Edgar Bingham cautioned.[31] It is important to note that Bingham implies that the "real attachment to land" sentiment had been present among mountaineers before development had occurred.

One of the best-known regional developers was a local resident named Jim Anthony. Born in upper South Carolina, Anthony began his career as a telephone lineman but eventually branched into real estate. After his first major successful gated community, Cliffs of Glassy on Glassy Mountain in Greenville's Dark Corner, he developed several additional "Cliffs" communities both on lakeshores and in mountain valleys, emphasizing a healthy lifestyle in well-manicured surroundings. One of Anthony's more controversial developments was the Cliffs at Vineyards community (figure 5) near the now-submerged confluence of the Big Eastatoee River with the upper Keowee River, now along the shores of upper Lake Keowee. Financially pressed during the Great Recession of 2007–2009, in 2008 Anthony was forced to declare bankruptcy and sell his financial interests in the Cliffs communities. More recently, he has become involved in helping his son develop another property in northern Pickens County.[32]

While the residents of the new communities range from young professional families to summer second homeowners, more than half are year-round residents from the northern and midwestern states, retired from a hectic corporate life. These newer arrivals bring new accents and new values—and new tax dollars and new employment opportunities. These newcomers defined their developments as "communities" because they provided a supportive and active environment for residents. On the other hand, the socioeconomic homogeneity of the communities directly contrasted with that of the locals outside the developments, leading to significant disparities between those within and those outside the gates surrounding landscaped lawns.[33]

One Eastatoee Valley inhabitant offered an example to explain the difference. One morning she and her husband were walking their dog down the road threading through the valley (figure 6), and a group of bikers raced past wearing skin-tight black racing gear and helmets. The woman described them as ignoring the couple completely, just racing past as if they did not exist. Neighbors, she explained, would have stopped and chatted. When asked, she viewed this oversight by the bikers as a metaphor for the relationship between inhabitants and relative newcomers, who race through the valley without slowing to admire the scenery or talk with the locals. Another Eastatoee Valley resident described a time when traffic on a county road that led into the valley and also into a gated community had been blocked temporarily by a minor accident. All the valley residents got out of their cars and visited with their neighbors, while the gated community residents remained locked in their individual vehicles.

Compounding the social exclusion that many inhabitants feel toward these newer communities has been their physical exclusion, even from formerly public lands. Greenville County physician William McCuen, in an epilogue to his local historian wife's book about the Dark Corner, grumbled about one of Jim Anthony's Cliffs developments. "A large part of the Glassy Mountain escarpment has been taken away from public use and turned into a gated community of many large luxury estates and a near world class golf course. It is a closely guarded community of the wealthy and is off limits to the ordinary people — even many of whom owned some of this land as did their ancestors before them."[34]

Emerging as a lightning rod for the conflicting meanings and uses of physical and social space was McKinney Chapel in upper Pickens County. Originally on a hillside near the junction of the Eastatoee Valley with the Jocassee Valley above the Keowee River, the chapel remained a community gathering place for over a century. After the valleys flooded in the late 1960s, the country road leading past the church then dead-ended into Lake Keowee just below the dam for Lake Jocassee (a gravel road continues into a narrow side valley). For a time, locals still could visit McKinney Chapel and the cemetery there as well as boat, picnic, and hike at the lake. By the 1990s, however, Jim Anthony had developed the Cliffs at Vineyards Community and restricted lake access, and after a long court battle Anthony's company sued to gate the public road leading through the development to the chapel. While Anthony granted permanent public access to the lake, the chapel, and the cemetery and the gate guards wave anyone right through if one mentions those destinations, many inhabitants today refuse to pass through the gates, disdaining having to "beg permission" to visit a public place and their ancestors' graves. "Nobody can tell me where I can and can't go," an Eastatoee Valley resident remarked. Another local woman continues to drive the former rural speed limit of thirty-five miles per hour through the gated community, ignoring the gated community's more recent signs permitting only twenty-five miles per hour.

By the late 1990s, most of the prime real estate along the shores of Lake Keowee had been either developed or purchased. The Duke Energy Company then decided to begin divesting itself of the undeveloped and less economically valuable lands higher up in the mountains around Lake Jocassee. The company held sixty thousand acres of land and eventually sold it in several allotments by 1999. Eagerly purchased by the states, the wilderness property formed the core of Gorges State Park in North Carolina and the adjoining Mountain Bridge Wilderness Area of South Carolina, enclosing the upper reaches of the Horsepasture and Toxaway Rivers, or the so-called Jocassee Gorges. "Some call the Jocassee Gorges purchase the most significant conservation land deal in the Southern Appalachians since the establishment of the Great Smoky Mountains National Park," environmental writer John Lane declared.[35] Today, this expansive area of mountain wilderness ties federal, state, and private land into a prime recreation area.

Conclusion

The Blue Ridge Mountains of the southern Appalachians offer natural beauty within a dangerous landscape. Both residents and inhabitants agree. Furthermore, residents recognize the strong ties that inhabitants feel toward this land of majesty and menace, and yet inhabitants remind others that they feel differently toward this land of their great-grandparents. In fact, inhabitants feel that this ambiguous land has become almost like a member of their family, and they connect with their ancestral past by connecting with their ancestral land. Ultimately, the southern Blue Ridge area is contested space— contested between inhabitants and residents, between menace and majesty, and between commodity and personification. Because meaning depends on cultural context, the same geophysical material can contain multiple and multilayered meanings. There truly is "something in these hills," and what that "something" is will be explained in the following chapters.

CHAPTER THREE

In the Middle of Nowhere
Resident Attitudes toward Land

Since the early nineteenth century, nonindigenous in-migrants have occupied and thus have described the mountainous areas of South Carolina, frequently viewed as a remote frontier removed from civilization. In this dangerous and yet beautiful frontier have lived dangerous and marvelous people, depending on varied perspectives. A symbolically complex and liminal region containing peoples sometimes feared and sometimes treasured, the mountain area remains an ambiguous place with ambiguous folk to most residents without generational ties to the land. Without these generational ties, residents view their lands as a material possession to be safeguarded or sold depending on the vagaries of personal preference or market pressures. Being "in the middle of nowhere" may be an adventure or a curse, but the phrase (uttered by a lakeside community resident) provides a revealing perspective for introducing the cultural meaning of landscape from the perspectives of most relatively recently arrived residents in the area.

Dangerous Landscape

Today, resident and visitor views of the dangerous aspects of the mountains have been enhanced by two major influences: the traditional views of the mountains and their occupants as "primitive ancestors" and the more recent James Dickey novel and subsequent film *Deliverance*. Popular media depictions over the decades have not improved upon these images and perceptions. While the region had labored under the "hillbilly" stereotype for over a century, it was Dickey's novel and the Hollywood depiction of the whitewater canoe trip adventure that dramatically enhanced the "dangerous" image of the area for the nation in general.

Journalist Horace Kephart, a visitor who eventually came to live in the Great Smoky Mountains of western North Carolina, helped to establish the area's "dangerous" metaphor early in the twentieth century (for reasons discussed in chapter 1): "Those who have lived literally close to wild Nature know her for a tyrant, void of pity and mercy, from whom nothing can be wrung without toil and the risk of death. To all pioneer men—to their women and children, too—life has been one long, hard, cruel war against elemental powers."[1] These "elemental powers" included geophysical ones (waterfalls, whitewater rivers, cliffs), zoomorphic ones (cougars, bears, venomous snakes), and human ones (weird or dangerous characters).

Kephart elaborated on the human dangers. "Homicide is so prevalent in the districts that I personally am acquainted with that nearly every adult citizen has been directly interested in some murder case, either as principal, officer, witness, kinsman, or friend." Odd or unusual residents also caught his eye. "Every stranger in Appalachia is quick to note the high percentage of defectives among the people," Kephart observed; "however, we should bear in mind that in the mountains proper there are few, if any, public refuges for this class, and that home ties are so powerful that mountaineers never send their 'fitified folks' or 'half-wits,' or other unfortunates, to any institution in the lowlands, so long as it is bearable to have them around."[2]

In effect, Kephart argued, because of the geography of the mountains, the communities "were cursed with a considerable incubus of naturally weak or depraved characters, not lowland 'poor whites,' but a miscellaneous flotsam from all quarters, which, after more or less circling round and round, was drawn into the stagnant eddy of highland society as derelicts drift into the Sargasso Sea. . . . The vast roughs of the mountain region offer harborage for outlaws, desperadoes of the border, and here many of them settled and propagated their kind. . . . Hence the contagion of crime and shiftlessness spreads to decent families and tends to undermine them." While "there are some 'dark corners' of the mountains, mostly on or near state boundary lines, where there are bands of desperadoes who defy the law," Kephart reassured his audience, "elsewhere anyone of tact and common sense can go as he pleases through Appalachia without being molested." One of those "dark corners," Greenville's Dark Corner on the Carolinas' boundary, "truly was home to another culture locked in another time," local writer Joshua Blackwell felt.[3] Kephart's travel book, *Our Southern Highlanders*, strongly influenced the American cultural image of the "dangerous" Appalachians for the next generations.

Natural Dangers

Even by the late twentieth century, the area retained its dangerous and androcentric reputation. Carolyn Heilbrun, a writer for *Saturday Review*, described the area as a place "where women do not go, where civilization cannot reach, where men hunt one another like wild animals and hunt animals for sport." A *Deliverance*-era newspaper article summarized the area's dangers for the film crew: "Getting to the destinations along the overgrown banks is impossible. Large snake populations, cottonmouths, rattlers and copperheads, make land travel even more dangerous than the river, charging its way down 40 or 50 miles of boulder strewn river bed. A stern warning was posted by the production office for all those who were lost along the riverbank. They were not to wander aimlessly, because the forests can swallow them up in no time. Plus a number of stills, for making moonshine whiskey, abound in the area and the owners of the illegal stills don't take kindly to strangers."[4]

Early in the twenty-first century, James Dickey's daughter Bronwen Dickey ventured back into the Chattooga country to revisit the places described by her father and older brother. Although enchanted by the scene, Bronwen Dickey's description of the route to the Chattooga River also portends danger, in part driven by the geographical and social isolation of northeastern Georgia or northwestern South Carolina: "The dirt road drops off steeply to either side, without the added security of guardrails. Radio stations come in infrequently, if at all. Walk half an hour into the woods, and you're away from ninety percent of the population. Walk an hour into it, and you leave behind ninety-nine percent. It's just you and the limitless indifference of a vast, tangled country."[5] Dickey's phrase the "indifference of a vast, tangled country" encapsulates the symbolic complexity of the place and its people.

Because of the steep-sided gorges, mountain roads are narrow and twisty and contain significant gradient changes as they plunge into and climb out of river valleys. The lack of streetlights and house lights along the roads renders these roller-coaster avenues dark and dangerous at night. Donna Trask, living in the Eastatoee Valley as a teenager, faced the social isolation of her girlfriends being unable to visit her after school or on weekends: "Their moms would not let them drive to my house after dark. You know they were kind of scared for them to be out on the road. And of course . . . the parents themselves would not have been comfortable driving up . . . here after dark!" "As soon as the sun start[s] to go," Shirley Patterson admitted about her more urbanized visitors, "they [are] ready to head back to the city. . . . This summer we just had a beautiful cookout; everybody had fun and everything. . . . But as soon as the least little bit of light was starting to go and getting dark, you should've seen the driveway. [chuckles] It just cleared out." In fact, a local woman quoted a neighbor who had a relative from the Low Country (South Carolina's coastal region), which is very flat. This relative was so afraid of the narrow mountain roads that "she would not ride in a vehicle up the mountain. She would get out and walk behind the car and make her husband drive in front of her because she was so afraid of them."

Often the igneous or metamorphic bedrock forms cliffs that frequently begin as a gradually sloping surface, slippery with water, moss, or leaves and soon plunge into a sheer drop-off. Beds of mountain rivers sometimes flow over these cliffs, creating magnificent waterfalls such as Upper Whitewater Falls (on that river) and Rainbow Falls on the Horsepasture River. Waterfalls are frequently places of injury and death, as fools or unfortunates try to scale the cliffs and fall or waders attempt to cross the river above the falls, slip on moss-covered rocks, and tumble over the edge. Although signs warn against such practices, every year newspapers report more injuries and deaths.[6]

I have personally witnessed how quickly tragic accidents may develop from apparently innocuous actions. Sometime around 1989, my wife and I were hiking with a group of friends along the Foothills Trail in upper Oconee County, South Carolina. We took a side trail to obtain a better view of Lower Whitewater Falls (figure 7), one of a series of falls along that river as it cuts through the mountains toward Lake Jocassee. We were trying to cross a sloping rock face about fifty feet above the pools at the top of the waterfall. As my wife tried to walk across, she stepped in a small rivulet, immediately lost her footing on the moistened rock, slid uncontrolled down a steep rock face for about fifty feet, and landed in a five-foot–deep pool of water, just above the lip of an enormous precipice. She was unharmed, but we have never done anything like that again.

In one of the deepest mountain gorges flows the Chattooga River, standing in for the fictional Cahulawassee River in *Deliverance*. In his autobiography, Burt Reynolds described the Chattooga River as "fifty miles of white-water hell and deadly waterfalls. . . . On a danger scale of one to six, the river is rated a five—the second-most dangerous river in the U.S. You aren't supposed to go down in a canoe unless you're an expert." "Every day we set out down the river," Reynolds continued; "we ate lunch out of paper bags on the riverbank, because once you started down you couldn't go back. And every day, no kidding, one of us was saved by the others. All of us got tossed in the water, bumped against the rocks, gripped by the current." In the scene where Reynolds's character slides down the waterfall, John Boorman (the director) tried the scene first with a dummy, but the effect looked too fake. Reynolds then volunteered to do the stunt himself and plunged down the falls, cracking his tailbone, almost drowning in a hydraulic, and emerging with his clothes ripped from his body by the force of the current.[7]

After the premier of *Deliverance* in 1972, the river became extremely popular for floaters but no less deadly. "Floating use on the river increased from an estimated 800 people in 1971 to 7600 in 1972 and continued to 27,000 in 1974. Sixteen people drowned in the four-year period. Rescue squads were kept busy hunting the lost, injured, and killed." Buzz Williams, one of the founders of Chattooga Conservancy (a private group devoted to the region's ecological preservation), described the river as a "killer river" to Bronwen Dickey. Williams then elaborated: "'Several rapids are considered "certain death" if you are unlucky enough to fall into them.'"[8]

The river's volume, coupled with the steep mountain gradient, creates an extremely powerful current, as National Forest rangers discovered. Describing to journalist Andrew Sparks how they lost both their boats to the river, Earl "Preacher" Parsons said, "'White water pinned the boat to that rock like cement. Nothing was holding it except the force of the river, but we couldn't even budge it with pry poles.'" They lost the second boat "'as we carefully let it down on ropes. It got caught under a falls and nothing would budge it. We lost everything and didn't even have a cigarette.'" Journalist Robert Cullen described another situation where four novices challenged the Chattooga. They got into trouble at "Big Shoals": "We hit the entrance right, but suddenly we were in trouble. The current was too strong, and before we could make our sharp left turn, we were swept into some rocks and pinned there by the foaming water. Within seconds, the canoe was swamped. We could not move it, and it began to bend. The river was capable of breaking it in half and leaving us stranded." They were eventually rescued by another party. On April 11, 1981, journalist Bob Harrell wrote, a private party of nine entered the Chattooga River at Earl's Ford; most were experienced whitewater paddlers. One of their party, Skip Holmes, stepped into a pothole at Bull Sluice and perhaps got hung up on something. The safety man below the rapids threw a rope, and the man's "hands were seen to grasp and hold. Then began a tug-of-war against the momentum of the river. It was no contest. 'We know he grabbed the rope,' said [a companion], 'but no amount of pulling would do any good.' Oconee County Coroner Ted Durham would later identify rope burns on Skip Holmes' body."[9]

Wilderness and deep coves hide animals, including large carnivores. While black bears are occasionally sighted at local bird feeders or outdoor dog dishes in the mountain or lakeside communities, cougar (or mountain lion) glimpses are much rarer—if they actually have been spotted at all. Buzz Williams, in his interview with Bronwen Dickey in 2008, claimed that a Forest Service ranger on the Chattooga had been chased by a cougar, although his colleagues thought it impossible and teased him about it. Williams did not think it possible; "'probably just a bobcat,'" he reasoned.[10]

Human Dangers

After the debut of *Deliverance*, a swarm of visitors overwhelmed area communities, local writer Dennis Duncan explained. "The relatively peaceful and undisturbed communities of Mountain Rest and Long Creek [in upper Oconee County] were virtually overrun by people from metropolitan areas going to the river. All too often 'outsiders' demonstrated little regard for the mountain ways of life which they encountered. 'Baptisings' by local churches had been held in the river for many years. There were instances where floaters shouted obscenities at congregations participating in worship services on the river. There were also instances of people shooting at boaters from the banks." Environmental writer John Lane added reassuringly that while "unpleasant encounters with the locals were not uncommon, . . . no murders or rapes of 'outsiders' were reported."[11]

The locals figured prominently in James Dickey's story (and later in the film), and he opened the novel with a rather neutral portrayal of them. The character of Ed asks Lewis what life in the mountains is like now:

> Some hunting and a lot of screwing and a little farming. Some whiskey-making. . . . These are good people, Ed. But . . . they'll do what they want to do, no matter what. Every family I've ever met up here has at least one relative in the penitentiary. Some of them are in for making liquor or running it, but most of them are in for murder. They don't think a whole lot about killing people up here. . . . But they'll generally leave you alone if you do the same thing, and if one of them likes you he'll do anything in the world for you. So will his family.[12]

A few pages later, Dickey's description of the locals turned darker. The character of Ed says, "There is always something wrong with people in the country, I thought. In the comparatively few times I had ever been in the rural South I had been struck by the number of missing fingers. . . . There had also been several people with some form of crippling or twisting illness, and some blind or one-eyed. . . . I wanted none of it, and I didn't want to be around where it happened either. But I was there, and there was no way for me to escape, except by water, from the country of nine-fingered people."[13]

In May 1971, James Dickey's son Christopher wrote, Hollywood came to the "country of nine-fingered people," and the younger Dickey recalled that period with a little apologetic regret as he reflected on the time. Early in the film, Ed (played by Jon Voight) "looks through the window of a little shack and sees an old woman whose face is covered with skin cancers tending a spastic child whose head lolls pitifully to one side. . . . Of course, Hollywood paid these people and treated them as gently as it knew how to do, but it was hard to get over the feeling as the lights went on and the cameras rolled that souls were being stolen here." Christopher Dickey continued: "Each day [of filming] moved the cast and crew a few more pages into the story, farther along the river, deeper into the woods. All the horrors were foretold. . . . The fact was, you didn't know what might happen up here." As the most horrific scenes of the film were acted out, Christopher Dickey observed, the relationship with the locals (from his perspective) deteriorated. "We were starting to hear from our trailer-park friends [with whom the younger Dickey stayed during the filming] that there were a lot of people in these mountains who didn't like this film we were making. And you didn't know who might get it into their head to teach some of these movie people a lesson. There were plenty of real mountain men out there, with real guns. . . . I was scared. Scared enough to leave. But I stayed, because more than anything else I was afraid to admit how scared I was."[14]

For the film's most infamous scene, director John Boorman wanted authentic characters. Burt Reynolds remembered an old acting friend, Herbert "Cowboy" Coward, who was hired to play the "Toothless Man." When told what his companion would do to Ned Beatty's character in the film, Reynolds reported, Coward replied that he had done a lot worse things than that in his life. Even Reynolds thought the other mountain man, played by character actor Bill McKinney, was "a little bent." In the days prior to the filming of the rape scene, Reynolds increasingly feared that McKinney might take the scene too far; during the actual filming, Reynolds felt that his fears had been realized, and he rushed in to intervene. "It's the first and only time I have ever seen camera operators turn their heads away," Reynolds wrote. At the end of the filming, Reynolds recalled, "all of us were completely spent. . . . It had been a long, emotionally and physically grueling picture. Like the characters we played, we had the sense of surviving something hellish, something extraordinary, something we might not ever repeat in our lives." By his own admission, Reynolds learned the hard way what the sheriff (played by James Dickey himself) admonished the film's character of Ed: "Don't ever do anything like this again.'"[15]

Today, many retail outlets in the mountains rely on the area's "dangerous" reputation to sell merchandise. In addition to the various manifestations of the Confederate battle flag and the Tea Party's "Don't Tread On Me" yellow rattlesnake flag (both also very popular with some inhabitants), merchants readily capitalize on the decades-old fears generated by *Deliverance*. Popular T-shirt slogans read "The river's thrillin' / Till you hear the squealin'" and "Paddle faster / I hear banjo music." The first imprint refers to the infamous scene (in both the novel and the film) where Bobby (played by Ned Beatty) is commanded to "squeal like a pig" and then sodomized by the mountain man. The other imprint reflects the film's impending sense of danger revealed by the opening chords of "Dueling Banjos." Note that the film had such an impact on American popular culture and, more specifically, on visitor impressions of Chattooga country that both imprints continue to be sold almost fifty years after the movie's premier and need no further explanation—everyone understands to what they refer.[16] Of course, the commercial and cultural success of the T-shirts also reflect the even deeper cultural stereotypes of dangerous, uncontrollable mountains inhabited by dangerous, unpredictable people.

Even if visitors overlooked or ignored a perceived threat from the locals, many assumed that locals had a glaring lack of concern for the area's beauty because of the "trashed" landscape; of course, visitors could have contributed to this pollution as well. In the years before the Chattooga was declared a Wild and Scenic River in 1974, journalist Andrew Sparks wrote an article for the *Atlanta Journal and Constitution*, commenting as a visitor on the locals' use of the river. Sparks quoted Darold Westerberg, forest supervisor in Georgia, who had recently run the river with some friends. "'Some kind of supervision will be necessary if the river is to remain wild. One thing is already bothersome: the number of camps set up on the banks by hunters, fishermen, and people who float the river. The sites are littered with cans and plastic and they smell. You can project four or five years hence and visualize people just wallowing around in their own garbage.'"[17]

Lakeside community residents had the same concerns thirty years later as they shopped for real estate in the Upstate. "And I think what really [bothered us] more than anything," Jack Benson admitted, "was the areas that you had to go through to get to your home. And I mean, 'cause everybody has their own idea of how their place should look. But some of them [locals]—I don't know how they live the way they do, because they don't ever clean up after them. And that . . . wasn't what we had aspired to. I don't know if that's being kind of picky, or not. But still, the area [out West] that we grew up in and we raised our children in . . . was super clean, and everybody, they took pride in their property."

As another woman and her husband explored for potential retirement communities in the Southeast, they considered the Upstate. But, the woman admitted to a group of her friends:

> I think I'll be honest. . . . There was a stereotypical image. . . . But you say South Carolina, and there is an image like, "Whoa!" [Another woman interjected: "Rednecks."] Yeah, rednecks, motorcycles, you name it now. . . . But, when [we first came to the state] . . . I got into this place [Bob's Place, nicknamed "Scatterbrains," a former motorcycle bar near the border between South and North Carolina (figure 8)], and I was a little afraid to go inside, but we went inside, because we are pioneers, right? . . . The place is absolutely filthy, and I'm not going to eat. . . . And all of a sudden all of these bikers come up and they have Confederate headbands on. I said, "I'm not going [to move to South Carolina]. That's it."

Of course, the speaker (and her audience) did move to the state.

About two decades ago, *Time* magazine writer Steve Lopez discovered Bob's Place as he ventured from North Carolina across the state line into what he termed "Bush Country" for an article about the upcoming presidential election. "The Roadkill Grill is an outdoor barbecue pit on the property of Bob's Place," Lopez wrote, "a rustic beer tavern where the Confederate flag flies proud and the 'Hillbilly Poem' is stapled to an outside wall." The poem read: "There's a place on this Earth my people call home / these hills and hollows everywhere and lots of room to roam / We're noted for our hard times and God's great creation [highlighting a contrast] / We're the people of the Hillbilly Nation." Greeting Lopez was local Tony Johnson, who (Lopez wrote) had lost his voting rights since he was an ex-con (arrested on weapons charges) and then mimed at shooting a friend in a passing pickup truck. Johnson warned Lopez that as he approached, Johnson had him in his sights as well. In May 2017, Bob's Place was burned to the ground; arson was suspected.[18] As of this writing, the place has not been rebuilt.

The dangerous aspect of the area magnifies even more as African Americans visit this assumedly white space inhabited by "odd tribes" of "not quite white" hillbillies like those from *Deliverance*. In an essay titled "Birding While Black," wildlife biologist Drew Lanham describes his experiences working in the mountains of upper South Carolina as a naturalist for the Department of Natural Resources during his graduate school years. During Lanham's experiences in the mountains, "someone at the university joked about my degree being awarded posthumously," he observed dryly. "I imagine a scraggly haired hillbilly," he elaborated, "who is going to require things I'm unwilling to give. Past incidents don't fade quickly from memory, especially when the threats of danger were real, raising a sour-slick tang of bile in the back of my throat."[19] In that same essay, Lanham described an incident where he and a white female supervisor were checking on small mammals in the Jocassee Gorges wilderness when they were approached by three local white males in a pickup truck. Lanham continued:

> I'd heard that people in the mountains didn't like strangers of any color. I was a strange stranger, and maybe not the person locals would think should be working with a white woman. . . . My stomach knotted. I wondered how long it would take the authorities to recover our decomposing corpses from the rhododendron hells where these hillbillies would dump us after they did whatever the f**k it was they wanted to do. [expletive deleted] . . . I was on an edge that I'd only experienced in very bad dreams. . . . I didn't relax until we hit the asphalt road that would take us home with speed.[20]

Note that in her earlier narrative of venturing for the first time into Bob's Place, the speaker had described herself and her husband (and probably including the rest of her audience, all residents of a lakeside gated community) as "pioneers." In her view, then, she and her upper-class white friends were the first to settle this frontier, apparently inhabited only by wild animals, Confederate flag–wearing "rednecks," and "scraggly haired" hillbillies, beyond the pale of civilization and hostile to any strangers, especially "strange" ones. In her view, her gated community served as a metaphoric fort, establishing a secure space for these upper-class residents protected by symbolic and actual walls from the surrounding untamed wilderness and untamed savages. She and her gated community neighbors are thus pioneers settling a dangerous landscape.

Magnificent Landscape

This dangerous mountainous terrain, full of dark and mysterious hollows, treacherous rivers, menacing wildlife, and threatening hillbillies, may also be perceived by residents and visitors as welcoming, beautiful, inspirational, and even magical. From the perspective of these people, the natural landscape contains extraordinary beauty—after all, that is one of the reasons they chose to move to or vacation here. One of the mountain valleys that retains much of the charm of the larger but now inundated ones is that of the Big Eastatoee River. Beginning in tiny creeks just across the North Carolina line, the river draws from larger named creeks such as Wild Hog, Rocky Bottom, Laurel Fork, and Reedy Cove, creating a cool, clear stream winding through a crescent-shaped valley of farm fields, pastures, and homes (figure 6); cutting rapidly through a narrow cleft between mountains; and ending today at the gated community of Cliffs at Vineyards and the uppermost portion of Lake Keowee, near McKinney Chapel (figure 5). The valley has been described by writer Eugene Sloan as "one of the most beautiful, untamed regions in America. . . . Scenic vistas are unbelievable and, in summer, when the tall corn grows in rich bottoms, it is a sight to behold. Wild flowers, some extremely rare, bloom unseen except to the few who know the vicinity." E. A. Wilkes, a Methodist preacher traveling the circuit in northern Pickens and Oconee Counties in 1893, described the area around McKinney Chapel: "The county abounds in beautiful scenery. . . . The people dwell on creeks, and drink water from springs hewed out of solid rock."[21]

The Chattooga River valley, although tarnished by Dickey's novel and the subsequent film, was praised by journalist Leo Thralls in a newspaper article, using an anthropomorphic metaphor contradistinctive to Dickey's theme of hypermasculinity. "My only disappointment to Mr. Dickey's thriller is the locale, i.e., the magnificent terrain of north Georgia's mountains. . . . The mountains are gentle—feminine almost—and the natural beauty is as unspoiled, as uncommercial as any in the East. That's the joy of it: the serenity, the absolute true communion with Nature." Dickey's daughter Bronwen, visiting the same area thirty years later, utilized her engaging prose to help her readers experience the mountains with several senses. "You can feel it when you leave the pavement in North Georgia. Even in the dead of winter, the air wraps around you with the smell of mountain laurel, hemlock, and rhododendron, a smell just a notch sweeter than that of fresh-cut grass. The world unfolds in sheaves of green and gray and blue and brown, then folds back up in layers of shadow."[22]

Those who now live in the communities along the shores of the lakes created by the dams also recognize the beauty of the place. In fact, the beauty of the place overwhelmed their initial hesitation about purchasing homes in a "wilderness" area relatively far from grocery stores, medical centers, and cultural activities. One woman from a gated community explained:

We get up in the morning and pinch ourselves half the time. You know, we look out on that lake [Keowee] and think, "Geez, God; thank you! Not only for Your creativity but for allowing us to enjoy it." And to be stewards of it is a big responsibility. . . . We don't want to burn and cut down trees and kill all the animals; we enjoy them. Yeah, there is a sense of danger in going out in your backyard and seeing "Bart the Bear," but— . . . just the joy of sitting out on your terrace or your screened porch and watching a *huge* Carolina moon.

Residents, including those of lakeside communities, recognize the contradiction between a "beautiful area" that also presents a "sense of danger." As Carol Benson admitted, "I'm not too wild about the bears. . . . It's a little bit scary because I like to walk. . . . There was a couple little fawns yesterday that were out on the driveway. A lot of people have trouble; they [the deer] eat their landscaping and things like that. . . . And of course everybody has a concern about the bears, because how do you coexist with them?" On the other hand, Doug Massey acknowledged that "it's sort of neat to see them. I mean, we've had, bears were walking around our house." Another woman exclaimed, "I love the deer! I even like the idea of seeing an occasional bear—I don't know why! . . . But the sheer beauty, and like I say, a little bit of the threat, of the danger, is part of it. It's kind of exciting to me."

Creating New Homes and New Communities

Surrounded by what lakeside community residents (or newcomers in general) recognize as cultural and economic differences between themselves and their mountain neighbors and exacerbated by the perceived natural dangers of their surroundings, residents in upscale communities frequently (but not completely) turn inward, within the security of their manicured grounds. While some residents join local community organizations such as the Lions and Optimist Clubs and others help at local institutions such as schools and libraries, most newcomers socialize primarily with their own kind. "When you retire and you go to a new place," Gary Lee observed, "you leave dear friends that you've developed over many years, and the question is how are you going to connect that way in something" new?

In order to connect, many newcomers create a sense of community "like we've become a family here, too," a woman in a gated community explained. "I never knew my neighbors [where she used to live]; we never wanted to know our neighbors," she continued. "And that was so different when we moved here. My daughters were totally surprised that we knew who our neighbors were." Another woman added, "especially those of us who live here full-time—we are just like one big happy family. And I think that that is mainly because we all are out here in the middle of nowhere. And when we came to this spot, we didn't know anyone so we had to become one big, happy family." Today, Gary Lee admitted, "we have I think a number of people here now that we feel just as close to as people we've had for years and years before."

During a group discussion in a gated community recreation building, one woman acknowledged that she and her husband had moved nine times in their married life, "so, when it came time to retire, where was home? We don't have a home! We don't have a home. So you had to come up and find one. And that's basically what we did. . . . We've established activities and routines and made it our home by what we do." From this perspective, then, a "home" is created by activities and neighborly ties rather than by a specific generational tie to a specific location.

The activities creating a home community may vary. "I think one of the things that brings you really close here are your building experiences," Doug Massey offered, "the building experiences [of the lakeside homes] for the people here; you all can empathize and sympathize with each other because you've all had great experiences, horrible experiences. . . . So that brings you together. And then I think you've got your interest groups: golfers, tennis players, wellness people, people that are boaters, people that are equestrians. . . . There's a lot that goes on, so that draws you together." Another woman admitted, "Most of our activities are centered right here."

In fact, the activities within these secluded communities generate a sense of home and community and also produce a newly created sense of family. When Carol Benson and her husband first considered moving into their gated community, she worried "was I going to die [from boredom] sitting up there looking at the birds. But there's just way too much to do." One woman explained, "We came here [to her gated community] for the golf course and the lake, and we will stay here for the people. We have found an amazing community of very welcoming people who are willing to do all kinds of things and share all kinds of expertise and—it's just been an incredible experience to be here. We came for the beauty of the area, and of course the golf course, and have just found so much more than that."

Pam Lee, a gated community resident, elaborated:

The [lakeside] communities are really what have changed the face of these areas. People from all over the country are moving here because of the communities. . . . And it's been wonderful. We have really loved being here. . . . The people [inside] are fantastic. . . . But as . . . more and more people are moving in here and the houses are getting larger and larger—we're talking eight to ten thousand square feet homes here—then I think people began to demand different things as they move in and invest more money. And they want a certain kind of life that may evolve to something else.

As wealthier gated and retirement communities continue to mushroom around the lakes and in mountain valleys, the residents of these upscale communities believe that their demands for improved infrastructure (e.g., better roads, utilities, and fire protection) impact their "redneck" neighbors in positive ways. For example, as developers build more expansive and more expensive homes, fire protection has improved, evolving from rural volunteer fire departments to more professional ones whose contracts, however, frequently require first responses to be within the expensive communities and (if possible) then to the neighboring locally occupied mobile homes and smaller houses outside the gates. Water and sewer lines reach farther into the mountains, replacing septic systems and well water. Rural roads may also be repaved and improved. Cell phone towers crown wooded hilltops. Internet service expands. Restaurants and upscale grocery stores open farther out in the countryside but with gourmet menus and offerings frequently out of economic reach for many locals.

Upscale residents acknowledge the growing economic gulf between themselves and those outside the gates. "Before we came," Doug Massey explained, "there were no haves or have-nots; there were just the haves. But then you get a point of comparison. . . . I've got my own little country store here, and wait a minute, who's the guy in the big Lexus? You know, and then you see eighteen Lexuses. And then you see these houses, these McMansions going up on the lake." When his wife asked if he had personally experienced this recognition of an economic division, Mr. Massey replied, "Oh, I sense it. I mean, I go to the local place, see, where I buy my gas. I can tell you he doesn't consider me one of his."

On the other hand, Doug Massey explained,

I think one of the challenges that communities like The Cliffs have is getting their story out because to the locals we're just a bunch of rich people that have come in here and taken over—because we can afford it. . . . Yeah, we have means. We've worked hard for them. But we also give a tremendous amount back, and that's a hard story to get across. . . . The privatization of this road [to McKinney Chapel] was a big issue. That creates community animosity. And now, you got to go through a gate to get to a road where you probably hunted as a kid and fished as a kid so that's—you try to balance that with, you know . . . we put our trousers on one leg at a time, and we try to give a lot back to the community.

"We all have a feeling that we need to give back, that we've been so lucky," Carol Benson recognized. "And you know, as much as we like to sit and look at the lake, we still want to be active. . . . We have a little elementary school [Holly Springs, recently closed due to consolidation] . . . that every spring, we all get together, and we teach the children after school, because there's a great wealth in retirement talents that are out there." For example, Mrs. Benson stated that her husband taught a "little woodworking class," she taught a computer class, and other neighbors taught quilting and photography. A retired pilot explained to grade schoolers how airplanes fly. "We do a lot of work with Helping Hands [local charity to help abused children] and United Way and a lot of those type things," Benson added; "it's more rewarding to us, than anything."

Another positive transformation is the greater appreciation for and financial support of local historical preservation efforts and overall interest in local history—at least some aspects of local history. "Well, I think we've also grown," Doug Massey admitted. "You know, we know more about this area than we probably know about our area at home, and I don't know why. . . . But we've certainly taken an interest in this, and the whole Cherokee history is pretty fascinating. . . . It's just something that sort of grabs your attention." Carol Benson added, "And . . . the different people that write about this area, and the books and of course, you know, the more history I can read about. Reading about how the lake was formed with Duke Power, and Keowee, and the Indians around here. I mean this is—it's exciting!" Of course, reading local histories about the protohistoric Cherokees, American colonial settlement, or the tragedy of land loss due to the lakes enables recent arrivals to learn a somewhat romanticized story of their new homes without acquiring a deeper understanding of the meaning of land shared by their current inhabitant neighbors.

While reading these local histories and in talking to some of their local service providers (plumbers, electricians, media repairers, construction and landscape supervisors), newcomers recognize the close ties to land that their "redneck" neighbors acknowledge, but their understanding of the reason for this sentiment may not be as profound as that of inhabitants. "No question about it," Doug Massey explained, "classic agri-philosophy—what the land gives you take and you give back. And then the next season you do the same thing over again. Oh yeah, that's pretty clear to us down here. You know, whether you're hunting or planting or reaping and then, the people that we've met, all the homesteads. . . . It was all about the land." His wife Sally added, "But you do start talking to a lot of the people that come in [to work on the house], . . . and they've lived here for a long time. . . . Their parents have an original cabin right up the road and talk about when they were here. . . . I've heard all these stories and, you know, you're not even aware of what you have cut off from these people."

With this sentiment, the Masseys reflect an assumption held by many newcomers. For example, geographer Yi-Fu Tuan, in his discussion of space and place, argued that "sedentary agricultural people" typically have a sense of "rootedness in the soil," and thus "pious feelings toward it seem natural." John Opie supported this perception, tying a "primitive" sense of place specifically back to the region's Scots-Irish heritage.[23] As chapter 6 demonstrates, however, inhabitants have a more complex explanation of their connection to the land of their ancestors.

Newcomers recognize the effectiveness of real estate developers (who created their communities) to overwhelm locals with powerful economic and legal resources, thus forcing them out of valued areas. As one long-term resident originally from the Northeast observed, locals "feel resentful of people coming in, like developers or people putting up a factory or something like that; it's because they will be taking away some of that possibility" for hunting, fishing, gardening, and sightseeing. Ultimately, newcomers believe the tragedy stems from the loss of "just having that freedom to do all these interesting things you do up here." Newcomers recognize the sacrifices that some of their "redneck" neighbors had to make in order to allow developers to create their wonderful communities in their beautiful lakeside or mountain settings. Sally Massey admitted, "We could really understand where people were coming from when we came into this community because we're the ones coming in building and taking over their land where they could hunt and fish and swim and, you know, go to the gorges." Another woman added, "Well, when some of us came we got into the middle of this controversy about the gate [controlling access to McKinney Chapel]. . . . Because I remember the first time we talked to the guy from DirecTV he had nothing to say good about [her gated community] . . . because we were taking the very land that he and his buddies used to hunt on away from him."

The propensity to hold onto family land or homeplaces, even after they appear to be economically worthless, puzzles newcomers. Apparently abandoned homes or trailers, boarded up or covered with kudzu, dot the mountain landscape. Yet, extended families vigorously defend and own these places for generations. Social worker Jack Weller perceived this practice as a source of family stress. "In Appalachia great quantities of such land have been left by fathers and grandfathers to their children, who now hold the property jointly. Those who want the land for themselves cannot buy it from the others, who do not want it but don't want to see anybody else in the family have it. Thus it is passed down to each generation's children, the ownership being spread thinner and thinner while the land and buildings stand unused."[24]

"The child knows the world more seriously than does the adult," geographer Yi-Fu Tuan asserted. "This is one reason why the adult cannot go home again. This is also one reason why a native citizen knows his country in a way that cannot be duplicated by a naturalized citizen who has grown up elsewhere. Experienced spans of time, at different stages in life, are not commensurable." According to Tuan, then, newer residents of these developments cannot perceive the land in the way multigenerational local residents perceive it.[25]

"Once stripped of sedimented human meanings," archaeologist Christopher Tilley observed about land, and thus "considered to be purely epiphenomenal and irrelevant, the landscape becomes a surface or volume like any other, open for exploitation and everywhere homogeneous in its potential exchange value for any particular project. It becomes desanctified, set apart from people, myth and history, something to be controlled and used." Viewing land as desanctified, devoid of memory, and open for exploitation fits what Tilley described as a typical Western view of the land, a view shared by general American culture. According to anthropologist Margaret Rodman, Marxist urban geographers have also examined the contrast between "entrepreneurs concerned with exchange values [speculation] and residents concerned with use values."[26]

Although in a few ways the residents I have interviewed in the gated communities represent a group of people somewhat distinct from typical Americans, my intention here is for them to reflect the common American attitudes toward land and (more specifically) the southern Appalachian Mountains and their inhabitants. Marxist geographer David Harvey argues that under capitalism, "everything under the sun must be . . . subject to commodification, monetisation, and privatisation." "Nature is necessarily viewed by capital," Harvey continues, "as nothing more than a vast store of potential use values—of processes and things—that can be used directly or indirectly (through technologies) in the production and realisation of commodity values. . . . Natural use values are monetised, capitalised, commercialised, and exchanged as commodities. . . . Nature is partitioned and divided up as private property rights guaranteed by the state." In Harvey's view, capitalism reduces nature into exclusively "functionalist aesthetic values." Increasingly, Harvey notes, consumers "treat their home as a short-term speculative investment rather than as a place to create a solid and settled life." Land that does not add financial value is seen as wasted and is thus potentially acquirable for "improvement." Because of "vulture capitalism," though, development may be uneven, and thus capitalism may "feed off the destruction of ways of life in whole territories if necessary." Eventually under capitalism, David Harvey continues, "dispossession and destruction, displacement and construction become vehicles for vigorous and speculative capital accumulation as the figures of the financier and the rentier [property owners], the developer, the landed proprietor and the entrepreneurial mayor step from the shadows into the forefront of capital's logic of accumulation." Inevitably, Harvey concludes, "affections and loyalties to particular places and cultural forms are viewed as anachronisms."[27]

From this perspective, then, to many area residents (as with most Americans), land is an economic commodity that may be partitioned, measured, and sold. As a commodity, valuable for certain commercial and aesthetic characteristics, land is secular in that it is not infused with spirituality. Land is also a place for activities but is atemporal in that social actions and generational time are not directly connected, because landowners move multiple times from place to place and the same physical place may be owned by serial strangers. Questions such as "where are you from" are often difficult to answer or are answered in vague terms ("from the Midwest"). Land reserved for uses other than commercial ones "needs" to be developed, and such development may create islands of relative prosperity like fortresses surrounded by frontiers. And those outside the fortresses, holding onto family lands for noncommercial reasons, appear to be quaint, anachronistic, "contemporary ancestors." From the perspective of residents and visitors living within general American culture, land may be both menacing and majestic; it may be home, but it is not anthropomorphically alive.

Conclusion

These resident perceptions view the history of the region as focused primarily on that of the Native American occupation with less recognition of the more recent period, especially of the late nineteenth and early to mid-twentieth centuries. When discussed, that period is often romanticized or barely acknowledged. Thus, lakeside community residents recognize the "distant" history of Native American occupation of the lands they now occupy, but residents can rest comfortably knowing that they had nothing directly to do with Cherokee removal from upstate South Carolina in the late eighteenth century. On the other hand, more recent displacement of locals is perceived as the loss of the land's utility; that is, the tragedy of land loss is seen by newcomers as troubling because locals lost the *use* of their lands and not for any deeper symbolic reasons.

This concept of land value as measured by utility also explains the newcomers' created sense of "community." To residents of these restrictive developments, a sense of community is formed from shared mutual activities (such as constructing a house, golfing, boating, or socializing) as well as a sense of the shared insular life as frontier pioneers within upper-middle-class secure enclosures "in the middle of nowhere." While newer residents hear from their local contacts about the personal importance of the landscapes now covered by the lakes and recognize that the submerged land was "valuable," that value is determined by a typical American cultural value of utility as measured by what could be done on or with the land (farming, hunting, or fishing) or in economic terms (market value). Many newcomers also perceive the local connection to land as somehow "primitive" or even childlike, an ancestral tie to land paralleling that of other smaller-scale agricultural societies. Since inhabitants have a difficult time expressing to themselves what the land means to them culturally, they would have an even more difficult time explaining their perceptions to newcomers and expecting newcomers to comprehend and appreciate those feelings. Consequently, then, residents view land as typical Americans would or as they *expect* inhabitants do, not as the inhabitants *actually* do. Inhabitant perceptions of land are presented in the next three chapters.

CHAPTER FOUR

A Pretty Primitive Feeling

Inhabitant Attitudes toward Land

"A pretty primitive feeling" accurately reflects the ambiguity of the meaning of the mountain landscape from the point of view of inhabitants. Assuming "pretty" to be a synonym for "very," the phrase indicates the sense of wildness and danger associated with the mountains (and their occupants) of upper South Carolina. On the other hand, placing a comma after "pretty" and assuming that the word means "attractive" combines both themes of menace and majesty together. Inhabitants recognize the beauty of their home but with an even deeper sensorial perception than their resident neighbors. At the same time, as members of their own culture, inhabitants also acknowledge the dangers in their landscape but perhaps see them in more detailed ways: the natural ones of undeveloped mountainous wilderness, the faunal ones of venomous reptiles and large-bodied predators, the human ones of eccentric or lawless neighbors, and even the supernatural ones of unexplained sightings, sounds, or events. Like residents, inhabitants acknowledge and mediate this contrast between menace and majesty, but inhabitants process this synthesis with much greater detail than their resident neighbors.

Anthropologist Melinda Wagner, interviewing locals in the southwestern Virginia mountains and utilizing a slightly different methodology than I use in this book, discovered the exact same sentiments. Among other techniques, Wagner and her colleagues calculated the time locals spent talking about their natural surroundings and then analyzed the results. Based on her team's research, Wagner found that for locals, "nature is used, nurtured, admired, feared, and kept at bay. The length of time residents spend talking about nature and the detail they use in their talk symbolize its significance in their lives."[1] The same is true for the well-established folks in the mountain counties of South Carolina.

Beautiful Landscape

Perhaps since its submergence has been best documented, the Jocassee Valley and the neighboring Horsepasture area have been widely described and often romanticized. Debbie Fletcher depicted the Jocassee Valley she visited every summer as "the nearest place I knew to heaven on earth." Fletcher remembered that the valley "had a dusty road which followed every bend in the river as it wound its way into an enchanted land. A pristine valley tucked peacefully away in upper Oconee County, Jocassee's life was the Whitewater River. . . . It was always a joy to be back!"[2]

"I mean, there's no lake that's ever been made that can compare to a square foot of that land up there," Ralph Glenn echoed. "There are parts of it [that] were almost other-worldly. . . . In the summer [it] had this sort of high-humidity, deep, deep green sort of moist feeling about it." The Whitewater River was "such a clear water that you weren't sure about the depth," Brenda Kendrick reminisced. "I mean, you'd think just walking in ankle deep, and you'd be knee deep. It was a beautiful valley, beautiful area," Kendrick sighed.

To the north and east of the Jocassee Valley was the Horsepasture area, described by writers Gerald Orr and Ann Tankersley: "The Horsepasture is a natural formation up near the North Carolina line—a spectacular amphitheater ringed almost completely by the cliffs of the Blue Ridge Escarpment. . . . Beautiful waterfalls spill like lace down the sides of steep cliffs."[3] Before it was flooded, "they called the Horsepasture 'The Garden of Eden,'" Brian Alexander explained, "and when Duke Power come in here in the '60's—as far as my opinion is, they 'rurn'd' it all." "You wouldn't believe what was done away with," a woman who once lived near the Horsepasture asserted; "it was the next thing to paradise" up there.

"There was a place . . . up Horsepasture; it was called 'The Narrows,'" Mike Davidson remembered. "And it was solid rock. . . . And two rivers come together there. . . . And we'd go up there and camp. . . . And you just didn't get no prettier than that water right up there. . . . You know it was unspoiled, very few houses in the valley. . . . People'd go in there and camp, but nobody lived back in there. . . . But it was just gorgeous. And like I say, you could drink the water, it was so pure." Kayte Lessor lived in Sapphire, North Carolina, and helped protect the river above the lake. "'I've never been to a place as wild as the Horsepasture seems to be,' she said. 'It's a different kind of river. It's narrow and really wild. . . . It's something that's been there millions of years. It's so beautiful, so wild and untamed.'"[4]

Jerry Vickery lived along the upper Keowee (downstream from the Jocassee Valley) and remembered the river near his home:

The river was such a wonderful place. Getting into it was like entering another world. . . . Playing in the river made our world right. It gave us purpose and appreciation for nature. It gave us quality family time where we learned to take care of one another. It taught us respect for the land and how to work it without spoiling this wonderful river. . . . In places the laurel and ivy would form an arch reaching almost all the way across the river from bank to bank. At this time [1950s] the river was so clean that you could drink water from the river itself. . . . This river, to me, was the closest thing to Heaven on this earth.[5]

The Chattooga River, now protected under the federal Wild and Scenic Rivers program, enchants locals or those who have become so. "'It's magic out there,'" whitewater river rafter Dave Perrin told Bronwen Dickey, "speaking of it [the Chattooga River] with the tenderness one usually reserves for a first love," Dickey added. Perrin, Dickey noted, began his career decades ago "as a longhaired raft guide, and like them, the river got under his skin."[6]

While the Chattooga flows freely through a narrow, rocky gorge and while the wider Jocassee, Horsepasture, and upper Keowee Valleys are now underwater, the Eastatoee Valley preserves (on a smaller scale) some of that same river valley beauty (figure 6). Country veterinarian Gerald Orr described the "beautiful Eastatoee Valley" as "one of nature's grandest places: a mountain-rimmed stretch of meadowland carved out by the clear, rocky waters of Big Eastatoee and Mill Creek."[7] A long-term inhabitant of the valley described her valley home in intimate detail:

And, sometimes you come in [to the valley] and there's this marvelous sunset beyond you, and you think, well, this is the best place in the world to live. . . . I have a special curve up there on the mountain that I've always been enchanted with. . . . It has hemlocks and mountain laurel and birch trees . . . and in June when the rhododendron bloom in there it looks like snow falling because there are all those lovely white blooms. . . . And when it snows, it's a wonderland to me, just perfection. . . . And in the spring and summer, I always roll my window down when I'm coming beside the little branch that runs right beside the road so I can hear it and hear the shoals as the water rushes off over them.

Ryan Trask, the woman's neighbor, added, "Eastatoee [Valley] has always been special. The water, the mountains, the trees, everything . . . ; it's kind of separate and apart. And you're blessed if you can spend time in it. And so as a little kid, it was one of my favorite places on earth to go. . . . It smelled different, and it looked different, and it felt different. It's a pretty primitive feeling, I guess." Another Eastatoee Valley inhabitant appreciated the "purity of the mountains," because "everything's just running off. All of the waste and everything is going that way"—downstate. Another valley dweller concluded, "You know, if I die tomorrow . . . it was worth it. You get out here and get up in the morning and you get to [look] . . . at a scene like this [view from his front porch]. If you get to do it a few days, that's more than most people get to do in a lifetime."

Above the valleys along the Carolina state border, the unflooded lands are remote and almost wilderness. Regional naturalist Dennis Chastain described this area as "'almost primeval. . . . You can go back in hemlock groves in there where three men can't reach around the trees,' he said. 'There are huge oak and poplar cove forests. It's one of the few places in this region where you can at least get a sense of being in the wilderness. I compare it to Yosemite.'"[8]

Locals often connect the land's beauty to their predominantly Christian faith. Bernard Quinn explained: "Especially when the sun is there about almost down. . . . You can kind of look like you're going to get close to . . . the Good Master. . . . You can see some of His workings. We don't know nobody else who could do all that! . . . To see them hills going down and coming up, and the little curves in the mountains and the roads and all. That's fascinating to me. . . . I'll drive up there [to the mountains] . . . just to see that. Especially in the fall when the leaves are turning; yeah, it's beautiful."

"My sister-in-law and I took a ride into Asheville [North Carolina] to see the foliage," Shirley Patterson recalled. It was "absolutely picturesque. And as we was riding, I was pointing out . . . the vibrant colors. . . . And she said to me, 'Those are God's paintings.' [pause] And that stuck to me—those *are* God's paintings. Those trees in all different colors, all different shapes, all different sizes. All this He gave for our beauty. . . . These are His paintings. He goes out there with His paint brush . . . and He paints all these beautiful colors. And we ride through the foliage, and we just take it all in. . . . He gives us something different every season, to take in." Brenda Kendrick supported Patterson's observations: "'God, I know you made this. . . . It's just an awesome feeling. . . . This area is so changeable. . . . It's beautiful in the spring. It's gorgeous. But then in the fall, . . . brilliant colors—I don't think I've ever seen such brilliant colors. And it's just like, I thought, you know, if I could paint, I'd love to paint this. . . . I love to go to the beach, but there's nothing like the mountains." "It might be just the feel of the wind and the smell of the air, you know?" Marsha Baird explained. "I've always loved the mountains. . . . And there's something about the beauty of that look that makes me catch my breath. And it changes always. . . . It changes the clouds in the mornings and the fog in the evening and the sunsets. It's always changing, and it's just always something different to look at."

"I love the mountains," college student Kayla Radcliffe admitted. "I mean, since I was really little I was just like, 'Wow—those are really, those are awesome!' . . . So, growing up I knew, I mean I loved living there. I loved the animals, I loved the plants, and being able to go out in the woods to see these things. . . . Honestly, I feel like I'm kind of indebted to it."

In this quote, Kayla Radcliffe tried to explain her "indebtedness" to a physical place, a place many inhabitants have described with the intimacy of detail that lovers know of each other's faces. Inhabitants provide not only descriptions of valleys and cliffs and rivers (descriptions residents and visitors would also be able to provide), but inhabitants then add more intimate details, such as specific rapids, road curves, hillside hollows, rock formations, and even individual trees. The connection to the places arises through multiple sensory experiences—the sights of fall colors, the sounds of falling water, the smells of rhododendron, the tastes of spring water, and the touch of moist earth. Moreover, inhabitants also recognize that the seasons transfigure these sensory experiences, enhancing the area's diverse beauty month by month and then returning to familiar sensations again year after year. Inhabitants feel both a physical and an emotional connection to these places, crediting a spiritual creative force as the designer for their cherished surroundings. Inhabitants see the same physical reality as their resident neighbors, but inhabitants do more than see—they experience their surroundings with all their senses and connect this sensorial experience to the supernatural as well. The resident's perspective of the land's economic utility and value (and beauty) cannot compare to the inhabitant's perspective of that same land's spiritual and emotional experiences toward that beauty. This "indebtedness" that inhabitants feel to their land acknowledges this connection.

Dangerous Landscape

Travel narratives as far back as the early nineteenth century have described the Appalachians in dichotomous terms, as a "landscape that can be at once horrific and sublime."[9] Inhabitants recognize that the same land to which they feel such powerful emotional and spiritual ties also hides a great number of dangers emanating from the natural landscape, from specific animals, and also from some of their neighbors. "There's something in these hills," Joe Sherman wrote proudly in his essay about his alma mater, and James and

Margaret York (upper Pickens County) echoed to me his exact words almost forty years later but with a more ominous and ironic twist. "There's always been something in these hills," Mr. York offered during an interview. "No matter how far you go, there's always something in the hills." But in contrast to the majestic meaning Sherman had intended, Margaret York then elaborated: "Liquor making, chicken fighting, [and] dope growing."

Natural Dangers

Just as residents and visitors noted the ambiguous danger of impenetrable darkness in a wilderness area, inhabitants recognize this as well. Benjamin Craig, who lives with his wife Denise at the upper end of a narrow hollow in upper Pickens County, acknowledged that "it's fairly dark here. . . . You get a little bit of moonlight and some starlight and stuff like that. . . . So we rode over there [across their property] in the truck. . . . And I turned off the truck and stepped out and I said, 'Good God Almighty! I can't see my hand in front of my face!'" Cynthia Niles, who lived for years at the end of the road in another narrow mountain valley, recalled a time when "there was one guy, they were from Greenville. . . . And . . . it was about dark and there was a knock on the door and I went . . . to the door and this woman, her husband had run off the road and she had a three-year-old child with them, and the baby had got throwed out on the bank. And, she had gone down with the truck, and her husband, she said the windshield was broke out and that's how she got out. And her husband drownded."

Steep mountain slopes could even collapse on the narrow, winding roads. Claudia Alexander remembered a time when she was about sixteen and attended a church across the North Carolina state line. "I can remember hearing this big rumble," Mrs. Alexander recalled. "Didn't know what was going on. And they had a landslide up on that road. . . . And that whole mountain slid off in the road, you know. . . . We would drive up there and [her brother] would park his car and we would walk over those big rocks [to get to church], and then either the preacher or one of the deacons or members would pick us up and drive us on up to the church and bring us back."

One of the inherent dangers in steep, forested mountain slopes is fire. One retired forest ranger, Peter Abney, elaborated. "Mountain fires are dangerous—very dangerous." The challenge, Abney continued, is that mountain hollows act "just like a chimley; I mean it's got a draw to it." Another retired forest firefighter, Charles Watson, remembered a time when his team "went over a ridge to get the ridge 'tween us and the fire. And just before I went over the ridge, I looked back, and that blaze [was] coming—Lord, it was a hundred fifty foot tall. I was wondering to myself . . . what hell looks like, when I looked back over my shoulder. And so much smoke blowing over that it was like being out on a moonshiney night. You see how to walk, but it's just like moonshine."

One of the consequences of upper-class real estate development projects is that newcomers often want to live on the tops of ridges and hills, unlike earlier settlers who lived near sources of water on flatter tillable floodplains. These new mountaintop homes require narrow, twisty roads and steep driveways to access the houses. Retired firefighter Watson cautioned, "Now, they [are] going to lose some houses, because you take a lot of these developers, . . . they build these houses up on the side of that mountain, and if a fire ever starts on the southwest side of them houses with that upslope draft, they couldn't get enough fire trucks up that mountain to water it out. No way in the world."

Besides fire, mountain dangers may also come from water. Journalist Mike Hembree described the rivers flowing through and down the South Carolina Blue Ridge. "The Whitewater, Thompson, Toxaway, and Horsepasture are a quartet of wild rivers, each unique, . . . like marching sisters they stride across some of the roughest countryside in the entire sweep of the Appalachians, much of their wild beauty hidden from view because of an environment that often is stark, forbidding and dangerous."[10] These four rivers tumble through narrow gorges, and inhabitants respect their power. One man recalled the narrows on the Horsepasture, where the powerful river funneled through a fifteen-foot channel. "I mean swift," he observed. Then he continued the story: "And it was a Lowe boy that lived . . . in the Horsepasture, and they was seining [fishing by long net] and he got in that swift water and it sucked him under and drowned him."

Eventually some of these mountain rivers formed the more placid Keowee, still powerful especially in the upper reaches. Doyle Porter remembered that "one Sunday after church, our whole family went . . . for a riverside picnic. Of course, we children played in the river. . . . The river was one of the most pristine and beautiful mountain rivers in all of South Carolina. However, it was also very dangerous. There were potholes in the river that a person could not see before it was too late to avoid stepping or falling into them."[11]

"We learned to respect the [Keowee] River," local author Jerry Vickery observed. "We were not afraid of anything in or around the river. We knew every inch of the river . . . every sinkhole, every rapid, every sand bar, and every whirlpool. Although we had confidence in our ability to handle any situation that might occur on the river, we still knew the dangers of the river and respected it. The river was our life, but we knew that it could also take our life."[12] Another man related that "I was always afraid of that river. I almost got drowned in it. . . . I got in deep and couldn't find the bottom. And I started yelling and [a relative] come and got me, pulled me out to where I could touch the floor again. . . . It scared me when I found out I couldn't find the bottom."

Inhabitants only cautiously venture into the even more fearsome Chattooga River. "We've had a lot of deaths up there," Josephine Chavis related, "a good many deaths. . . . This boy I went to school with drowned. . . . [Before federal restrictions,] people would just go, you know like Sunday afternoon, or sometime, and drown. But now most of the way they drown up there now is going down, you know, on those [rafting] trips. . . . People just love it, but I'm scared of the water. I never did learn to swim."

"When the movie [*Deliverance*] came out, that's when just the general public was like, 'Oh, let's go buy a raft at Kmart and go down the Chattooga,'" professional rafting guide Amy Driver observed,

> and then that's when all the trouble, the drownings and so forth, started. . . . We [her natal family] had come down I guess for the summer, and they [her family, starting a rafting company] went up to the state park and they offered free trips, and . . . nobody came. Nobody. Not one person. . . . Even now, it amazes me how many locals [avoid the river]. . . . We started bringing the [local high school] ninth graders up here as a team-building activity for the class. And it was still amazing to me — this was '95, '96, '97; there were parents that didn't let kids come because that river's too dangerous. . . . You ask kids if they ever been canoeing or kayaking or rafting, and most of them don't. They'll say they've been fishing or camping or hiking, but a lot of them haven't been rafting. And there are a lot of locals that haven't and won't, even with the [perfect] records that the three [regional] outfitters have. [laughs and knocks on wood]

But there have been a lot of drownings on that river. Journalist Phil Garner wrote a story for an Atlanta paper shortly after *Deliverance* was filmed and interviewed Claude Terry, an amateur river guide: "'You don't beat the river,' said Terry, "'you work with it.'" Another guide reminded his Atlanta newspaper interviewer that the Chattooga has "'got a reputation as a river that's capable of killing people,' [John] Hicks says, 'That's good, because it is.'"[13]

"My next-door neighbor got drowned, actually, on the river," Oconee County resident Bruce Anderson admitted. "He was just—he was young, probably thirteen, fourteen years old. He . . . got over in the wrong spot down there and got pinned up under a rock. And he couldn't swim very well, and he got under a rock and he drowned. And we've had some other local people that have been talked into going to the river and ended up getting drowned. And you won't find many of the local people going to the river because of that."

Amy Driver, a professional guide on the Chattooga, explained that some of the more dangerous rapids are Five Falls, Bull Sluice, and the apparently benign but deceptively deadly Woodall Shoals.[14] Bruce Anderson, resident of Oconee County, described Woodall Shoals:

If you go out there at Woodall Shoals today and look at it, why it doesn't look bad. But there's a lot of the hydraulics in there. . . . I've spoke to several guides that have been through the wrong spot, and some of them said they were very fortunate that they got out of the wrong spot, because you just can't fight the river. You got a thousand cubic feet of water a second flowing by a spot, you're not going to be able to move. You know, you're going to get pinned in there. And a lot of people've drowned because they were not cautious enough. It didn't look dangerous and they got in the wrong spot. But it's still a good river to fish.

Bull Sluice also looks relatively easy but can be dangerous too, Amy Driver explained. "Yeah, I had people fall out there all the time. . . . I was down there two weekends ago, when out of three trips two boats flipped." At lower water levels, potholes are revealed. "Somebody drowned in that upper . . . pothole. 'Cause when the water's high, there's just so much force of the water going in there that you can't physically get out yourself."

Driver vividly described the passage through the Five Falls on the Chattooga:

Before you enter the Five Falls, right above that is where they filmed the pig scene in *Deliverance* at Camp Creek [Last Chance Pool]. . . . And then Entrance . . . drops off like a seven-foot or five-foot drop. And then . . . with Corkscrew you enter from middle, and then you're going to make a left-hand turn and then it kind of corkscrews down. . . . And then you got a big pool . . . [and] you go right around the corner and that's where Crack in the Rock is. . . . Guests walk [portage around due to the danger]. . . . And then Jawbone is a pretty long rapid; we set up three safeties [safety ropes] in Jawbone. . . . That's the last chance rope before you hit Sock 'Em Dog. . . . And this one, you . . . go off a drop to the left; there's a big pool, then you make a right-hand turn, go off a big slide, which then aims straight at a rock called Decap[itation]. . . . And it's a really nasty hole at higher water level. . . . And then you're at Dead Man's Pool.

Perhaps the most infamous of the Chattooga River drownings was that of sixteen-year-old Rachel Trois on May 29, 1999 (also fictionalized in Ron Rash's novel *Saints at the River*).[15] Trois, vacationing from Pennsylvania, had been trying to cross the river above Raven Chute (on the most dangerous Section IV of the river) and got swept into the narrow, trough-like rapids and was pinned in a pothole underwater by the tremendous force of the river; it took divers until late July to figure out a way to recover her body. Since the river was federally protected, officially nothing could be done to modify the natural landscape (such as building a dam to stop the water's flow to allow for recovery). Eventually a compromise was reached, thanks to the intervention of U.S. senator Strom Thurmond (R-SC). On July 28, the day of the planned recovery, some of Rachel's bones were discovered in eddies downstream. "I was down there the day that they found the few bones that they did find," Amy Driver reported. "And when they actually were able to stop the water enough to look, they—there was a stick that was probably about that big around. It was wedged in the rock, and her bathing suit top was wrapped around it."

Driver remembered an even more gruesome incident:

The worst was the kayaker that drowned in Left Crack [in the Rock]. . . . The river narrows down in Section IV, and there's one stretch where it gets really narrow and there's basically three small channels: left, middle, and right. And . . . there've been a lot of drownings there. . . . And there was (you probably don't want to tell anybody this) but anyway, the . . . rapids down there are right behind each other, so there's not much leeway to get over. And he [a kayaker] was swimming upstream, so he'd drop into it backwards; immediately broke his back, head to feet. . . . And then, when they were pulling him out, he came out in pieces.

Because of the relatively impermeable igneous or metamorphic bedrock coupled with the rapid descent of the water, most river valleys in the area also have waterfalls and cliffs, tempting to climb but dangerous for waders, swimmers, and hikers who venture too close to the edge. "As beautiful as our waterfalls are, they also hold hidden dangers," the official web page for Transylvania County, North Carolina, warns.[16] In both North and South Carolina, about once or twice a year people fall to their deaths. Others, trying to wade across a river upstream, slip on rocks, lose their balance, and are swept over the edge. Brian Alexander and his wife Claudia recalled a time when "I went fishing up there at Howard Creek. . . . I was on [wading in] a set of shoals up there, and next thing I know I slipped and I went about fifty to eighty feet *down!*" Claudia Alexander immediately continued. "Oh, he was skinned all to pieces. Scared me to" — Mr. Alexander interrupted: "I put my hands around my head and a big old rock hit my shoulder — like to knock me out and I went in a big ol' hole of water over my head, and it took me about three hours to get out of there."

Because of exfoliation, the very hard igneous or metamorphic rocks erode into bare, curving expanses that gradually seem to curve off into open sky or straight down, creating smooth slides for tumbling creeks and rivers and similar slides for those getting too close to the slope. Examples include Table Rock (Pickens County) and Bald Rock (Greenville County). Some creeks create long water slides, rivers tumble down "turtleback" falls, or steep cliffs form "glassy" mountains (due to the sun shining on the dripping water). These open expanses of rock form tempting palettes for graffiti artists.

Perhaps one of the more familiar graffiti-covered slopes is that of Glassy Mountain, just outside of Pickens, South Carolina (a different peak than the same-named one in northern Greenville County). An isolated monadnock with a north-facing granitic slope, the rock face long has tempted local high school daredevils, who painted their graduating years in numbers as large as they dared under the cover of darkness (figure 2). One of the culprits confessed, "We took four other guys up there with us, and they were so scared. . . . They didn't want to stand up on this mountain, and we . . . had already did it once, so we'd already lost all our fear; we were just going around, painting where we needed to. I know I almost slipped and almost probably hurt myself very badly. . . . It was still *really scary*, because you felt like — it looked like how it was curved, it would drop off after a certain point" (figure 9). This particular group of amateur artists was apprehended, questioned, and ultimately released by a game warden who had discovered them because some of the artists had flashed their spotlight on private homes at the foot of the mountain; the occupants then called the county deputies.

Since many people traditionally made a living by timbering, this activity might also result in horrific or painful accidents. Garvin Bradshaw related two tales. "We was cutting timber down there. . . . That tree went over, and that thing split up and come back and jumped off and busted his [brother's] ankle there and broke his leg there. I had to tote him out of the woods. He said me a-toting him hurt him a whole lot worse than it did, the limb breaking it. He said that every time that I stepped it felt like a toothache." Another time Bradshaw's father had been cutting fence ties, and "they were unloading them when one of them ties fell off and hit Daddy on the foot and broke his toe right in two. . . . Well, Daddy got pretty well drunk that day, and he . . . come home and Momma got to go pull his shoe off, and that bone had come through his toe and stuck down in the bottom of his shoe. . . . Well, whenever she pulled his shoe off, he passed out. It hurt him so bad he passed out. . . . They finally got his toe straightened up."

Animal Dangers

In addition to the dangers from the natural environment, inhabitants also acknowledge dangers from animal life, especially venomous snakes and large-bodied carnivores. The rugged mountains hold several species of venomous snakes, including timber rattlesnakes (*Crotalus horridus*). Douglas Edison knew where to find them. "But now if you wanted to see a rattlesnake, go to them berry patches. See, birds would come in there and feed, and them snakes would be there a-waiting on them." His friend Robert Davidson elaborated. "Grandpa . . . and [a relative] was picking berries, and Grandpa found a rattlesnake and he told [the relative] to get him a stick. . . . And [he] was out there looking for a stick and found another one [another rattlesnake]!" "We was in there picking [blackberries] one day," Joshua Flowers related. "Well, I looked and I saw a snake, and one of my aunts was coming over that way and I told her, I said, 'Don't go over there next to that bush over there,' I said, 'there's a rattlesnake under there.' And she says, 'Shh—don't say anything! They'll [the other pickers] get scared and want to quit!'"

Snakes also hid around old cabin sites, as Charles Watson discovered. "Going down to where my Grandpa Watson first built [his cabin] right up there. And the old chimley off of that house had done fell over, and just old boards and stuff laying around there. . . . And I don't know why that snake struck, but he struck and went in front of me and . . . [I] whirled around and looked back, Lord there was a pile of snake big around, looked like a[n] automobile tire. . . . Ain't no telling how big that snake was. I believe it was the biggest 'un I ever seen, and I've seen a lot of them."

"[A neighbor] said his brother invited him up one night to spend the night with him at a sawmill shack," Garvin Bradshaw narrated. "And he said he went up there, said along that night in the bed him and his wife were laying in the bed, and he said he felt something on the foot of the bed, and he just give it a big kick, like that, and he said a rattlesnake started singing [buzzing the rattle]. He kicked a rattlesnake off the bed! . . . But he said he never spent the night with his brother since!"

Besides rattlesnakes, copperheads (*Agkistrodon contortrix*) also posed a threat, as Garvin Bradshaw discovered. "I was laying in the bed down there [family home] one night, 'bout 11:30. . . . Well, I heared something under the bed. I thought it was a house cat. I pulled that light on, and there was a copperhead, slid out from under the bed, about that long. . . . I grabbed a shot gun and got to hunting for that snake, and we had a glass window over there laying up against the wall about that far from my bed. And that snake had done got up on the glass window and started up on the bed. I shot glass, window, snake, and everything!"

"Some hikers got lost over here [in the mountain wilderness]," Charles Watson recalled. "We was over there trying to find them; they'd been gone several days. . . . Well, we was tracking them, and . . . I heard something, sure behind me, and I looked back, and Lord there was a copperhead as big as my arm! It was the longest one that I'd ever seen; he was chasing me. I reckon I'd walked over the top of that thing. But I had on snake leggings, and those saved me, . . . and good heavy boots."

"Them old water moccasins'll [*Agkistrodon piscivorus*] make you sick," John Summers asserted. "I got a place on [the] side of my leg now where one bit me. . . . Me and [a friend] was on a pontoon [boat], and we pulled up in there below Bad Creek [on Lake Jocassee]. Was going to cook our fish, you know. . . . And I just had one foot on one rock and was letting them fish scraps go down—you know, just cleaning the fish? And I didn't see that old snake down there. . . . And that thing got me right there in the heel of the hand."[17]

Venomous snakes have peculiar properties, according to mountain folk beliefs. Garvin Bradshaw provided examples:

Daddy had corn in that bottom over there. . . . And on Sunday morning he'd always go out and look at his corn patch. . . . They had a pile of rocks right at the lower end of it [a field]. And they had a big rattlesnake crawled out there, and he killed that thing. . . . And he brought that thing on up to the house, and he had a[n] apple tree standing right behind the house about that big around and it had a fork in it. And he hung that rattlesnake up in that tree, let it hang there all day. And in about two weeks' time that tree was just dead as a weed. That poison, I reckon, soaked in that tree and killed it. Everybody said that's what done it.[18]

"You know them things [rattlesnakes] can charm?" Garvin Bradshaw explained:

Got over there at the bridge, there was a rabbit running along the edge of the road. . . . [A neighbor] caught that rabbit, and we went on up there to [run an errand]. . . . We got right back . . . where we picked the rabbit up at, had a rattlesnake same place where we picked the rabbit up at. [The neighbor] got out and took a lug wrench and killed that rattlesnake. It wasn't two minutes that rabbit died. When he killed the rattlesnake, it killed the charm. A lot of people don't believe that, but it's happened. You kill a snake, you killed its charms.[19]

Children had to learn early where to walk and where to avoid. "For whatever reason our Reedy Cove home was a haven for these poisonous snakes," Douglas Alexander recalled. "We learned at a very early age to look before we put our feet down. We saw copperheads in the garden; in the woodshed; in the outhouse; on the back porch; in the kitchen and everywhere else. . . . None of us nine kids ever got bit."[20] Denise Craig recalled that her "mountain grandma" cautioned her to stay in bed in the mornings "until she had the time to come look under the bed in case there was a snake under there. . . . And I remember . . . having a snake in the kitchen that Grandma had to kill . . . before she could fix breakfast!"

At her Pickens County mountain grade school, Kayla Radcliffe remembered dangerous animal sightings:

Like there was a really exciting point when I was like in third grade because there was a *snake* on the playground. And this kid [who saw it], . . . he's like, "Yeah, I saw the snake, and it crawled right between my legs and I almost peed on myself!" . . . And when there'd be a bear sighting in the area all the teachers would be extremely scared because the fence [around the playground] isn't complete—there's like this twenty-foot stretch where there's no fence. And all the teachers would be like, "Oh, man—there's been a bear in the area. We need to keep the kids on this side of the playground."[21]

As Radcliffe's grade school teachers and classmates recognized, black bears (*Ursus americanus*) are frequently sighted. Shirley Patterson related a story: "I have a neighbor up here, and he has some, you know, the boxes with the honeybees in it? . . . So, he was on his porch, and he saw the bear come up and just grab the whole honeybee box and just carry it down in the woods. And he got his binoculars, and he [the bear] just tore it apart, and . . . he's just sitting there just taking those combs of honey out and just having himself a good time! So . . . why do people want to live out here? [laughs]"

"We've seen a bear eating our corn," Benjamin Craig declared. "It probably weighed about 250–300 pounds." Denise Craig continued: "He had made a pile, and he was leaning over, just eating that corn, just relaxing like he was lounging. . . . And he looked at us, and we looked at him. . . . But he did get up and mosey [move slowly] and look between the corn back at us. . . . When we came back, we turned in and had the lights on down the cornrow, and he was back there behind the corn. But, and he was looking at us like, 'Are you back?'"

A bear's proclivity toward corn includes the intoxicating taste of moonshine mash, as friends Norman Cleveland and Robert Davidson discovered. Sometime around the year 2000, Davidson's son Mike narrated, his father and Cleveland were processing grain for alcohol production somewhere in upper Pickens County, and a bear got into their mash. Although warned not to shoot the bear because it was not hunting season, Cleveland did anyway; they buried the bear in the woods to hide their crime. The Department of Natural Resources officers somehow discovered the crime and fined Cleveland $5,000 for hunting bear out of season because the men could not reveal to the officers the true reason for having "hunted out of season."

While exciting to see, bears also may be dangerous, as young mother Donna Trask recognized. "Well, you know, I'm not too worried about the bear. But I will say this, that, you know, when [our daughter] was little, we put our swing set where it is for that reason. We didn't want it in the back of the yard because we'd had trouble with bear then, and . . . I didn't want to be in here fixing supper and her outside playing too far from the house. . . . When she was real little, you know, . . . two, three years old."

Cougars (mountain lions, panthers, or pumas [*Puma concolor*]) may be extremely rare today but create an unforgettable impact on locals.[22] For example, Benjamin and Denise Craig, living adjacent to mountain wilderness, have "heard a panther . . . and it sounds like a woman screaming for her life," Mrs. Craig reported. Her husband continued: "And we were, I had gone to bed early and [my wife] was still up, and I had the window open in there, and I heard this blood-curdling scream, you know. . . . I'm thinking, well, should I go check and see if somebody's hurt or something, you know? . . . But I got to go back there [in the wilderness] where you can't see your hand in front of your face!" Mr. Craig decided to remain in the safety of his home.

Some adults remembered stories about cougars from earlier generations. For example, Douglas Alexander's grandfather had been setting trap lines for small mammals to trap, skin, cure, and sell their furs to a furrier in New York, and one morning he noticed that all the animals had been ripped from the traps. "About the time he figured out what was happening, he heard it. That high-pitched, almost feminine scream that only a panther could make. He knew that without a gun he only had one option; turn around and get out of there as fast as possible." The panther tracked him for a while, staying "just behind him just far enough not to be seen." The next day, he and a friend went back up and discovered a mother panther and her two cubs, so they frightened the trio back into the Table Rock Watershed where the cubs could be raised in peace.[23]

Other adults vividly remember hearing panthers only decades earlier as children themselves. For example, Doyle Porter remembered that he and his father and brothers

> went on a fishing trip to a place called the Horse Pasture [sic], which was a large part of a gigantic wilderness area in the northwestern mountains of South Carolina. . . . Sometime in the wee hours of the morning, I was awakened by a very loud, piercing scream that seemed to be coming from just a few feet away. It was pitch-black dark, and I could not see a thing. The same noise also awakened everyone else in the camp. . . . I heard Dad say that it was a "painter." (That was his way of pronouncing "panther.") I knew a panther was a very large, wild cat, big enough to eat me, and I was as scared as I have ever been in my life.[24]

Jeffrey Donnelly remembered one trying to get into his childhood home:

> One came to the house one night, and they scream, you know (they say they scream kind of like a woman), and [was] trying to get in the house. I guess they had some fresh meat; they'd [his family had] killed a hog or something, and I guess it was smelling it or something trying to get in the house. Momma had got the rifle down or something, a shotgun, and she was going to try to shoot it . . . if it came in. . . .

But those cougars or panthers, . . . they would come to your house every so often. In fact, I think my grandmother shot one in this house. . . . Shot it with a shotgun; trying to come in the window. I guess they were hungry, too.

Before the ease of modern rabies vaccines, domestic and feral dogs infected with the disease were greatly feared, obviously for the disease but also perhaps by the apparently mysterious transformation of an animal normally loved and cherished but now metamorphosed into a beast hated and feared. Children seemed especially vulnerable, since they might approach a strange dog without hesitation. Ryan Trask admitted that "that was one of the things as a kid I was scared absolutely to death, because I heard my dad and granddad and others talk about it. If you got bitten it was over — you got rabies." James Edwards remembered his parents cautioning him and his siblings about two dangers as they left the house to play outside: "'Well, watch out for snakes and mad dogs.'" Joseph Yeats recalled merely cuddling his puppy that had been seen with a rabid dog; as a precaution, Yeats had to have the twenty-one shots, one per day. Ryan Trask described an episode where a young boy leaped onto a porch to escape a rabid dog, and a neighbor "shot it out from under him." As a child, Douglas Alexander recalled driving off a dog attacking his younger siblings. "As he [the dog] ran away I saw a sight that I had never seen before. The dog's eyes were as green as emeralds; he was foaming at the mouth; and every hair on his body was standing up. Mad dog." He and his oldest brother tracked the dog; it charged them, and they shot it four times before it dropped dead at their feet. "The sight of that mad dog and the horror of what we all went through will live in my memory forever," Alexander professed.[25]

Despite the dangers in the area, young parents Donna and Ryan Trask reflected on the relative safety they perceive in the upper South Carolina's mountains. "I've always felt very safe here," Donna Trask related. "I've always felt more safe here than I would living in town. . . . I mean, we've had bear on our porch and in our yard. That's always more exciting than it is dangerous. . . . Snakes, maybe, snakes in the summertime. But we get a lot more peace and quiet and privacy, which is one of the best things." Her husband then compared their life to that of a colleague who lives in downtown Greenville, and Donna Trask responded, "I think that's scary!" Her husband quickly added, "That's exactly what I said. . . . 'I'd prefer to deal with a timber rattler or a black bear than those crack dealers that run through your neighborhood any day!' I said, 'You ought to be the one that was scared!'"

While residents and visitors from Horace Kephart to James Dickey have described the terrifying locals, even inhabitants acknowledge some truth to the stereotypes (compare the perspective of historian Gordon McKinney, who argues that Appalachian residents are not more violent than other sections of the country and that incidents of violence may be traced to "social forces" that mountaineers could not control). "You had to be tough or you'd die!" Patrick O'Connell asserted. "If you didn't die you'd wish you was dead. Yeah, you had to be tough. . . . It was a tough country." At first reading, John Lane felt that Dickey had unfairly characterized mountain people in *Deliverance* but was corrected: "'Those people are out there,' a long-time resident of the Chattooga watershed said to me once when I suggested naively that Dickey had created stereotypes in Lonny the banjo boy or the Griners or the mountain man who brutally rapes the outsider from Atlanta. 'They're just not the *only* people out there.'"[26]

One of the more unforgettable characters created in the Dickey novel and portrayed in the dueling banjos scene in the film is Lonny the banjo boy, a boy with symptoms of Down's syndrome. There is also a very brief glimpse inside a mountain home where an elderly woman attends to an obviously mentally handicapped child. The two scenes together remind readers and viewers of what Horace Kephart had mentioned earlier about mountain people caring for their own mentally challenged relatives rather than institutionalizing them due to the power of family ties.[27] Thus, even though Dickey portrayed fictional characters, "those people are out there."

One South Carolina mountain woman explained:

Back then, if you had a child that was handicapped, or mentally retarded, . . . you kept them at home; you didn't take them to an institute. They lived there. And I was just a little kid, and I noticed at this home, I noticed this beautiful doll, and I . . . reached over and started touching this doll. Well, I heard something in the next room go "bump, bump, bump!" and a scream, and it just—I just froze. And it was a girl—I would say late forties, early fifties [in age], and she had fell down. She walked on her knees, and she crawled; . . . she ate like a dog. You know, they put food in a plate on the floor, and that's how she ate. But she fell out on the floor, and she was coming to me. . . . She mumbled, and she could do guttural sounds, and she'd say "baby." That she could say—"baby"; I was getting her "baby." She didn't like that.

Patrick O'Connell provided another example from his work experience as a telephone lineman:

I was way back in them mountains, and a neat little old log house over there. . . . I went over there to use the telephone, call and see where I was at. And I asked him [the owner] could I use it, he said, "Yeah—come on in." Well, there was a man laying there in a hospital bed, and I walked in that house; he had towels wrapped down his arms. And he seen me and he got upset, and he started gnawing hisself, started gnawing his arms and things. And he didn't have a back of his head—just from his ears up was all he had. He'd been laying there thirty-five years in that bed. He was borned that way. And she raised that boy. He didn't have no back of a head. And I had to leave; I didn't use the telephone.

As in many other cultures, mental illness may be interpreted through a lens of the cultural understandings of the local groups themselves. Drawing upon a long-established Euro-American witchcraft (and Christian) world-view, an Oconee County family interpreted what may have been mental illness as evil possession; in fact, the "possessed" woman believed that as well. Garvin Bradshaw and his sister Claudia described their aunt, who, Mr. Bradshaw asserted, "tried to be a witch. . . . [A neighbor] had a car stuck over at the foot of the hill one time. And Aunt [the possessed woman] come by and laid her hand on it, and it never did run no more. He swore she put a spell on it. It never would run no more, not a lick." Claudia continued: "She would not touch anything that had a picture of Jesus or God on it. . . . He [their father] had to do all her like, bill paying, 'cause she wouldn't touch currency or coins. And I had a picture on my bedroom door of Jesus, and she would wake me up in the middle of the night, for her to go to the outhouse . . . and make me open the door because she would not touch the door 'cause it had Jesus's picture on it."

"She lived right over yonder where that outhouse is," as Garvin gestured. "And if she went anywhere she had to backtrack herself. . . . She had to come back out the same way she come in. . . . And she would—if something didn't run, and she didn't touch something, she'd . . . go down to the branch [small creek], she'd pull her clothes off, wash them clothes off, and put them right back on . . . just as wet as they could be. . . . And I've seen her lay down over there in the road and just kick like a dog with a running fit, and I've seen her take her fingers and just tear at her face and blood'd be running all over her."

Claudia then asked her brother, "Didn't you say when her daughter got married, she walked that mountain, hollering like a panther—?" Garvin interrupted:

She went over that mountain there . . . tried to get her daughter to come back, and she wouldn't do it; she got lost on that mountain that night. She didn't have no flashlight, and she was squalling like a painter [panther] all night long. Everybody knowed her, and they wouldn't go to her; she stayed on that mountain all night long. . . . She was a mean woman, boy. . . . She'd never have nothing on the opposite side of her. . . . But now she'd come up that road there, if you put a line across there, or a dogwood limb, she wouldn't go back there and move it. . . . A dogwood limb. See, that's what they claimed Jesus was crucified on.[28] And she would never go by it. . . . And if she was at the table, she'd wait till the last person got up, and whatever piece, glass, fork, spoon, whatever they laid down last, she'd get up, pick it up, turn around with it, and then lay it back down before she'd leave. . . . One time she got mad at Granny, run her off, and Granny come down here to Daddy. . . . Daddy, he come up there [and told her to behave]. . . . And she struck at Daddy and run. Daddy run her down in that holler [hollow], and he slapped her; he slapped her plumb[29] up under the brush pile.

According to both siblings, their aunt acquired her power from another witch "somewhere down around Seneca [South Carolina]," Garvin Bradshaw told his audience. "I've heared Momma tell that a many a time. . . . If she seen the chicken eat corn, she'd grab that chicken, take a razor blade, and slit its throat and let the corn fall back out[30]. . . . I've heared Momma tell that a many a time. . . . People wouldn't have nothing to do with her! No, they wouldn't have nothing to do with her."

Other characters, perhaps with other mental or behavioral issues, also had reputations. For example, Mike Davidson described the local fellow who served as caretaker of the Jocassee Girls' Camp during the off season. "He was a little man of stature," Davidson recalled, and "was not scared of nothing. Cursed! You never heared nobody curse like him in your life. . . . He was a mean old cuss. Golly. I bet he didn't weigh a hundred and ten pounds. . . . Man, was he mean. Matter of fact, he shot a guy up there one time. There were some guys going in there hunting going across that property there at the girls' camp and he told them, 'You touch that gate and I'll shoot your ass.' They thought he was—they touched that gate, [the caretaker] shot him. . . . Didn't kill him."

Probably the best-known feisty character of upper South Carolina was Bob "Scatter" Johnson, the late owner of Bob's Place and the adjacent cookout area called the "Road Kill Grill." Often, customers referred to Johnson by his nickname, "Scatter," and so the bar became informally known as "Scatterbrains" (figure 8). Many upper Pickens County inhabitants told stories about him. Before he owned the bar and grill, Johnson had been a painter in Pickens, along with his brother. "Good painters," a man recalled, but "they just wouldn't work. . . . He was so crooked he'd have to screw his own britches on!" Margaret York first explained the nicknames: "Anyway, somebody said, 'Well, how did it [the bar] get called Scatterbrains?' She said, ''Cause Scatter'd scatter your brains, that's why!' I thought that was right[31] funny."

"Now he was a character, I am telling you," Harry Edison offered. "Two of the stories that I can remember about him was—you remember when *Gunsmoke* [television series from 1955 to 1975] came on? Well, Matt Dillon would always draw and shoot. Well, one day they said Scatter was standing there, had his gun in the holster. Well, when Matt Dillon drew his gun, Scatter pulled his out and shot the TV! And he said, 'I told you I could outdraw Matt Dillon!'" James York recalled a time when "we stopped there to get us a beer and shoot the bull with Scatter a few minutes. Well, we's sitting there talking, drinking a beer, and this fella 'bout your size, glasses, got him a beer. . . . That fella took about one drink, and Scatter just hauled off and just slapped that man and knocked them glasses off. . . . He said, 'I don't like you. I never have liked you.' Said, 'You get out of here!' He got his beer and he got him on the road." Edison told another story in an earlier interview:

He [Scatter] took a drive shaft one time and made like a bazooka. He would drop a cherry bomb down in one of them holes in one end of it and throw a beer can back in there and . . . that beer can went across [laughs] the place. . . . Everybody has a story on Scatterbrain. . . . These guys came in there one time and they was going to be roughnecks, you know. Well, Scatter he just pulled his pistol out and shot a hole through the roof there, and they left in a hurry [laughs]. . . . They had a few scrapes up there at Bob's Place.

"Anything could happen, it's happened right there at Bob's Place. That's a *bad* place!" Patrick O'Connell assured his audience. "I seen them get shot, get busted in the head with clubs, and everything else." At Bob's Place "there was always a fight," O'Connell stated. For example, Douglas Edison narrated, "these guys come out of North Carolina. . . . And there was a set of triplets grew up just up here above Bob's Place. . . . And these guys took a knife to them boys, and liked to kill them, one or two of them. And they say old Scatter was saying, 'I've told you I'm too old to fight you; I'll just shoot you.' . . . He was shooting at them. He could've killed them. He was a good shot. But he's hitting them in the rear and stuff like that. . . . He put a stop to that fight, right in a hurry."

Apparently, James York was an eyewitness to that fight or at least to a similar one:

I went up there [Scatterbrains] one night. . . . Well, there's another fella started in the building, and he was on one side of the door and I was on the other. And about time he got right even with me a fella from the inside came through with a knife. . . . He come by and he ripped that boy, just about cut him in two. I mean, he was fearing for his life. He's pouring out blood. . . . He wasn't after nobody else, but he seen that boy coming through that door and he went through and he sliced him in two. And that started off a-fighting I ever seen. Scatter got his gun and shooting. . . . And the law finally got up there, and they about run him off, little skinny deputy. . . . I thought he was going to shoot all three of these. . . . And I ain't never heard any more problems.

Harry Edison described a fight between his mother's youngest brother and Edison's nephew, both men about the same age. "They were up there one time, and they were drinking and got into a fight, and my mom went up there and she went up on the porch and she just scolded them and she said, 'You boys ought to be ashamed of yourselves, you up here fighting, you such good friends like this.' And both of them started crying and big old hug!"

Robert Davidson, who had been raised in the area, frequented the bar. Even before Scatter owned the place, it had a reputation: "Oh, it was rough! . . . There was some good fights up there, yes sir. That Pumpkintown [a nearby crossroads community] bunch that I was talking about, they'd go up there, and this other bunch'd come in there and all that; they couldn't get along three minutes! They just had a grudge; they just couldn't get along. There was two of them big old boys up there . . . one night a-fightin', and they said they fought just like two dogs and just fought till they give out. [chuckles] . . . Never had a bit of trouble, myself. I pretty well knowed how to keep my mouth shut." Inhabitants appreciated the adventures and excitement at Bob's Place "more than we do the [Cliffs at] Vineyards," Benjamin Craig chuckled.

Bob's Place and its eccentric proprietor were so renowned that Douglas Edison remembered a time when

> the first election for President [George W.] Bush, the first time he run for president, this guy from . . . *Time* magazine, he ended up up there. And Tony, the son, was sitting on the porch. And . . . Tony was just really pulling a trick on him. Tony said, "I had my gun pointed at you when you come up through there." Make out like he was going to shoot him and all that stuff. . . . But people were not too happy around Pickens, you know, about making the *Time* magazine, because they thought it made it look bad around here. But Tony, he just thought it was funny.

Denise Craig remembered that Bob's wife had told the reporter that she was going to vote for Bush "because he was cute. And another person said that he couldn't vote because he was a convicted felon. . . . So, I mean it just made South Carolina sound *so* wonderful!" As mentioned in chapter 3, on May 21, 2017, an unknown arsonist burned Bob's Place to the ground. To date it has not been rebuilt, and no one has been charged.[32]

As discussed in chapter 1, the manufacturing of untaxed liquor has a deep traditional foundation in South Carolina's mountain counties (figure 10). John Summers admitted:

> And there's a lot of people up here, that was their source of living, you know. . . . My daddy made it [moonshine]. I mean it was just a family tradition for us. . . . My daddy had . . . three [stills] going here at one time. . . . And it was just right across the hill right there. . . . I was a watchman for them. . . . I walked the woods with a shotgun. . . . And if I seen anything here, I'd shoot one time. . . . I's about thirteen, fourteen years old, somewhere along in there you know. It wasn't much pay, but back then fifty cents was good pay.

Vince Aiken described visits to Sugar Likker Road in Reedy Cove (upper Eastatoee Valley) as "'just like going to the liquor store.'"[33]

One woman and her family sang gospel songs at regional churches, homecomings, and revivals, and she remembered that

> my dad [also a county sheriff] got a call about the revival [in Eastatoee Valley] if we would come and sing. My dad was very hesitant. . . . He

got off the phone, and he was talking to my mom and he said, . . . "that's some mean people up there"; said, "they're bootleggers and chicken fighters, and I've had to go up there several times for murderers." . . . Well, my mother said, . . . "If you're doing God's work, He's going to take care of you. I don't have nothing to worry about." . . . So the revival started, and it lasted six weeks. And the bootleggers, a lot of them got religion, and the chicken fighters, and they changed their ways.

In fact, the woman recalled, after the revival she and her family were invited to a chicken supper, and "when we got there we had every kind of chicken; we had chicken and dumplings, chicken pie, fried, chicken stew, chicken you name it, we had chicken!"

Beth Lepre offered an alternate perspective. "People kind of look at the homemade liquor business and the still business as . . . funny and romantic. . . . But the idea that I got from my grandmother, and there was a lot of alcoholism in their families, is that, you know, when the men would go off on a drunk and stay drunk for a month and come back and here's the wife with twelve kids. You know it just wasn't really a romantic, funny thing to us."

Anna Muller interviewed two Pickens County deputies for a regional newspaper several decades ago, and one county deputy told her that "'most of the people who made whiskey lived around Eastatoee and Rocky Bottom and had no other way to make a living. They raised corn and made whiskey.'" Another deputy added, "'We put a stop to bootleg whiskey, but now it's been replaced by dope, and that's much worse. I'd rather have moonshine.'"[34]

Several people talked about the transformation from moonshining to marijuana and from marijuana to methamphetamine. In fact, Mike Davidson had known a bootlegger who switched from moonshining to marijuana production but still held to some old-timey traditions. "And I know this for a fact because I've done it. He sold his marijuana in quarts and half a gallons. I bought a many a half-gallon marijuana from him. . . . But he just packed it by half a gallon because he didn't know nothing about grams and ounces. . . . All he ever knowed was quarts and half a gallons like in liquor. And that's the way he sold his marijuana."

The shift from alcohol to marijuana, Charles Watson believed, has been due to the remoteness of the upper Pickens County wilderness: "A lot of it's growed around these lakes, I reckon, because you see a lot of boats over here where you know they'd be filling them up with gas and they'd have peat moss and rakes and fertilizer and you know they ain't going fishing with that kind of farming equipment!" Margaret York, who worked in the county sheriff's office, observed, "Pot growing was a big thing when I first went to work there in the early '80s, you know, people growing pot, and smoking pot. . . . They grew it here in the mountains." Local writer Joshua Blackwell blamed the region's use of illicit drugs on "remnants of Appalachian independence."[35]

During his lifetime, Mike Davidson has witnessed the transition from moonshine to marijuana to methamphetamine. "I remember the first marijuana that come to Salem. . . . I was twenty-one or twenty-two years old. Salem stayed clean for a long time—now I think it's one of the biggest meth places in the county. . . . Meth and whiskey is two different things altogether." A retired sheriff commented on the transition: "Well, drugs have taken over this day and time. . . . You very seldom ever heard of someone dying from getting some bad bootleg or something like that, but these drugs that they have this day and time is just terrible. And they'll do anything to get this meth. Stealing, that's probably eighty—eighty-five percent of the [county] crime is stealing to get drugs and everything. . . . They'll do anything to get it. . . . And there's a lot of money involved with it." Davidson agreed: "But these hills up here—there's so many kids on that damn crack and crystal meth nowadays. . . . These kids around here they'll . . . steal your false teeth if you laid them down. It's unreal. . . . Back in my younger day I smoked enough reefer . . . but it was different. I mean, we didn't steal for it or nothing like that—we growed our own reefer."

Perhaps related to the difficulty of traveling narrow mountain roads and the distances from county seats, the sheriff's deputies often could not assist relatively quickly in crime prevention or resolutions, and so frequently inhabitants took matters into their own hands (figure 11). Of course, inhabitants also explained this practice as being due to the Scots-Irish cultural value of independence or to the borderland or frontier values of retaliation. John Summers offered an example:

> I had some old cars up there on the hill, you know. . . . Well, I thought I heard the hood of one of them old cars shut. . . . And when he [a trespasser] come out the door [of a storage shed] he had a whole case of the [blasting] caps, a whole case. I hollered at him. When he come out [of] the building, I take him out [shot him] through the lip, right arm right there. . . . That broke him sucking eggs![36] I didn't kill him, but I fixed him good. . . . I ain't ever seen him again, so. He was just going through the community, stealing, you know. . . . I mean once word gets around, they ain't nobody bother you.

Nearby in Eastatoee Valley, Ryan Trask acknowledged that "there has been somebody in the past several years who lived in this valley who did some things that weren't acceptable. Stole some things. But one thing that everybody knew is—he's not going to steal anything in here! . . . He didn't have the courage. He would've been killed. He went elsewhere."

Women frequently handled their own problems too. In her Eastatoee Valley home, Donna Trask admitted that she has had to confront trespassers, but "you just take care of it. . . . I have never shot anybody. Or at anybody!" Jeffrey Donnelly told a story of a relative: "She was kind of a tomboy, I guess, and some guy—he met her out on a trail somewhere she would fight just like a man, they said. He said something to her and she'd beat up on him. He took her to court and [the] judge was going to fine her five dollars or something or he did fine her five dollars. She said, 'Judge, you may as well fine me ten because if I catch him out I'm going to whup him again!'"

The isolated rural area, coupled with the prevalence of gun ownership and the propensity to handle matters extralegally, sometimes leads to potential accidents. Joseph Yeats, who lives in a small valley in upper Pickens County, was relaxing quietly at home one night when suddenly bullets started flying through his home while his wife cared for their new baby:

> She screamed, you know. Well, I run out there in the yard and . . . bark hit me in the face. They'd fired again and hit the old willow tree right above my head. Well, I thought they were serious, you know, and I hollered for [my wife]. She handed me my rifle (she'd already got it and had it loaded). Well, somebody come between me and the headlights, and I had a bead right on them. . . . I raised up and shot over their head. Well, they tried to back the car up, and I just opened up behind the car. . . . Those boys come out and they were scared so bad they couldn't even get a word. . . . They had a rabbit in the road out there, and . . . they were shooting at that rabbit and the bullets was hitting the house here, you know?

As numerous informants have mentioned, crimes like robbery and drug (or earlier, alcohol) manufacturing, coupled with the area's traditional reputation for lawlessness or for resolving disputes extralegally, inevitably led to more serious crimes such as murder. "My uncle killed a man . . . which, you know, I'm not proud of it, but—," Douglas Edison admitted, "and I think it was—I have heared from my dad that it was over a liquor still. . . . They had one together, and they fell out, and just whichever one got to the other'n first, one that was going to die." Denise Craig admitted that her great-uncle killed his brother and sister-in-law by beating them with a hammer, "and then he cooked up some breakfast." Alice Flowers, also a relative of the murderer, declared the motive to be "because they wouldn't give him money for alcohol." "And I think he was a little off," Mrs. Craig concluded.

"Trouble was sort of an emblem of the territory," journalists Mike Hembree and Dot Jackson wrote. In an interview they conducted with Paul Bowie from Eastatoee Valley, Bowie described an incident in which "one man nearby [to Bowie's one-room school in the Horsepasture] had cut off another man's head with a straight razor. Another had sent an enemy to heaven with a double-bitted axe. Guns bulged in pockets, and knives were standard equipment. Yet, Paul observes, the crimes were crimes of passion; 'I never did anything to anybody, and I never was afraid. We had no law back in there, and we needed none.'" "'Very rarely, there would be a bad fight or a killing, a crime of passion; dependably,' says I. C. [Few], 'it would be over a likker [sic] still, a woman, a dog or a property line. And the aggressor rarely denied the deed, relying on the Law [sic] to agree that the victim needed thrashing, or, if the vengeance was fatal, that he just ought not to have been let live.'"[37]

As an example of a potential victim who "needed thrashing," Ralph Glenn related a story about Paul Bowie, by then in his eighties:

And he went down to go across to his field he was farming across the [Eastatoee] River, and there was a guy blocking the bridge with his pickup truck, down in the water fishing on Paul's land. . . . So he got out and politely told the man to move his truck so he could get where he was going. Well, the guy not only started arguing with him, he . . . pushed this eighty-something-year-old man down on the ground. And Paul got up and said, "I'm going back to the house. I got to get something. Hope you're here when I get back." Of course, the guy got the message and he left. Paul would have killed him right there on the spot if he'd been there when he got back.

As another example, reporter Herbert Connelly collected a story about a Christmas Day 1928 shooting on Little Cane Break in upper Pickens County. According to the narrator, two men were working in a lumber camp, and occasionally their wives came for weekend visits. One weekend, one man's wife came but the other man's wife did not. The men started celebrating with locally produced moonshine, and the man with the wife who was present at the time got too drunk to perform sexually. The frustrated wife turned to his roommate, who willingly obliged. As they were making love the other man sobered up and grabbed a pistol, and in the struggle the sober man turned it on the drunk, who was shot and killed. The next day the sheriff sent two deputies to the camp to arrest the murderer, but "'I told them the facts and Nance's wife listened in and declared I was telling the truth. I remember, the deputies looked at each other and thought about the circumstances. One said he didn't see the necessity of taking me in, looked like an accident. They shook hands all around, got in their Model-T and rode back to Pickens. . . . We killed off the last bottle of [the victim's] whiskey and returned to North Carolina. Never went back.'"[38]

Garvin Bradshaw related a tale of another love triangle:

> Well [Smith, pseudonym], he was going over there and meeting that girl. . . . Well, anyhow he went to the house that day and, well, [Smith] killed [Jones, pseudonym]. And cut him up, got a chopping axe and cut him up and put him in a trunk and put him in the back room of the house. . . . Well, the preacher come up to . . . eat dinner with them one day over there. And the preacher got to smelling something. He got to hunting, and he found that in the back room where they had him. Well, they tried them and [Smith] told them what he done. He said they hit him in the head with a hammer. And . . . they give him eight years in prison and give that woman eight years down in Columbia. . . . Well, there was a preacher went from Seneca and went to Columbia got that . . . girl out, brought her down there to his house and raised a kid by her.

A pugnacious attitude began in childhood and progressed, locals admitted. "Now they was a *mean* bunch in Rosman [North Carolina]," Robert Davidson remembered from his childhood early in the twentieth century: "They was a mean bunch in Rosman. It was four years before they got to keep a red [traffic] light in Rosman! Them boys from the mountains would come down there, be drunk, 'bout drunk, and they'd come down there and shoot the red light out and take off and go back to the mountain. . . . That went on for years and years. But they didn't know no better! They was just growed up mean, that's all there was to it. Just a damn bunch of mean-ass boys, that's all."

"Mean-ass boys" proliferated in the mountains. Perhaps to generate publicity for the *Deliverance* film, in July 1971 Keith Coulbourn interviewed Bill McKinney, the actor who portrayed the sexually aggressive mountain man in the film, for the *Atlanta Journal and Constitution*. In the interview, McKinney (born in Tennessee) said, "'I know these mountain people and I know they're full-brimming over with violence all the time. When I was growing up as a child they picked on me, humiliated me and beat my ____, you know.'"[39] Up in Eastatoee Valley, Ralph Glenn admitted that

I had been aggravated and bedeviled by a kid on the [school] bus. . . . And I had had enough of them [five brothers] that they were escalating in severity at that point and I didn't need any more of it. And so, I realized on the way home that day that I wasn't going back to school [the last day]. . . . And that little bastard [the tormentor] started in on me again, and right back up here on Eastatoee Community Road. . . . I walked back there and I beat . . . that boy so hard that I about killed him. When . . . the bus driver stopped the bus and got me unwrapped from around that boy's neck, he fell over in the floor and was having trouble breathing. And I remember when . . . the bus driver put me up in the front seat, and I had five of them back there wanting to come break my neck. And they all . . . swore that there'd be vengeance over the summer. And I told them to come on down, I'd set my German shepherd loose on them.

"Nobody'd pick on me! Nobody done pick on this boy," Patrick O'Connell assured his listeners,

'cause we had never done nothing but hard work, you know—stout. We were strong. We didn't have to worry none. Had one [classmate] one time on the [school] bus. . . . Worked him over pretty good. . . . He come back there and I killed him! And my first cousin was driving the bus, and he pulled to his driveway, and [one student] of Rocky Bottom take him out the emergency door at the back, laid him on the side of the road, his sister's standing over him, and drove off and left him. And there wasn't nothing said about it. . . . We was all mean in high school—too mean to learn anything. We stayed in more fights than stayed in class!

Girls too readily defended themselves. Elizabeth Nelson provided a personal example:

In the fourth grade I got taller than all the other girls, and there was one boy in the class that was taller than everybody else. . . . And so he was the last person in the back of the class, and I had to be put in front of him because I was the next tallest person. And he'd sit back there and pull my hair [laughs]. . . . And I'd turn around and say, "Stop it!" And he'd keep on pulling and I'd turn around and say, "Stop it." Or I'd look at him right hard. And he'd keep on pulling, and finally I just turned around and smacked him! And at that point, . . . our fourth grade teacher saw us and said, "Okay, you're both gonna stay in at recess and write a thousand times 'I will not misbehave in class.'" And we did!

As a high school girl, Claudia Alexander defended herself and her female classmates against a male bully. "I whupped one guy good," she explained, for "talking dirty to other girls, and then when I went to sit back in my seat he started on me and I told him to shut his mouth and he wouldn't." The bully shoved his desk into hers, and Mrs. Alexander retaliated in kind. "And then he came up to me . . . and knocked my books off on the floor. All I did was I slapped the fire out of him, like 'You will not treat me like that!' So I guess I got my daddy's little bit of Irish blood because I felt like I was defending my honor. . . . I was scrappy!"

As schools consolidated into larger, more professionally administered units in the late 1950s, juvenile assertions of independence and lawlessness evolved. One university student reflected on his own high school years in the early twenty-first century:

> There's not much to do [in Pickens], so you'd usually go to a movie [on] Friday nights or Saturday night. And then you'd always be looking for something to do after like ten, eleven o'clock. . . . It usually had stealing in it somehow or another. . . . One time we had a big group stealing . . . golf balls, and we got the bright idea to go drive around and throw them at signs and other things. . . . We invented this one thing, we called it "cobbin'," and it must be one of the most country, hick things you can do. There was a corn field near my house, . . . so we pull over the car, run over in this cornfield; so we pick some corn, bring it back, and so we'd have like armfuls of corn. . . . So we started a tradition of picking, stealing corn, and then going and throwing that at stuff. . . . We always tried to find some girls that didn't know what snipe hunting was; we never could find any [girls], though.[40]

Despite the reputation of the area, Margaret York, who lives in the shadow of the destroyed Bob's Place in the Eastatoee Valley, appreciates her home:

> This area through here has always been a lesser crime area. . . . You'll have some house break-ins or somebody steal your lawn mower out of your yard or something like that. You know, some come through and does some malicious damage like beating your mailbox up. We had somebody shoot our night light out not long ago. Just stupid stuff like that, but nothing really, really where you got to be worried about coming in and out [of] your house and something happening to you. . . . House

break, like I say, is the biggest thing up through here, I would think. And every once in awhile I'd catch somebody growing a little pot in these woods or something. Other than that, as far as really being a bad area, it is pretty safe considering the rest of the country, I think.

Supernatural Dangers

Danger may lurk in the dark, timbered wilderness, in the swift mountain rivers, with the wild, dangerous animals, or with a few unpredictable or violent human residents. But danger may also lie outside the realm of nature completely. Mountain residents also have described supernatural events, not life-threatening or life taking but nevertheless frightening.

Early in my interview with Gregory Clayton as he was reviewing his work history (including making moonshine at times in his younger days), we both heard the sound of a rattling plate that came from within his house (figure 12), audible enough to be recorded digitally. The noise seemed to me like a pet had stepped on an empty food dish, but Clayton's face registered mild surprise. He interrupted the interview and said simply "Haint."

"Well, now I hear things, you know, when I'm outside," Clayton admitted:

There's all kind of noise inside the house like that un [one] was awhile ago. . . . A lot of times I'm out here, working around and . . . I lock the door so I know that there ain't nobody in the house. And I hear a noise; I just let it go. Don't never find out what it is. . . . It ain't happened in a while, but I have been in bed, and it felt like, just felt like somebody sat down on the bed. There wouldn't be nobody there, but feel like the bed go down, and that's the only thing that's ever bothered me any. Some of the kids, they claimed they seen some— seen people upstairs. . . . I ain't going to say if they was a-dreaming or really seen it or what, but some of them . . . wouldn't sleep upstairs on account of it. I know you can hear different sounds up there. And in the end, nobody ain't slept up there in a long time, but they still hear sounds upstairs. Like somebody a-walking, or rocking in a chair or something. . . . As long as they don't bother me, I'm going to let them go. If they are a ghost, I don't know.

Garvin Bradshaw, an inhabitant of Oconee County, knew many ghostly tales. He related one from his childhood:

Daddy said one night they was living over here behind [the neighbors]. He said his daddy was off a-working. . . . And he said he was sitting over there one night long about nine or ten o'clock, setting around the fireplace. . . . Went around to every one of the kids, and when he come to the momma, he asked her was she scared and she said, "No, I'm not a-scared of the devil." Said time she said that, there was a racket started in the chimney column, a rumbling, that went right out toward the barn, and said it done that every night as long as they lived there, till they left. And said long about four o'clock it'd be something like turning loose like a sack of flour from out of the top of the house and hit in the wall, and they said far as what it was they never did know what it was and never did find out what it was.

"That was a ghost," Bradshaw assured his audience.

"Now let me tell you Granny's favorite story," Stephanie Jamison offered, about her grandmother Anne Flowers:

Granny and [her sisters] were sleeping in the bed. . . . They would lay across the bed so there'd be more room, but their legs would hang off. . . . Grandma and them were laying in the bed and she . . . felt something on her toe. Well, she kind of just looked down and didn't see nothing so she rolled over and went back to sleep again. Granny said it felt like something grabbing her big toe and just kind of pulled it up like that. And so she just pulled her foot in. And it wasn't long after that she noted . . . one of her twin sisters jerked her foot in. So that next morning while they were cleaning up the kitchen, doing dishes, Granny said "[Sisters], which one of you-all pulled on my toe last night?" And they said, "Lawd, [Anne], we didn't do it," and [one sister] said, "I thought you pulled my big toe" and Granny said, "I thought you pulled my big toe."

The woman's aunt continued: "And Aunt [the other sister] is laying in the bed (she hadn't never got up), she's laying in the bed, and she said, 'well, my big toe got pulled too!'"

"We was coming around up here at the old Wiggington House one night," Garvin Bradshaw narrated,

and me and Daddy and [two other men]; they was nobody lived in that house whatsoever. We went there coon hunting and it was kind of foggy and rainy, and we come down by there, and they heard the door opened and shut back just exactly like there was somebody opened that door and shut it back. And we still don't know what that was. [A neighbor] said one time he was up setting up there at the fireplace . . . about eight or nine o'clock at night. Said old man [Willy Smith, pseudonym], he was staying with [Jones, pseudonym] up there, two men, two old bachelors. And said Willy got up and come in there and said, "[Jones], there's somebody come across the bed while ago where I was at in yonder." [Jones] says, "You don't have to worry about that." Said "Old man Jim Wiggington" (see, old man Jim used to live there). He says, "Old man Jim come down here every night, smokes with me and goes back upstairs." Old man Willy never did spend the night with him no more. That was the last night he stayed up there!

Donna Trask related a story about a building on their property in Easta-toee Valley:

When we first bought it [an old house], you know, a lot of the people up here, the neighbors and all, they— . . . some people said it was haunted. . . . They had said that when her [the former owner's] second husband . . . died, that they brought him back to the house and, you know, that was an old tradition to bring people back to the home. And I don't know if that's why it was haunted or what, but— . . . . We actually had an experience. . . . One time when [my daughter] was little (she's two or three), we were down there and you [her husband] had her in the house, didn't you? And she wanted to know who that lady was that walked by!

Her husband continued: "We had about a hundred pound solid white boxer . . . who would attack anything and fight anything, and he wouldn't go in the house. He'd get to the door and he'd start shaking, just trembling. And you could kick him in the tail or throw him in there and he'd turn around and run out just as fast as he could!"

Garvin Bradshaw added another story from across the state line. "Old man [Wilson, pseudonym] set up yonder in North Carolina; he said there was a house up there, said people'd move in it today and they'd move out tomor-row. He said that night about nine o'clock he said there'd be a baby start cry-ing like in the lower end of the yard, and he said that baby would cry right up to the fireplace. And when it got to the fireplace it'd quit crying. And he said when they found out what was wrong with it, there'd been a baby killed there and burnt up. . . . Now I guess that'd be a ghost."

Bradshaw also related a version of "The Vanishing Hitchhiker":[41]

And the road was coming down from Little Eastatoee, and there wasn't a house in three miles there, and it was just a-pouring rain. And a woman was walking right down the edge of the road there; she was dressed in white all over, and she didn't even have a flashlight nor a[n] umbrella. I went down the road, and I think to myself, "I'll go back and pick her up." And there was something told me not to go back, and I didn't go back. And I's telling somebody about it a little bit later on, and they said, "You ain't the only one that's ever seen that there." Said, "That's been seen several times." And after a turn of about two weeks [a neighbor] had that car wreck. . . . I believe that was a warning. It was either a ghost or a warning, one.

Bradshaw differentiated between ghosts and warnings:

Old man [Jones, pseudonym] used to stay with Daddy a lot, right down here. . . . On Sunday night he didn't come back, and we were setting there eating supper. And had a bird come in the kitchen door. It flew right down to where [Jones] set at, flew around two or three times, and went right back out the door. Next time we seen [Jones], find him dead laying on his porch; fell dead of a heart attack. And there's a warnings, and people don't understand what they are until after they done happened. And I ain't going to say what they ain't ghosts, but I'm just telling you.[42]

Michael Valentine remembered as a child visiting his paternal grandmother with his father. Father and son would walk across the fields several miles to her home and then return. One time on the trip back from visiting the old woman, Valentine and his father both saw a ghost cross the road in front of them. They interpreted that vision as a premonition of her death, which followed shortly after this episode.

Alice Flowers and Stephanie Jamison, the daughter and great-niece of Joshua and Anne Flowers, related multiple supernatural stories about the elderly couple as well as about themselves. For example, Stephanie Jamison remarked that "Granny [Anne Flowers], . . . before she died after Grandpa died, she said he would come see her. He would crawl into the bed, and she could feel the bed dent, and he'll be behind her, and she said she could just feel him like wrap his arm around her." Alice Flowers then added, "Yeah, and she could hear him breathing now."

Mrs. Flowers continued:

When [my daughter] was four years old she had an imaginary friend . . . and she called it Satchel. . . . And so I just played along with it, and I thought she's very creative. And so, and then one day I didn't have to set the plate for Satchel and she said, "No, he left," and

I said, "Okay." So nothing was ever said again about it until about five years ago. . . . And she said, "Where did I get [the name] Satchel?" . . . And so she got on the computer and looked up the meaning of the name "Satchel," and it means "guardian angel." And they say sometimes that kids can see their guardian angels because they're not prejudiced and don't have the stuff that we have. . . . And that's another thing that we got from Momma.

Whether warning, angel, or ghost, Stephanie Jamison told another story about Anne Flowers. "So Granny was sitting on her couch, and she said I [Stephanie] had dosed off [while watching her and Joshua Flowers, a stroke victim], and she said all of a sudden she felt somebody [smack sound] slap her hard on the leg to where it made a mark on her leg, and she jumped and looked and Grandpa [Joshua Flowers] is standing straight up and down and . . . she said he was wavering [potentially falling]. And she said, 'I just ran and grabbed him and knocked him down,' but she said something or someone woke me up; she said she don't know who it was but they slapped her on the leg to wake her up to help Grandpa."

Ms. Jamison continued:

But we all prayed for Daddy a lot [after he died]. 'Cause [Flowers family members] were very religious and we're devout Christians. . . . And she [his wife] was praying that he was at peace. She said, the next day she's sitting there on the sofa, she heard a ruckus out the front door so she went to go get up to go to the door, and she said . . . before she could get to the door my dad come through the door, walked through the den, turned and looked at her, and smiled and walked on through the kitchen and out the back door. And she said that was him letting me know that he's . . . in peace and not hurting anymore.

Ms. Jamison stated, "Now I always told Granny I dream," and explained that

when something was going on in my life I would always talk to my dad, and he always helped me in making my decisions. . . . I told Granny I've been having dreams about my dad, and they're so real, I can—you know people have smells. . . . I can smell this other scent and [snaps fingers] I'm with Granny, you know. And my dad had this distinctive smell, and in my dreams *I can smell him*. They're so vivid; they're so real. It's like he's right here with me. And I told Granny that and she said, "[Stephanie], he's visiting you in your dreams." . . . And just right before my . . . total hysterectomy I was—I talked to my dad. Like I'll sit here and I'll just say, "Okay, Dad, this is going on," you know. "I wish you were here to give me guidance." Well, right before, or two nights before, I'm [dreaming that] . . . me and my dad are standing right there in the middle of the road. He had on his khaki jacket and his blue jeans and his Velcro tennis shoes. . . . And he had on his white-and-blue plaid shirt. And . . . he hugs me. . . . And we're like holding hands, and he's like he's being pulled away and he said, "You're going to be just fine; you're going to be just fine." And . . . I went into the surgery calm; I mean I prayed about it but I knew I was going to be alright because my dad told me I was. And by God I was, was I not?

Alice Flowers concurred and added:

But since I've been down here [in her house] I can feel him [her own father] sometimes. And I've only glimpsed—like I was sitting where you are watching TV and I saw in my bedroom somebody go by the door and you know, you just see the flash, but you know who it is. So we just believe that. . . . I was the seventh child and last daughter of Momma; [Jane, a pseudonym] was my only daughter. So it skipped me, it skips a generation, so Momma had it and I don't know who back, 'cause she didn't know. But she'd always had this kind of, we'll call it a sixth sense.

Stephanie Jamison has the same gift, and she provided an example:

This past weekend we were in . . . the old Rabun County [Georgia] Hotel. . . . The woman took us upstairs and showed us to our room— nothing, nothing. I walk in this one room, I got the heaviness so bad and I'm like—I *knew* this hotel has a ghost, or a spirit—I call them spirits. . . . And I knew it was a woman, and I sat there and I said, "[Alice]," I said, "I'm having a heaviness in my chest." And that woman turned around and looked and she said, "Well, I know y'all like history." She said, "You know, this—we're haunted by a lady." And I said, "Yes, I know." . . . I can go places and sense stuff.

When I asked her if that heaviness on her chest ever had an evil feeling, Ms. Jamison replied,

I've only had one time where I have gotten the heaviness and I felt like you have *got* to get out of here! And that was an antique store [in] downtown Easley, and [my cousin] had the same experience in the same room. . . . I can go to the threshold; I can't go in because there's something bad there. I mean, it's something in that room. I can usually go to the area where it's at, but if it's negative—if I feel—the pressure gets so bad where I'm like, [pause] "Can't breathe!" So I walk away. I walk away.

Alice Flower's daughter had another strange sense of evil:

She lived up at Table Rock on her first marriage. And after a rainy day we'd go out and pick up arrowheads 'cause they would just wash out of those woods. . . . And most of them are of the stone that you see up there, but this one was black, jet black. . . . And so she just didn't think anything of it and just threw it in with the rest of them. But when she came home that night, they didn't have a yard light, they didn't have the porch light on. And when she pulled up in the yard she said that she could feel the hair start standing up on her head. . . . So she got out and from where she walked up the steps it was really dark until you got to the front door. . . . And so she went over and she grabbed ahold of the door knob . . . and turned it. Well, something wouldn't let her turn it. She couldn't get the door open. And she said that she just took a deep breath and she thought, "I got to have lights," so she shoved [the door open] and flipped the light switch on. And it helped some, but then they kept hearing things and feeling things. . . . She finally figured out what it was. So she took that black arrowhead out and put it in the yard. And she—I tried to get her to give it to me; I wanted to mail it to some people! [laughs].

While ghosts and premonitions may not be explained easily, inhabitants recognize that some apparently supernatural experiences undoubtedly have mundane explanations. For example, during his discussion of ghosts Garvin Bradshaw also remembered an episode when a man had fallen off a rearing horse and had been killed. The body was taken back home for the wake:

Well these people, they went and set up all night that night there with him, and this little boy said he had to be sure and . . . he had to go right back where that man got killed at. And he said he had to go through a pasture, and he said he wasn't going to look, and he said when he got to where that man got killed at, he looked. And he said there he was, dressed in white. Said the longer he stood there, he could even see the necktie on him and everything. And he said he just froze there. Said when he come to hisself, a white-faced calf had got up and come up right to him and licked him. Said that's when he come to hisself. That's what the ghost was. It wasn't a thing in the world but a white-faced calf. You can get out here and you can find you a booger[43] at night; you'll be a little bit scared and start out here by yourself a-walking at night, and you can find a bush out there and you'll make a booger out of it. I've done it a many a time.

As a younger woman, Anne Flowers explained how she had debunked a ghost story:

> After they bought that place up there on Eastatoee, she was scared, just her and [her husband], staying up there by herself. . . . And she said, "Now, [Anne]," she said, "I have found a booger up here—or heared one up here." . . . Said, "It goes just like somebody rolling a barrel across the floor." You know, that old house was old and . . . I don't know how many people had died in there, and [the owner] was superstitious. So, well, we went on up there and spent the night with them. . . . And it was in the front room—and there's a fireplace there. And we just got into bed, about to cut the lights off, laying there, and directly I heared it start. . . . So I just eased out of bed, got over there about the middle of the room, and I . . . could tell it was coming from the fireplace. Well, I just walked on over there to the fireplace, listened; I stuck my head down there. It was chimney sweepers [birds called chimney swifts, *Chaetura pelagica*]! . . . Up in the chimney. They had a nest up there. . . . I says, "Come here." I says, "I think I found your booger!"

Conclusion

Like any member of the family, the South Carolina mountains convey a great deal of natural beauty that inhabitants recognize and, in fact, embody through their senses. They see the intimacies of their natural world, they smell the flowering mountain laurel, they taste the frigid spring water, they touch the cool plowed earth, and they hear the sound of rushing waterfalls. At the same time, inhabitants recognize the inherent dangers of this special place. They treat with caution the whitewater rivers and slippery waterfalls, guard against the venomous snakes and unpredictable predators, and avoid as best as possible the eccentrics and the criminals. As (predominantly) Christians, some also acknowledge the potential presence of spirits beyond Earth. Like a family member who may be both entertaining and eccentric, the ambiguous space of the mountains generates feelings of menace and majesty to the area's inhabitants, who perceive those traits more fundamentally than most residents. But inhabitants also establish a more emotional connection to the land than residents do. How this cultural process occurs is outlined in chapter 5.

FIGURE 1 Table Rock Mountain. Photo by the author.

FIGURE 2 Glassy Mountain (Pickens County), with high school graduation dates visible on the rock. Photo by the author.

FIGURE 3 Oconee Bells.
Photo by Sue Watts.

FIGURE 4 Chattooga River. Photo by the author.

FIGURE 5 Upper Lake Keowee, looking toward Cliffs Vineyards Community. Photo by the author.

FIGURE 6 Eastatoee Valley. Photo by the author.

FIGURE 7 Lower Whitewater Falls. Photo by the author.

FIGURE 8 Bob's Place (Scatterbrains) before the fire. Photo by Bob Spalding.

FIGURE 9 View from the top of Glassy Mountain, looking toward the Blue Ridge Mountains. Photo by the author.

FIGURE 10 Moonshine in a
Mason jar. Photo by the author.

FIGURE 11 Warning sign, upper Pickens County. Photo by the author.

FIGURE 12 "Haunted" homeplace, residence for two generations over sixty years. Photo by the author.

FIGURE 13 Cluster of homes. Homeplace (third generation in residence) and (clockwise) family homes for a grandson and two daughters. A son's house is behind the center tree. Photo by the author.

FIGURE 14 Slave cemetery, Soapstone Baptist Church, upper Pickens County.
Photo by the author.

FIGURE 15 Holly Springs Baptist Church Cemetery, upper Pickens County.
Photo by the author.

FIGURE 16 Beech tree and boulder, upper Pickens County. Photo by the author.

CHAPTER FIVE

A Deep Relationship with the Land
Connecting Inhabitants to Land

While both wondrous and dangerous, the mountains of South Carolina also convey a deeper level of meaning for those who would be considered inhabitants. To these long-term dwellers with multigenerational ties to land, the mountains, and more specifically the lands these people occupy, mean something much more vital than mere property regardless of the scenic or financial value. Through a complex process of cultural envelopment, inhabitants become intimately connected to the land they occupy. This chapter seeks what Clifford Geertz described as "a grasp of what it means to be here rather than there, now rather than then, without which our understanding will be thin, general, surface, and incomplete." This chapter offers a "thick description" rather than a "thin" one of the process by which readers may begin to perceive what it means to inhabitants to be "here" in the South Carolina mountains.[1]

Names on the Land

One of the cultural mechanisms by which people connect to the lands they occupy is through the application of place-names. Place-names redefine geography by designating and delimiting it. As anthropologist James Weiner observed about the Foi of New Guinea, "A society's place names schematically image a people's intentional transformation of their habitat from a sheer physical terrain into a pattern of historically experienced and constituted space and time.'" "By the process of naming places and things," archaeologist Christopher Tilley continued, "they become captured in social discourses and act as mnemonics for the historical actions of individuals and groups." Place-names "serve, like a verbal fence, to enclose an individual place as a spatial self," anthropologist Charles Frake explained, and are "markers and delimiters of place," "tokens used to negotiate and mark positions in social interaction," and "worthy of a story." More specifically, as Keith Basso noted of the Apaches, place-names are powerful because in part they call up "thoughts of fabled deeds and the singular cast of actors who there had played them out." In the southwestern Virginia Appalachian Mountains, anthropologist

Melinda Wagner and her research team found that "settlements and land-forms are named for people who were a part of the county's history. . . . Place names symbolize the genealogical, the geological, and even the botanical landscapes." "In a fundamental way," Tilley argued, "names create landscapes."[2]

Place-names in upper South Carolina reflect these same characteristics. Sarah Jane Wooten, Claudia Hembree's sister, told the latter that "'a popular thing to do was to go for a walk or hike. We had no car but most of the places we walked to was just to see them because Daddy had told us about them. The trees, streams and even the fields and foot paths all had a story behind them and they all had names, some of which we thought were funny.'"[3] As Sarah Wooten observed, walking through a landscape populated by place-names and listening to stories about those places and the people for whom the places were named connected future generations to those places and to the past generations through the tales. Joshua Flower's Uncle Bill "knowed these mountains like a man knowed his backyard" because of his extensive walking.

Perhaps most noticeable in the mountain counties are place-names of Native American origin, although the more contemporary legends supporting many of these place-names are suspect. Local historian Lillie Blue volunteered the origins of some of the area's better-known Native American place-names: "Jocassee means 'place of the lost one' from an old Native American legend about a winsome maiden, Jocassee, who loved a young warrior, Nagoochee, from a rival tribe. The romantic legend claims Jocassee jumped into the river when Nagoochee was killed and, instead of sinking, walked across the water to meet his ghost. The name Keowee means 'the place of the Mulberry.' . . . Toxaway comes from the Cherokee word meaning 'a noise as the thunder.'" On the other hand, local historian Fred Holder argued that "the Legend of Jocassee is clearly nothing other than the invention of [mid-nineteenth-century writer] William Gilmore Simms. He simply used names from a geography of South Carolina which he happened to be working on at the same time he wrote the story of Jocassee. Our local historians have conveniently managed to forget (or perhaps because they have never even read the original story), that in addition to a local name [Eastatoee] meaning the clan of the 'green bird' or 'Place of the Green Bird,' he has other local names equated with alligators. . . . Had we remembered the Alligator Clan, we would have had to have long since dismissed the story as nothing more than a creation of Simms," since alligators were (and are) not native to the upper part of South Carolina.[4]

Besides the Native American place-names, perhaps the best-known Euro-American one is the "Dark Corner" of upper Greenville County, reflecting the theme of danger in the mountains. "The fabled Dark Corner has a special fascination," local author Alexia Helsley wrote. "The name evokes a mindset and a way of life—forgotten and forbidden." To explain the place-name, local historian Mann Batson offered this familiar tale: "The story is that during a political speaking, in the 'Dark Corner' area, a cart was used for a platform on which the candidates stood while making their speeches. Some of the local citizenry, not agreeing with what a candidate said, picked up the shafts of the cart and shoved it down a steep hill with the candidate in it. The speaker, skinned and bruised, got up and said the local people were living in the dark. . . . This incident no doubt occurred, but the cognomen 'Dark Corner' was in place many years prior to this incident."[5]

Perhaps the second best-known local place-name belongs to a now-inundated area called the Horsepasture. Local historian Pearl McFall traced the name back to Cherokee times, when "herds of wild horses fed on the bush pastures of cane and wild pea vines and the Horse Pasture Valley now in Pickens County was their favorite range. These horses are believed to have come from those brought in and left by the Spaniards who came with Desoto [sic]." Others claimed the name traces back to the American Civil War. Douglas Edison explained: "And I've heared legends about it. . . . I've heared that back in the (I don't know whether it's the) Confederate War, they hid their horses in the Horsepasture, and up on the Musterground, you know, is where the fighting was. Now that, that might be some Indian story, I don't know." Because local naturalist Dennis Chastain has found the name on an 1813 map, he discredited the Civil War origin story.[6]

As former Jocassee inhabitant Sarah Jane Wooten mentioned earlier, however, virtually every place had a name and a story. Gregory Clayton related that his deceased wife's "grandmother was a Brown. This is a[n] old Brown place, you know, the Browns. I think when they give out land, the Browns come in here. . . . You see that big mountain up yonder? . . . That's Brown's Mountain." Anne Flowers described the mountain near her home: "This one [mountain] up here? We call that the Walker Mountain. There's a Mr. Walker used to live up there. . . . That's all I knowed to call it." "Grandma and all, she was raised on Cain Mountain up there," Charles Watson reminisced. "She was Cain Chapman's daughter. In fact, there's a mountain up there named after him." Abner Creek, on Sassafras Mountain, is named for Abner Chastain, and John Field and Cabin Field were named for Upstate pioneer John Lewis.[7] "Just about every old place in there is named after somebody," Charles Watson continued. "There's a Dick Branch in there named after Dick Dotson. Ann Reed Place—that was just up to the right of Laurel Fork Creek." "That first hollow, that little old branch there" out of Eastatoee Valley, Joshua Flowers recalled, "they named that the 'Harley Hollow.' . . . He killed a lot of squirrels out of there, big time."

Joan Randall, who grew up in Jocassee Valley, had a footnote to the Jocassee legend. "I hadn't read it [Jocassee legend] in a long time. Well, she's supposed to have got drownded in—they called it Thirty Foot. It was right below the house where we lived. There's somebody that said they had put a pole—thirty foot long—and it never did touch the bottom. . . . Well, further on down the [Whitewater] River from Thirty Foot there was Long Hole; and on down there was a Patterson Hole. Now, I heard that that was a sinkhole, but I don't know—I never did know nobody go in swimming there."

Cynthia Niles had heard a local legend about the naming of Cashiers in Jackson County, North Carolina:

> He [a relative] would summer up there, in North Carolina, and winter down here. So, he would take his horse, which he called Cash, up there in the summertime and bring him back down here in the winter. Well, when he got ready to leave from up there in the wintertime, one winter, he couldn't find Cash. So, he had to leave without him. And when he went back the next year, he was looking for him to be dead. But he found him, and so he started calling it Cash's Valley. . . . And so it went from Cash's Valley to Cashier's Valley. Cashier's Valley's named after a horse.

Land as Resource

While place-names emplace people onto landscapes, people may also connect with their places by using them for their livelihoods. In addition to the traditional resource-extracting methods of timbering and farming and the distilling of alcohol from grains, the land provides economic support through the extraction of other valuable materials. In part this sense of utility stems from what Ryan Trask described as the "fiercely independent people" in the mountains who desire to use their land as they please, following the Kentucky way and remaining on the edge of global capitalism (see chapter 1). As Colleen Zimmerman explained, "I think people . . . like the things they do. They like to hunt and they like to fish and they like to garden, all the things that you can do on the land. . . . It's being able—just having that freedom to do all these interesting things you do up here."

As Mrs. Zimmerman mentioned, many locals fished in the free-flowing streams coming out of the mountains, always connecting a trip with a story. For example, Joshua Flowers recalled his times on the Horsepasture River:

But after I learnt to fish, well, it hurt me when they dammed that old river up. I'd go leave here with a half a dozen minnows, catch them out of the Oolenoy [River] and dig me a few worms. I wouldn't bring back a load of fish. But I'd bring back a mess[8]. . . . Trout, river trout, and catfish is what we went for going in, but we ain't never been able to catch us one nowhere that's as good as the flavor up in . . . the Keowee River. . . . And you can catch a mess just about any time if you knowed what to do.

Well into the twentieth century, fur trapping of small mammals continued in the wilderness of the Blue Ridge forest lands. Garvin Bradshaw, from northern Oconee County, remembered that "my daddy . . . used to trap a whole lot. He'd go catch muskrats, minks, and he'd bring them to the house and skin them, stretch them on a board. And . . . [another person], well, he'd buy fur and he'd take them down there [below Pickens], and he'd sell that fur. . . . He'd get his money back out of it, maybe double his money."

In addition to timber, the forests provided many types of botanical resources. A common tradition, Bradshaw's sister explained, was to obtain the family's Christmas decorations from the forest but in an unusual (but locally common) manner. "We always had a little Christmas tree 'cause the house was so little. . . . And Daddy just got one 'bout that big so all he had to do, he'd take his gun and shoot the top out of a cedar tree and would bring it. . . . And he'd shoot us out some mistletoe out of trees."

Trees also provided bark for tanning, Anne Flowers noted, and Robert Davidson described his "granddaddy" using "a good pair of mules" to haul out chestnut oaks (*Quercus montana*) for bark. "He run a whole crew, . . . two or three men," cutting and peeling bark for tanning. Trees also provided saplings for baskets, Claudia Alexander explained:

And I would watch him [her uncle] as a little girl, and he would go out in the woods, get these little round sapling trees, bring them in the backyard, shave off the outer bark, and then take this little wedge thing and hammer. And he would split it and make them real thin. . . . And I would sit out there under the shade of the trees in the backyard and watch my uncle make baskets. . . . And he'd make fish baskets, laundry baskets, bottom peoples' chairs; . . . and some people would pay him to do that. . . . He did pretty good.[9]

Before the chestnut blight eliminated the mature trees, they provided not only timber but also nuts, feeding both people and livestock. "The chestnuts herein talked about were free," inhabitant Buck Newton wrote in his recollections, and "they were plentiful and all you needed to do was go into the woods and gather them. . . . These nuts were all through the mountain until the late teens and early twenties. A blight of some kind came and killed them; strange how plentiful the trees were and within a few years they were gone— not one to be found anymore."[10] Douglas Edison remembered that "a lot of them old mountain people on above us would go to town and peddle. . . . And there's a lot of chestnuts in them mountains, and they'd pick up chestnuts and sell them." Harry Edison added, "See, back then up until I guess in the '20s you had the chestnut trees, and they just turned their hogs and the cattle loose [to feed on the chestnuts]. I've seen some of these old chestnuts still lying back in the mountains. Those are huge trees. It is such a shame that those things were killed off."

Besides the nuts from trees, there were also "great big huckleberries," Robert Davidson recalled. "But we'd go up there and pick huckleberries and then [a neighbor's] young'uns'd climb that mountain, that rock cliff and go up. [laughs] . . . Had a trail up through there and it was just straight up. You just had to get out and crawl through there, but they'd go up there and go to the [neighbor's] place and pick huckleberries and stuff like that," Davidson observed.

"And we used to break ivy [mountain laurel, *Kalmia latifolia*]," Garvin Bradshaw remembered:

It's a green bush out in the woods. . . . They started buying it up here in North Carolina and started buying it back in the fifties and I broke it for three cents a pound. . . . Her [his wife's] daddy bought a brand-new Jeep pickup and paid for it from breaking ivy. That's the way he made a living. . . . Him [another person] and [my brother] decided they'd go break some ivy, and we laughed at them. When they got their paycheck and showed us what they got, we quit cutting locust timber and we went to breaking ivy. We went to making some money then. . . . And they . . . ship it to New York and they make Christmas wreaths out of it and stuff like that. . . . We done anything to make a dollar. Times was hard back in them days.

Mike Davidson added that "I know some guys that are my age [early sixties] that've never done nothing else. . . . Their whole life, that's all they've ever done. And make good money at it. . . . It'll start probably September, and it'll run until about April. Then during that time they'll cut boxwood, or — and there's different mosses that they gather. There's something or other [in the forest] that they can be getting all the time."

For example, Garvin Bradshaw sought "Grub root [*Chamaelirium luteum*]. It's a little ol' root that grows out in the woods. It's got two leaves on it, and they call it grub root. And he'd [his father] sell that for so much a pound. . . . They say they make some sort of medicine out of it." Anne Flowers "used to go with my momma, and we'd go and dig bloodroot [*Sanguinaria canadensis*], and star grass [most likely *Aletris farinosa*]. . . . They would dig it and they'd wash it, dry it out, her and one of my aunts. And . . . then they would ship it somewhere another and sell it. Sometimes they'd have a big sack full. We'd been all over them mountains back in there." Such collecting intimately tied people to place as they came to know the resources in every hollow and on every ridge.[11]

Anne Flowers's husband Joshua also collected ginseng (*Panax quinquefolius*). "You'd carry it back here to them filling stations . . . right above Cherokee [North Carolina]. . . . In summertime you'd sweat to death, digging ginseng back there on them hills. . . . I sold it for thirty, thirty-something dollars a pound, what I sold. But it went to about a hundred dollars a pound. Right before I quit digging, it was way up yonder. But the government got in there and got at them, but they never did get too much of it stopped." In fact, Mike Davidson noted,

> I went up to a guy's house yesterday, and he gave me a piece of ginseng. He had like five pounds of ginseng up in North Carolina. . . . Ginseng right now is bringing eight hundred and five dollars a pound. . . . You know, the best ginseng in the world is grown here. The Chinese grow it, but it's not near the potency as what we have. . . . I don't think you can dig the stuff on . . . government land. . . . And these boys, they sneak in there on government land, you know, and dig that stuff. . . . There's different companies that buy it. You just send it to them, and they send you a check.

Asserting another intimate connection to land, locals prided themselves on fresh spring water. Mountain people "are emphatically partial to the taste of their own spring or well, be the taste that of sulfur, soapstone, limestone, freestone, or merely clear and cold," Berea English professor James Raine had discovered almost a century ago. "People could discuss long and hard the merits of a particular spring," folklorist Michael Ann Williams noted of western North Carolina, and "people from the region still tend to be sensitive to the taste of water." James Edwards explained:

> Next to land, good water is a typical family's most prized possession. . . . To have good water means more than money. . . . All the old cabins and homesteads were built next to springs or a good source of running water. . . . It was something always subject to bragging rights. Like my great-great-grandfather that lived up in . . . Little River section of Transylvania County [North Carolina]. He . . . had a great, beautiful spring there that was all lined with rock and under a big hemlock. But he would always tell everybody that came there what fine water he had. Says, "Coldest water in the world." Says, "It always stays two degrees below freezing!"

In her mother's "last days," Elizabeth Nelson would "catch water for her" from a local mountain spring "because that's the only water she liked." Even today, her neighbor Ryan Trask added, "a lot of people fill up jugs [from that same spring] and take them back to town or home." As with (perhaps too) many other traits, David Fischer attributed this interest in the taste of spring water to a Scots-Irish borderlands past.[12]

In Eastatoee Valley, Beth Lepre prided herself that

> Momma and Daddy had gravity flow water. . . . Back, way up on this mountain [behind her] there's a spring, and the water comes into the spring and then my momma actually, and daddy, put a big culvert, and then the water goes into the culvert and then it gravity-flows to my house. And . . . they used those systems until [pause] nineties, when we had that dry snap and everybody's water went away. That's what we used. And we always had enough water. . . . The bad things that would happen is it would freeze sometimes and break, and then we'd have to walk the line and see where the water, where the ground was wet. Or a spring lizard[13] would get in there and get turned.

Although unethical (and, depending on the owner's permission, maybe also unlawful), the looting of Native American artifacts from mountain land is another form of income generation and of connection to a place and its history. Recalling his school days, Ralph Glenn justified the practice. "Indian stuff always fascinated us. . . . I used to find a lot of quartz down there [at the end of Eastatoee Valley], had magical powers. . . . Sometimes you find musket balls. . . . I've got just boxes and boxes of this stuff. I would walk across those fields in the afternoon and pick these things up until I couldn't put them in my pockets anymore and had my hands like this [full]. . . . And I'd trade it off at lunch the next day for an extra apple from somebody." James York, a local antiques and collectables trader, admitted that he "always loved the Indian stuff—arrowheads and tomahawks and all that stuff. . . . I've got Indian rocks that we've got out and found, from all over—from Table Rock, from up here [upper Oolenoy Valley], from everywhere around here. . . . I got into selling these Indian rocks. I sold two old rocks the other day for five thousand dollars."

Brian Alexander confessed that

> before they flooded Keowee and Jocassee, I used to go up there and find big pieces of Indian pottery. Matter of fact, I've got some in there [another room in his house] right now. I've got some axe heads, the gambling stone they used to gamble with, some arrowheads. . . . I'd dig down about that deep and find the fire pits where they'd burn. You'd find pottery and you could find bones in there and then you'd find pieces of pipe, and you'd just find all kind of stuff up there. And I watched one man dig up an Indian up there. And you'd find Indian beads up there. . . . I used to find all kind of Indian artifacts up there.

"When Duke Power built the dams up there," Margaret York remembered,

> we used to walk around where they, you know, was clearing. We found a lot of arrowheads back then, but I don't think they even let you look nowhere anymore. . . . Nowadays, if you try to look on anything that belongs to the government, there's no way you can look on it. They'll fine you good for it anymore. So we don't look. . . . We used to get out and walk, us [she and her husband] and the kids. We'd get permission from people, that we'd walk along the creek banks or whatever. And we found a lot of stuff in different places like that.

Structures Built from Land's Materials

Another means by which people connect to their land is by using the land's products to construct their own homes or personal living spaces, often with their own hands.[14] Moreover, inhabitants take a great deal of pride in this fact. Theodore Franklin, for example, explained that the large rectangular stone blocks lining the path toward his house had come from a nearby quarry and had originally formed the chimney of his family's 1870s homeplace. In years past a fallen tree had damaged the older home and chimney, but the rocks had been salvaged for the pathway. Marie Ellison and her husband live in a century-old home that was originally a two-room cabin built by "homesteaders . . . with their hands, so it has a lot of history to it." Julie Jackson related a story originally from her grandmother that a relative "cut the timber off the land to build that [her] house. Took it to Pickens and had it milled and built the house for four hundred dollars." Her brother added, "The finished lumber they hauled from Easley up here in a wagon. The whole thing cost seven hundred dollars for the house. And this was in nineteen five, which was a lot of money in nineteen five." As Gregory Clayton walked through his home, he explained to me that he had cut and split the logs from trees on his land; the logs were about six inches wide. Peter Abney built the home in which he lived "in 1949. I went up yonder and cut the trees, carried them to the sawmill. Or I had the sawmill come get them and cut the framing for this house. . . . That's the way you done it."

Norman Cleveland lived in a home where Robert Davidson's

> grandmother, she was raised right here at this old walnut tree . . . right here on the bank [of the Eastatoee River]. . . . And she drove the nails out of that lumber and stuff when they moved it up there. . . . And they built that house and lived in it till they died. . . . They said they . . . built that old brick house; . . . them bricks was made right there and built that brick house after slaves was in here. It's that old. . . . They made them bricks right there. . . . They had a liquid form and they set up in that shape.

Although in a more urban neighborhood, Pamela Williams still lives in a house built by her father:

> My dad made the block—the cement blocks. . . . He came home from work every day, and he built the form and had a pile of cement and a pile of sand; . . . every day he'd mix that up, and he'd make six blocks. The next day he'd pour those out, or during the summertime of course, he'd make six more. He did that for about two years. He mixed six blocks. Now, can you imagine how I would feel about selling that house? I don't think so! . . . No. Not in a million years.

Ownership of Family Lands

In fact, the homeplace, or the place where one arises, carries powerful emotional and symbolic importance for those in the South in general and in the southern Appalachians in particular,[15] demonstrating the fact that from an inhabitant's perspective, property ownership and value are measured in more than financial ways. "When writing about Appalachia," geographer Donald Davis observed, "one must always consider the role of home and place in the lives of mountain residents. The fact that the terms 'home' and 'place' in Appalachia are collapsed into a single word—'homeplace'—speaks volumes about the role of the mountain landscape in shaping Appalachian identity." The southern Appalachian homeplace, folklorist Michael Ann Williams argued, "is not a symbol of the distant past or of many generations of a single family. Rather, it is a symbol of the individual's own past and the individual's immediate family." A homeplace, then, "is where a person feels rooted, whether the roots are distant in time or recently sunk," anthropologist Karen Blu concluded.[16]

Pickens County inhabitant James Edwards explained. "But I can't stress how much land gives a sense of place and belonging to people from the South in general and especially the mountain folks. They always feel like if they, I always have a home to go back to. No matter where they got to, they could always have a homeplace. If you listen to much bluegrass music and mountain music, you hear that as a theme a lot about the old homeplace, and mom and dad back at the old homeplace." As James York recalled, "I was born and raised up in an old slab house about two rooms." The place "wasn't as big as, hardly as big as this thing [a single-wide trailer]. I got a little bit older, and we moved into this little white building out here [in his yard]; it used to be way down towards town. . . . They was going to tear it down, but Daddy had it moved up here and then I had it moved again. But that was my second home, I guess, in that white building out there."

Today, Margaret York (now widowed) lives on that same property in a modified trailer near her late husband's homeplace, which more recently had served as a storage facility for his antiques and collectibles business. This particular use of a former home, Michael Ann Williams explained, is typical. "A homeplace may double as a barn for the housing of livestock or the storage of hay or farm equipment, or it may serve as 'junk house' for miscellaneous possessions. These functions would seem to devalue the meaning of the homeplace, but this is not necessarily the case. It is a testament to the complexity of the house that such diverse functions, if not in conflict, can coexist."[17]

Homeplaces also have complex meanings, anthropologist Karen Blu cautioned:

The emotional tie obviously may be concurrent with ties of kinship, marriage, or friendship, and it may be connected to relations of status and intellect as well. . . . Few home places are simple. . . . One group's home place may be another group's home place, too, which can be a terrible problem if multiple claimants have different views of what should be done with the home place, how people should act while there, and who should be allowed to live there. . . . Alternatively, one group's home place may be a territory where other people live who do not see it as a home place but merely as a residence.[18]

The multiple meanings of the homeplace not only engender misunderstandings between inhabitants leaving vacant the original homeplace and residents or visitors who see an unoccupied structure but also spark disputes within extended families as well. As folklorist Michael Ann Williams discovered, a great deal of angst and legal entanglements ensue from quarrels over inheritance over the homeplace (but see the work of anthropologist Allen Batteau, who interpreted the clashes as class-based).[19]

In order to prevent such difficulties, Williams discovered,

in many cases the homeplace functioned most effectively as a symbol when it was simply not lived in. An empty house is a potent symbol of the past. The house is also a better symbol of the family who once lived there if another family has not taken up residence. One child may own or be designated to maintain the homeplace, but it still functions as *our* home. For this reason many families keep old houses empty but do not truly abandon them. The house does have a use. Its function as a symbol, however, has taken precedence over its functions as a shelter or container of social activity.[20]

Cynthia Niles described the challenges of preserving the Watson Family homeplace. "And, their house, . . . never anybody lived in it since. It's just like they go and clean it and it's just like that they left it. . . . And see, nobody's lived in it but her; . . . and they [children] never had to do anything with the house, rent it, or anything like that. They just keep it for Momma and Daddy. . . . None of the grandchildren moved in it or anything. I don't reckon they want anybody to live in it."

The relationship between the homeplace and family property demonstrates the paramount significance of family property itself. Folklorist Michael Ann Williams explained:

The fact that the homeplace remained the property of the builder or his widow during his or her lifetime often made the intergenerational transfer of ownership difficult. Inheritance of land, on the other hand, was basically egalitarian. The individuals interviewed [in her study] uniformly agreed that land was ideally divided equally between the male heirs, or more commonly, between all the male and female children. This pattern had several important ramifications. The continual dividing of land made it difficult for families to keep large tracts of land intact and impeded the development of a stable rural elite. . . . Those who chose to stay would usually build a new house on their own land near the homeplace.[21]

As Kayla Radcliffe explained, "Family connections are used a lot to get housing. Like one of the couples I was talking about before, . . . they now live on the land where [my] mother and father lived when they first got married, and that's because their mother and father owned the land there. . . . So it just gets, like hand-me-downs. Hand-me-down houses." "Well, mine was handed down to me," Garvin Bradshaw admitted:

My daddy's was, my granny's was. It's been a hand-me-down all the way down. . . . And I've got mine willed to my kids, and my wife's got a life interest in it. Nobody run her off; if I die, she got a place to live here long as she live. . . . It'll be a hand-me-down right on down. It may be a hand-me-down right on down till there ain't even room for a grave. My daddy and them, they had eighty-five acres; there's four of them. . . . Well, they had eight kids. . . . That left eight to divide the land between, so that give them all two acres and a half apiece, more or less. . . . So, I think it should stay in the family. That's the way I feel about it.

Pamela Charles noted that "my two daughters live on the homeplace. And my sister's two girls, they live on the homeplace. And two of my brothers, . . . their boys, both live, have homes on the homeplace. And then some of the grandchildren and they have a family that Daddy gave us all property." At the time of her interview, Elizabeth Nelson still lived in her family's homeplace. "We always lived here in this old house which was my grandparents' home. And it's the house my dad lived in his entire ninety-one years. . . . I know that my grandfather's aunt and uncle lived here when they were first married, and then my grandmother and grandfather lived here when they were first married. . . . So, part of the house is well over a century old." Because of a conflict with a sibling, Nelson had to abandon her homeplace for an adjacent home, and now the old house sits empty.

Maintaining control of family land, often through multiple generations, is critically important for mountain families. Anthropologist Patricia Beaver discovered that "the family network is the community, and family identity is synonymous with place. Family, and thus community identity, is bound up with community historical events and rootedness in the land." Environmental historian John Opie added that "the plot of land the mountaineer knows so intimately is his fixed place, the central axis of his life. It is his reality."[22]

James Edwards provided an excellent example from upper Pickens County:

> In that general area is where our ancestor, our ultimate ancestor Philip [Edwards], settled in 1783. . . . I was actually born in that little area there, and that's considered the springhead, I guess, of the [Edwards] clan. . . . But anyway, after the [Revolutionary] War, you know, this land, upper Pendleton District [now in part Pickens County], was opened up to settlement by the Revolutionary War veterans. . . . So, about 1783, supposedly he came to where he got a grant of land there where [Edwards]town is. . . . But he was the founder of the [Edwards]'s Chapel Methodist Church and was one of the first preachers there. . . . Philip had a family of thirteen kids, and each one of them, most of those stayed . . . in this area, and most of them had ten kids, or a dozen kids, so over a period of about ten generations there's quite a number of his descendants in this area.

James Edwards then elaborated on the symbolic importance of owning ancestral land:

> I still own an acre and a half of the original [Edwards] land. . . . But it means something to me to be able to go out there and grow a garden, a garden on that land that I know my father worked, and my grandfather, and my great-grandfather, going back five or six generations. So it's not land I ever intend to part with, but I hope to pass on to my son, so he can continue it. It's, I can look up the road a little ways and see the spot that I was born, the house I was (well, the house is gone), but I know where I was born, and my grandmother's house was across the road, and it's still there. I can still have that tie to it. The church . . . it's been a part of our family for all these years.[23]

"Landownership traditionally has provided a margin of economic stability and embodies family solidarity and unity," anthropologist Patricia Beaver recognized.[24] Claudia Alexander elaborated. "My dad would say, 'As long as you got a piece of land, you got a home.' . . . And he would never go borrow money and you'd have to put your land up? Oh no, you don't do that.

That was like a sin or something." Consequently, Mrs. Alexander admitted, her father's house might have needed some repairs, but "Daddy would never borrow money on the land to fix up what he did have, the little house. . . . You know, you ain't gonna lose your land for material things." David Ellison commented, "Well, I could have sold that piece of property [family homeplace] fifty times [claps hands]—that quick. . . . I wouldn't sell it no kind of money; no, no, it's not for sale. Period. I could get a handsome price for it, I could. But I want the boys [his sons] to have it. I worked hard for it, see. I plowed those mules I was telling you about. Worked hard, picked cotton. I know how that property— . . . how I got it. So that's why it's not for sale. Something come hard, you take care of it." "Like, we could make a lot of money selling our property, but we've never wanted to, and Grandpa didn't want to," Elizabeth Nelson reflected. "And once it's gone, we could have the money and we could buy other places, but it wouldn't be the memories and it wouldn't be the beauty."

In these comments, notice how both Claudia Alexander and Elizabeth Nelson consider their family land to be something *more* than a material possession; for example, one does not trade or lose land *for* material possessions, and "land" differs from "land with memories," the latter being much more valuable but not in a material way. Given the choice between material possessions and family land, Ralph Glenn observed about his Eastatoee neighbors, "they'd take the land." As Peter Abney explained, "In other words, money is not everything; sometimes you've got to have values above money. I don't know hardly how to explain it."

Claudia Alexander tried to explain how difficult and sometimes heartbreaking it is to transfer family land and the homeplace:

My sisters that died, their children that didn't want to buy the land, *family* bought it because we wanted to keep it in the family. . . . I had to sell my homeplace where the old house was at, and it like to kill me. I cried and cried. I tried to sell it to my brothers, but they at their age didn't feel like they needed it. . . . My first cousin bought it! . . . That's my daddy's nephew—straight bloodline, so I was happy. . . . My daddy did that on all the land deeds; he didn't want any son-in-laws coming in and selling the land out from under his children. . . . Babies always got the homeplace. I don't know why; I guess it's the last piece of land left, but mountain people—the baby of the family always got the homeplace. . . . But that way it stayed in the family. And that's the way it's always been handed down—in my daddy's name.

So my niece has got it now, but she's got it going to go to her children. . . . But at least it stayed somewhere in the family.

"Yeah, I think they ought to keep old places long as they can," Gregory Clayton agreed:

I still got the piece of my granddad's old land up yonder, Carson's Creek, next to Caesar's Head. Been thinking about going up there and making me a place where I can take my camper . . . when it's hot down here [upper Pickens County] and stay a weekend or something. But I believe anybody ought to keep their old—their ancestors' land. There ain't many that're doing it now. . . . There ain't many places left like this one [his house, figure 12]. They about all gone; the people let them go. I don't know what'll happen to this one after I leave.

Peter Abney thought that "land and families is scarcely[25] vanishing. There's a lot of land that's not family owned anymore and it's hard to find a piece of property now because if a family owns it, they don't want to sell it. And the family tries to keep it for their own. . . . Especially mine, because they see the value of it. We've done discussed it. . . . What property's up in here that's owned by families—unless a[n] older one dies out, it won't be for sale." In fact, Abney related a story in which some of his family's traditional land had become available due to the death of a neighbor, and he was going to buy it back at a land auction. People in the community "knew what was in the back of our mind, and they didn't bid against me. Jim Anthony was the only man that bid against me." Abney outbid Anthony, and the land now belongs to his son and daughter-in-law, and a granddaughter "has already got a double-wide up there," Mr. Abney proudly proclaimed.

Peter Abney's grandson, a college student, reflected on the importance of his family's land:

I'll probably live here my whole life. . . . Unless something really big comes up I can't *imagine* selling the land just 'cause I value it. And once it's gone, it's gone and money you know it runs out, so then what do you got left? Nothing. But the land will always be here if you keep it. I do too much stuff on it to let it go right now, so I couldn't imagine selling it, honestly. . . . Up the road where my cousin lives up above there . . . is state-owned land so you can hunt up there; I ride my four-wheeler up there. There's a stream that runs through there you can fish in there; there's occasional trout. . . . I don't know what about it—you don't want to leave. I couldn't sell it.

Forrest Sanders, also a college student, admitted that

my grandparents, like they're real reluctant to sell their land. . . . Like, my grandparents ended up selling some land to remodel their house. . . . And my grandpa, he got *so* mad, because he had sold it with all these rules and regulations on it, saying, you know, you can't put more than so many houses up on it. . . . I think they built two houses on it, and he was *furious* because they had built these houses on his *land*. . . . He was raised—like where his house is now, across the street and over, maybe a hundred yards or so, was the house that he grew up in.

Brenda Kendrick thought this sentiment varied by individual, though. "It just seems like some children are closer to the land or want to stay on property that's belonged to the family for a long time, and there's just, I guess, just a difference in children. My oldest son would love to have my old homeplace where I grew up. He's always said, 'I'd love to live over there.' I don't know. I've told my cousin or my brother-in-law if his children decide to sell it or if his daughters decide to sell it to let me know. . . . All the kids would like to have it."

Kendrick reflected on her grandparents' home, tying the house directly to memories of her family in that place:

We lived at the old homeplace when my children were younger, and they can remember going down to the river and playing in the river. You know, it's just childhood memories, and they'd like to keep it. Sometimes it's just not possible, you know, keeping it in the family, but it's good that you can. . . . I have cousins that own the property where my grandma and grandpa lived. That was just a special place to me, because I remember them. . . . It makes you closer because we lived, say, maybe a mile from my grandma. . . . I can remember going to my grandma's and spending the night, you know, in that old house. . . . I can remember going up there when I was a child; that's where grandma, my granny, and granddaddy would be sitting, one on each side of that fireplace, in their little chairs, you know. It was just a special time just to get to go to granny and granddaddy's house and spend the night.

Occupying Family Land

As informants have noted, it is critically important to not only use and own family land but also continue to occupy it. As family-owned land is subdivided into smaller and smaller parcels generation after generation, clusters of family members come to live near each other (see figure 13). Cultural anthropologist Allen Batteau found that "in the early years of marriage, children often live close to the husband's parents, and . . . the typical living arrangement is for parents to have some of their children living in houses clustered around their own, in a small hamlet. . . . This is the domain of householding—a set of relationships based on coresidence, commensality, and fixity of place. Its emphasis is on independence, sharing within an independent unit; yet the continued dependence within a family, carrying through even to the establishment of new domestic units, is also clear." Social worker Jack Weller observed that "whole hollows or bottoms have gradually filled up with the houses of kin settling close to each other." Thus, historian Harry Caudill explained, "on practically every creek and stream the inhabitants are a tangle of cousins, aunts, uncles, nieces, nephews, parents and grandparents. In some communities the blood lines are so few and so intermixed that the most patient genealogist might lose his wits in attempting to unravel them."[26]

"Many parents fear their young married children will move on soon and sell their property to others," anthropologist F. Carlene Bryant discovered. "Even those who have moved away are sometimes given a parcel of land in case they wish someday to return," folklorist Michael Ann Williams noted. "In keeping with tradition, new ranch houses and mobile homes encircle the bungalows and other dwellings built by the parents' generation in mid-century," Williams added. Consequently, anthropologist Karen Blu argued, "to an extent, the family nexus is visible, plotted onto the land in the clusters of houses nestled close to one another." "Most people live on or own land in the community settled by and inherited from their family founder," Bryant observed.[27]

Moreover, since families have moral reputations and since land and family are linked, even one's morality is tied to place. For example, when Claudia Alexander was dating, she knew that her boyfriend would be acceptable to her father merely because he shared a last name with a locally prominent World War II veteran. Mrs. Alexander's father-in-law added that "most people back then [an earlier generation] were as good as their word, simply for the very reason you had to be. If you got the name out that you wouldn't pay your bills and debts or wouldn't keep your word, that was fatal for a person" or an entire family; such a reputation would "affect them all." As with (perhaps too) many other cultural traditions, historian David Fischer attributed these clusters of kin in mobile buildings, associated with family reputations and physical places, to be "from the Old Country."[28]

"Place, in this sense, is a part of a larger world view, an outlook on life which is communal rather than self-centered and individualistic," historian Ron Eller explained. "One's attachment to place in the mountains is an attachment to family, kin and neighbors, to shared experiences that imply responsibility beyond the self and provide linkages between the past and future."[29] "I was born," John Summers began,

> born right out here out on this hill. And we lived up on the hill there . . .till my daddy built this house. . . . Every one of them [grandchildren] wants to live here. Everyone lives here. I got five grandkids up the hill here. . . . Youngest grandson wants his own place here. . . . My oldest was wanting that up there on top of the hill. And the oldest granddaughter, she's wanting to put her double-wide in up here in this patch of woods right here above us, so we'll probably do that. So far we know three of them's definitely wanting to live here. Yeah, and if that's what they want, that will be arranged.

In an interview before his death, Peter Abney proudly proclaimed: "I was born in Pickens County . . . about three mile[s] from here. So the only two places that I've ever lived, is here [his current home] and there." "We still got kids around," Abney said. "Most all of them live close. I've got one son that lives in . . . North Carolina, and he's got two sons. . . . So he's the one that don't live close by, but the rest, yeah, we all live close, close around. I think we all live in Pickens County. But see my son and daughter live over there; son lives about a half mile down the road." When someone once asked Alice Flowers whether she was from Pickens County, she replied, "I'm about as much from Pickens as you can be. You know I was born in the bedroom my mother died in." And my "daddy's mother" served as midwife for my birth, she added.

Peter Abney's adult daughter Nancy Daniels remembered her childhood and the benefits of living close to kin. "Well, I grew up right where my daddy still lives. . . . My grandmother just lived in the house that's still standing right over here. And we had two cousins who lived on out past her. So, we had lots of fun. My brother and I and our two cousins would meet at my grandmother's yard and play every single day. . . . But we all just grew up right around here together." Marie Ellison's childhood friends "were my little cousins that grew up down on the same river branch we did, and there was two sets of them and they were all my age, . . . and all were girls. And we played . . . at playhouses . . . and looked in the woods for different wild-flowers and just little things like that." Depending on circumstances, these relationships often continue into adulthood. "One of my cousins that we played with all the time just still lives right on up the road, and the other one lives down toward Pickens," Nancy Daniels stated. "We just remain very close all these years."

Alice Flowers, the youngest daughter of Anne and Joshua Flowers, described one downside of such close resident kin for children:

> But I know that our little road, [Flowers Road], just about everybody on that road, especially when I was growing up, were kin folks. . . . I grew up being able to go from house to house to house, you know, and Momma didn't worry about us that much because she knew everybody that was on that road. . . . I was as apt to get a whupping in Aunt [Cate's] yard as I was at home. . . . If you was doing something wrong they whupped you right there and told you. And then they called your momma and you got another one when you got home.

Another downside of living in an area surrounded by relatives is finding someone to date as a teenager. Edward Daniels complained that this is a problem "for me 'cause I'm kin to everybody! [laughs] I mean honestly, there is *nobody* that I am not kin to that's like my age." His mother Nancy Daniels agreed that he would have to drive a distance to meet potential dating partners, and her son Edward added, "I'm not talking about going somewhere, I'm talking about trying to find somebody that—like date somebody that lives around here is about impossible." His mother concurred, and then Edward joked, "We don't live in West Virginia!"

In describing his immediate surroundings, Mike Davidson demonstrated the very close relationship between his sense of place and his sense of kinship:

> When you go across the hill over here . . . on the left-hand side there, . . . my nephew lives on the right, and then my sister lives there, and then my cousin owns property there. And you go on down the hill . . . and my aunts live all on that property on the left, . . . and my cousin lives there, and then my great aunt lives there, and my cousin lives out that road, and my brother-in-law's sister owns the property up that road, and you go on out, my oldest sister owns thirteen acres at the end of it. . . . My family's only one that lives there. . . . Been that way for 150 years.

As a consequence of the close association with land and kin, Brenda Kendrick recognized that "there's a deep relationship with the land. . . . Like my grandfather. He had four children. . . . He left the land to his two boys and gave the two girls money. . . . I know one of my uncles, his children are still on the property. My other uncle just had the one child, and I think maybe she sold part of hers, but she still has part of my granddaddy and granny's old place." Even in more recent generations, Kayla Radcliffe noted, "They [local people] don't move around a lot."

But occasionally people must leave, for a variety of reasons. "Families that were originally here is getting less and less, and their children has moved off," Margaret York worried, "and they've sold their place, and then it's been broken up into subdivisions and housing. You know, it's disappearing. It's disappearing pretty fast." Many inhabitants, from multiple generations, reflected on the monumental decision to leave their parents' home and enroll at a college or university or to leave the area in search of a better job. While many American parents and children struggle with emptying the nest or seeking one's fortune in the world, these challenges create visceral social and emotional conflicts for many inhabitants from mountain counties.

For inhabitants, departures might open eyes to new possibilities or feed a desire to explore the world (intellectually and actually), but departures might also sever a deep bond between family and land. Kayla Radcliffe admitted that her parents

> wanted me to live at home and drive out and back to Clemson [as a college student]. . . . And I don't know if it's because of them pushing or what, but sometimes it's—it does feel kind of like an indebtedness. . . . I'm actually in her [aunt's] will to get the land that she has. And I don't know how I feel about that, because honestly my plans aren't to go back to Pickens. I don't—I really don't think I can live there and be happy because it is so closed off. But there's this little like guilt thinking I can't. You know, I feel bad about this. So there is a kind of a pull there.[30]

This "kind of a pull" felt by Radcliffe actually reflects a colossal tug of war between the centrifugal force driving some out of the area to discover a wider world or better economic opportunities versus the centripetal force pulling inhabitants back to care for aging relatives and to occupy family land, regardless of economic consequences.[31] As early as 1899 William Frost criticized the tight-knit mountain communities as limiting, for "the children grow up with almost no examples or analogies of life outside these petty bounds." Because of the love of place common to mountaineers, scholars Angela Cooke-Jackson and Elizabeth Hansen discovered, sometimes they "stay in places where there is no hope of maintaining decent lives." Writer James Vance acknowledged the pull to stay in place but believed that the path to success in American society leads out of the mountains (especially out of mountain "culture") permanently. Most likely, as geographers Holly Barcus and Stanley Brunn summarized from the scholarly literature, mountain people reflect a continuum between those desiring to leave and those desiring to stay; mountaineers also recognize the ambiguous consequences of either decision.[32]

Many college students from the mountains struggled with these opposing forces of family/land versus fortune/world. As noted earlier, Kayla Radcliffe accepted the fact that "my dad's going to not like it [her moving away after college]. My mom understands. . . . [but my dad is] . . . very uncomfortable about me leaving; he was very uncomfortable about me moving here [university housing], and it's just thirty minutes away. So it's actually, it's a really big challenge, because, I mean, I don't want to hurt his feelings and be like, 'I don't want to live with you anymore' but I can't—I can't basically handicap myself career-wise by staying there." Radcliffe continued:

> Middle-aged, like people like my dad, or my mom, [are] so settled in where they are, and not leaving, but—like my Aunt [Cate]. She would never leave. . . . So it just depends on what the incentive is to get out, and most of them don't have it. They like what they have [and] they don't see anything better. . . . For me, it was something that I didn't start experiencing until I was in high school. . . . I became more realistic about what I had to do and where I needed to go to learn about things I liked. And then I realized, you know, I can't get that here. . . . For other people, some people did leave out of rebellion. . . . And then other people do it very reluctantly.[33]

A generation earlier Elizabeth Nelson had enrolled at the same university as Kayla Radcliffe and felt the same pull as Radcliffe did but discovered a different life lesson. "I guess the fact that I had the opportunity to live on campus in college and see what other lifestyles were like and realizing, you know, I have it pretty good. And I think TV helped me, too, because you can see how so many different people live in so many different settings on TV. . . . And you know, I have a piece of heaven up here [in the Eastatoee Valley] . . . so I want to stay close to this and the people that I was raised with." Beth Lepre, Nelson's neighbor, also compromised while away at college. "I don't know of anybody [from her Pickens County high school class] that went way far away for school [university], I just don't. I mean, they may have, but I just wanted to stay close to home. I didn't want to go that far away. I just, my friends were here and Momma. I was close with my mom and dad, and I just was chicken and I didn't want to go that far away. And I could come home every weekend if I wanted to, you know; Momma would come get me if I wanted to come home."

Upon her college graduation, Lepre decided to value family and family land over uncertainty:

When I got out of college and started to work and started talking about having a place of my own, my mother, I guess, said, "Well, why don't we fix up the rental . . . for you?" And so my dad, . . . he fixed it up really nice for me, and I moved down here. And I didn't, I guess I just didn't want to go. You know, it sounds kind of sad, but I didn't want to go away from my parents. I just wanted to be with them. . . . I certainly needed them and they did a whole lot for me, but then it came to the point they needed me. . . . And I was able to retire early and take care of what I needed to take care of. . . . I just didn't want to go, but there was a reason down the road I didn't see.

After living in the Northeast for about two decades, Shirley Patterson also felt the need to return home to care for her aging parents. "My parents was getting up in age. And in my heart, in my heart, I felt the need, the responsibility, and the love to come back and spend some quality time with them while they were still up moving. . . . I felt a need to come home, to be with them."

For young adults seeking the American Dream but wanting to retain the Appalachian connection, this apparent contradiction may be overcome by life course flexibility. For example, contemporary college student Jason Taylor understood the desire of some of his college friends (such as Kayla Radcliffe) to leave the area for a wider world, but he had a long-term goal as well. "I really want to travel, travel around in my job for a few years just to get a feel for that. 'Cause I just want to experience the country more than anything, see what it's all about. And then I've always planned to come back, probably living in Dacusville" in upper Pickens County.

Several local residents had done exactly as Taylor planned to do—moved back home to complete their careers well before aging parents needed them. For example, Ryan Trask "worked as a stockbroker in a previous life [else-where in South Carolina], . . . and my wife was up here [Pickens County] teaching. . . . And I told her, I said, 'I am sick.' I said, 'I am physically sick, and I want to quit my job—tomorrow!' . . . And I remember saying to her— 'cause I was pretty lonely, sad at the time. And I said, 'You know, if I can't see Table Rock every day, I'm not sure I can get by.' That was just not literal, but if I can't see that, I'm just not whole." "I was living in Houston," Chris Jackson admitted, "had a job and all of that stuff, you know, that you have. And it dawned on me that this is not really where I want to be. *Why* do you live in a place you don't want to live, just because you have some job? They have them [jobs] everywhere, you know, if you're willing to work. So we moved back here and built that house on the side of the road." "'I took a notion one time to just live out there in Californy till I died,'" a western North Carolina mountain man told anthropologist George Hicks, "'but, you know, I couldn't. It just got so it'd make me sick to think about these mountains back here. I had to come back to this country.'"[34]

Those mountaineers who had permanently moved away for whatever reasons struggled with their emotions even when they returned briefly for visits.[35] Claudia Alexander remembered that when her older sister "would come visit she would cry when she'd leave because she'd say, 'I knew when I left those mountains there was nothing there for me. I wanted to go out into the world and make a life.' . . . I think it was hard. It was bittersweet. I think she knew there was nothing there for her. . . . But when she'd come to visit when I was a little girl, I didn't understand why she was crying so bitterly when she left. And a lot of times we talk about that now, and she says, 'I would love to come home and see you-all but it would just break my heart seeing that, how hard it was on Momma and the rest of us'" when she left again.

"'Do you ever miss it?'" Brenda Kendrick had asked her sister during a return visit home, "and she said, 'Yeah.' She said, 'I've always missed it.' . . . She said, 'There's just something special about coming back home to the mountains.' And she said, 'I'll always love it and it'll always be home.' But she said, 'We probably won't ever move back there' because, you know, they both [the sister and her husband] had jobs; they had family in Atlanta."

Elizabeth Nelson explained: "Well, to me staying within your raising (the old term) is important, just for my own personal sake. . . . I came back home to live. . . . There are others who've left this valley that absolutely hate it. . . . One of them's only about three years older than me, and yet her brother loves it here. He hasn't moved back, but he still has the land and the house and he comes whenever he can and he just absolutely adores it." For both Nelson and her neighbor Ryan Trask, their valley is "home." Trask continued: "Like a lot of people know every nook and cranny in their house and where this is placed. . . . I mean that's just, *it* is home. . . . The whole thing." Nelson then added, "The whole thing is home. It sure is. . . . It is a good comparison."

Living in the same valley as Nelson and Trask, Beth Lepre admitted,

when I met my husband and we got married . . . we looked all over all the land that Daddy had and we looked at some places really seriously, but I was just attached to *this place* [her homeplace]. So . . . we just added on here, which was probably more expensive. . . . That's what I wanted and like; one of my rules was my boxwoods out there, my *huge* boxwoods, that have been here since . . . I was a little girl. . . . I'm like, we have to build the house around my boxwoods. And we did. . . . So, you know, you just get attached to things, and I guess I was attached to the place but maybe more attached to my parents. You know, if they had moved, which they would *never* have done, but I don't know what would've happened then. . . . They just loved it here. I mean, they just—Momma grew up here and Daddy loved it here.

Ryan Trask, born and raised in Pickens County, contrasted the economic values of seeking one's fortune with the social value of remaining close to home:

I have a lot of friends that stayed here that valued their families and a particular lifestyle or their relationships or their sense of place that said, "No, it doesn't matter how much money I make or what I become, I can't be any happier than I can be doing this particular set of things." . . . People confuse per capita income with happiness or utility. And I think a lot of people around here got it figured out. And there are a lot of other folks that say why don't those dumb hillbillies . . . —gosh, doesn't he know what he could've done? And I think, no, that these people that some look down on figured it out early in life and the others are confused.

Early in his career, Peter Abney declined a promotion that would have entailed him leaving the upper Oolenoy Valley. "'Let me tell you something,'" he told his supervisor. "'I live up here. Neighbors tend to their business and I tend to mine. . . . If they've got a loaf of bread, I've got a half of it. . . . I don't think I want to give that up for a [job] title.'" When given a promotion at work, Ryan Trask was asked if he was going to move out of his mountain valley. "And I couldn't even fathom the question . . . , he said, "I can't imagine that! . . .

To be able to come home and work in the garden, or go for a walk in the woods, or go hunting, or spend time with your family or go out back to the picnic shelter and grill supper as opposed to going out somewhere."[36]

As I was leaving a home in the upper Oolenoy River valley, the owner, Nancy Abney Daniels (daughter of the late Peter Abney), offered me some of the ripe tomatoes on her back porch. She explained that they had come from her brother's garden, utilizing the exact same plot of land that her grandmother had used years before. Embedded within that tomato pulp or in the juice running down one's chin lies a direct connection to three generations of family living on and using the same plot of land for the same purpose. In that ordinary tomato germinated within the soil of one's ancestor, a perceptive inhabitant can taste and smell a plant from family land, remember in that sensory experience previous generations of tomatoes and previous generations of kin, and remember as a child eating tomatoes from that same garden received from a grandmother's loving hand, a hand now long quieted but never forgotten.

Memories of the Land

Imagine buying that tomato from a roadside stand from any of the clusters of homes in any mountain cove. Tourists would see the same vegetables, the same landscape, and the same collectivities of houses as inhabitants, but without the inhabitant knowledge of who lives where, how those individuals are related, and what their family reputations are, visitors would not comprehend the landscape (and its social implications and historical experiences) the way inhabitants already do. As historian Ronald Eller observed, "mountain people tend to be tied not only to a specific plot of land (the 'home' place), a specific mountain or a specific locality but to people (kin) and to memories (shared experiences)." These dense kin networks on adjacent parcels of family land establish strong social relations, and these relations can be extended back through time by memories of those who lived on those same lands generations before. "To know the landscape is to know and control access to that knowledge or to those experiences," anthropologist Angele Smith wrote. Through discussion of these experiences, anthropologist Keith Basso noted, "native views of the physical world become accessible to strangers. . . . Thus represented and enacted—daily, monthly, seasonally, annually—places and their meanings are continually woven into the fabric of social life, anchoring it to features of the landscape and blanketing it with layers of significance that few can fail to appreciate."[37]

In fact, "the addition of past memories increases the complexity and enjoyment of presently perceived settings," researcher Fritz Steele noted. As folklorist Michael Ann Williams argued, these narratives even may replace the physical entity of a homeplace should the latter disappear. Williams concluded that "it is not the property or the landscape, any more than it is the physical structure, that is important. The empty house site, or the empty house, is a symbol of the experience, or memories of the experience, of home. The power of the homeplace lies in its ability to evoke these memories. People who no longer have physical access to their homeplace seek solace in the power of narrative. . . . The entrance to the homeplace, I found, was through these oral narratives."[38]

Oral narratives connect people to places in intimate ways. "Fueled by sentiments of inclusion, belonging, and connectedness to the past," anthropologist Keith Basso argued, "sense of place roots individuals in the social and cultural soils from which they have sprung together, holding them there in the grip of a shared identity, a localized version of selfhood." "Animated by the thoughts and feelings of persons who attend to them," Basso continued, "places express only what their animators enable them to say; like the thirsty sponges to which the philosopher alludes, they yield to consciousness only what consciousness has given them to absorb. . . . Places actively sensed amount to substantially more than points in physical space."[39]

In fact, archaeologist Christopher Tilley observed, "human activities become inscribed within a landscape such that every cliff, large tree, stream, swampy area becomes a familiar place. Daily passages through the landscape become biographic encounters for individuals, recalling traces of past activities and previous events and the reading of signs—a split log here, a marker stone there." Through this process, Tilley continued, "places themselves may be said to acquire a history, sedimented layers of meaning by virtue of the actions and events that take place in them. Personal biographies, social identities and a biography of place are intimately connected." Thus, Tilley concluded, "places, like persons, have biographies inasmuch as they are formed, used and transformed in relation to practice."[40]

Inhabitants know these biographies of place intimately. For example, Douglas Alexander and his brothers "shared so many precious hours getting to know" the Reedy Cove area of upper Pickens County that "except for the native Cherokee Indians we saw more of this wonderful place than anyone else ever has or ever will."[41] As I walked down a stone path toward Ryan Trask's Eastatoee Valley home, I had to detour slightly around a waist-high bush growing between the stones and blocking the path. Trask explained that he could remove the plant (actually a walnut tree sapling), but since it began life as a wayward nut that had fallen between the stones as his young son cracked walnuts that he had harvested from a tree nearby, Trask wanted the tree to grow right where it was. Someday, he hoped, his son would tell *his* children the history of that tree.

As a teenager, Forrest Sanders felt a similar cross-generation connection. "The first job I think I had, back in high school, was throwing hay, for a guy out in Dacusville. . . . It was kind of interesting because my dad knew I was throwing hay, but then we were driving in Dacusville and I pointed out a farm, or a field, that I'd picked up hay in, and he goes, 'Well, I've picked up hay in that same field there. See, 'cause that used to be your uncle's house across the street.' So I thought that was kind of neat, I guess . . . , doing the same thing my father had done when he was younger." And in the same place, with connections to family, Sanders's statement implied.

"Before my son went off to college," Claudia Alexander recalled,

I took him down below the old house where I was raised. I took him down the old trail to where our old spring at the bottom of the hill [was] where I used to have to carry water from the spring (not a well) but I carried buckets of water. And I said, "I want to tell you something. You're going out into the world; you always know where your roots come from and where your family come from. And when you ever see anybody that's underprivileged, you think of your momma, and you'll think of people differently." And I don't think either one of my children has ever got away from that.

"I can live anywhere else," Brenda Kendrick admitted,

but there'd always be a special thing about coming back here, to the mountains. . . . I have not been back to my homeplace up there . . . since I had moved until a couple of summers ago. . . . And we [she and her sister] just walked all over the place and down toward the pasture, and you know, it just brought back memories of when we were children and when we lived there. Different things would pop up into your mind. . . . This was where Momma always had her garden, and you know just things that you kind of forget. And it was just good to go back and think . . . "Well, I lived here when I was a child; this is where I grew up. Where me and my sister used to have our fights and quarrels." And you know, it's just—it's good to go back sometimes, and just say, "This is where I was raised. This was some of my property." . . . It was just—that was a good day.

Journalists Michael Hembree and Dot Jackson related a poignant story of Marvin Gravely, visiting his old homeplace after the Jocassee lakes had filled. "In 1988, seven years before he died, Marvin returned with his son Will and friends Gene and Georgia Chapman to the home of his grandparents, the old Thomas McKinney homeplace near the mouth of Big Eastatoee. The hilltop farm site is accessible now only by boat; the house has fallen, and the road that ran in front of it has sprouted saplings. But the spring where his grandmother, Mary Emilissa Alexander McKinney, filled her water bucket was still flowing, at the lake's edge. And the beech tree where her grandsons carved their initials, in about 1916, was still healthy."[42]

Brenda Kendrick had specific memories of her family's homeplace. "I can remember going up there [mother's parents]. . . . And they used to have reunions there.[43] At the back of my grandparents' house was two or three big pair of trees, just across the back, and this huge place. We used to set up tables out there on just big planks, you know, and have all the [maternal] cousins and everybody; we'd have like a family reunion. . . . To me, that was just a special place, my granny and granddaddy's place was. I can see my granddaddy now; he had his own li'l rocking chair out on the porch."

Besides the homeplace and family lands, other places have special meanings as well because of the multigenerational ties to those particular places. Naturalist John Lane described Bull Sluice, the well-known (and dangerous) rapids on the Chattooga River. Just below the rapids "are at least three generations playing on the edge of the water, skipping stones, sitting, talking. . . . Their intimacy with and commitment to this river are admirable. I guess they might call it love. They've returned to this place with the regularity of migration, in spite of all the outsiders crowding them since the 1970s. In the old days, before the whitewater business, this deep pool and accessible beach below Bull Sluice acted like a community center—fishing, picnicking, even baptism."[44] Nancy Daniels's baptismal place on the Little Eastatoee River, also a locally favorite swimming hole, had been usurped by "drunks," especially on weekends, she complained, so her family had ceased going there. At her local church, nestled at the foot of the Blue Ridge (figure 15), a regional artist had replicated in a mural the old outdoor baptismal pool painted above the church's internal one.

Bodies Embedded in Land

The final way people connect to the family land they have named, used, owned, occupied, and remembered is through burial. As historians Michael

McDonald and John Muldowny discovered for the Tennessee Valley Authority Norris Dam project in upper east Tennessee, a mountaineer's sense of community embraced both the living and the dead. Families there had "a deep sensitivity to and an awareness of their existence as long-established social entities. This sensitivity was . . . nowhere more apparent than in the concern evidenced by the communities over the final disposition of the graves of their families. To the displaced and uprooted living, these graves were mute evidence of the continuity of their own existence, proof of the permanency of the past, and an irrefrangible link to their collectively shared communal and familial memories." "How much more personal can it be than to be born on a plot of land; grow up there; die there; and be buried there?" sociologist William Falk asked.[45] The interment of individuals into their family land permanently comingles their essence with that of their ancestral land, creating a physical, symbolic, and spiritual connection that inhabitants acknowledge, respect, and feel. A Blue Ridge African American woman connected to her ancestors while walking over her family's land, including the site of her husband's grave. As she explained, "And when I go up [to visit], . . . we walk the land. You're also communing with the people who were there way before you even knew anything about the land. . . . This is where they were, this is where your grandparents, where your great-grandparents, those people who saved it when they were enslaved. . . . Those lands have special meaning for me personally because my husband was buried there."

In this particular family cemetery, visitors leave the gravel road leading to the owners' home and instead follow a steep, poorly graveled road across a rivulet and into a small clearing completely encircled by forest and underbrush. Nailed to a nearby tree is a green and white sign, like a street sign, announcing the family name of the cemetery. Upon closer inspection of the ground, rough field stones emerge through the underbrush. In addition to the stones, two professionally carved granite slabs can be seen, including a marker bearing the name of the husband of the woman quoted above and another for the family's patriarch, born into slavery in the early nineteenth century. In a very real sense, this was not an overgrown and overlooked family cemetery but instead was sacred family property containing deceased family members, with their headstones and corporeal remains as much a part of the landscape as the trees and shrubs that grew from the graves and the birds that sang in the trees overhead. This is the place that has "special meaning" to the woman cited earlier.

In the Eastatoee Valley, Elizabeth Nelson described her family's cemetery on her family's land. "There are my great-great-great-great grandmother,

Nancy [Nelson], who was one of the first white settlers in the valley. Her grave is on Graveyard Hill right next to Uncle [David's] house. . . . And then there's lots of rough fieldstones as tombstones still there. . . . There's family there, buried there. I wouldn't mind being buried here when my time comes. I would love to be in that little graveyard. . . . That would be the place to be; looking down on this beautiful valley forever more." Gregory Clayton planned to be buried on the small mountain behind his home, next to his wife, and he hoped his children and grandchildren would be interred there as well. Local historian Jerry Vickery, raised on the Keowee River before its inundation, desired to unite physically with his home. "Although the lake is there now, this small place on earth will always be sacred to me. I have asked Bobbie [his spouse] and my children at my death to have my body cremated and sprinkle the ashes over Lake Keowee from where the Nimmons Bridge once spanned the river to the Craig Shoals, now deep under the pristine surface of the lake. I will return to the river and this time I will spend eternity."[46]

This connection becomes even more powerful when the family cemetery is associated with a family church, near family property.[47] "'This is a mountain church,' says Rev. Charles Leonhardt, who has served Gap Creek's [Greenville County] small but faithful congregation for a couple of years. Many of its members have deep roots here; the names on the rolls of the living also mark a century and a half of stones, out on the hill." One member of Pickens County's Soapstone Baptist Church's congregation reflected on the family cemetery associated with that church (figure 14). "Every one of them [ancestors] that's out there [in the family cemetery] that we knew as we grew up played a big part in our lives . . . because there were things they could tell us and we'd listen. So . . . that's another good feeling like . . . comes over you when you're there, you're close by."[48]

Conclusion

Unlike short-term visitors or longer-term residents, inhabitants develop a connection to their family land by placing family names on the landscape, shaping their living spaces from local materials, and using their family land (and commons, i.e., government) land as a source of material wealth. Inhabitants continue to own family land through multiple generations, occupy the homeplace or live nearby, cluster together, and tell stories about ancestors (and themselves) in those places. They appreciate, respect, and desire the literal embedding of family bodies into family land, thus completing a circle by becoming part of family land themselves and reinforcing the connection for future generations. Bodies transforming into family land bearing family names and supporting family buildings that are used, owned, and occupied by multiple generations of kin generate a process by which family land and family members merge, both symbolically and literally. This transformation creates a powerful spiritual connection between family and land and explains the deep emotional loss accompanying the physical loss of that land. Chapter 6 examines this transformative process and the emotional and physical consequences of that loss.

CHAPTER SIX

In Your Bones

A Spiritual Connection to Land

The consequence of the intimate connection between individuals and the family land they name, use, own, occupy, remember, and become generates a metaphysical synthesis between the elements of the soil, the humans on that soil, the kin ties between those humans, and the memories of past kin who lived on, labored over, and entered into that same soil. Above the ground, like a mist, floats a supernatural presence unifying and justifying these entities. For inhabitants, location becomes a part of one's identity and a part of one's being. Land and family and generations and memory merge, explained through a lens of spirituality. Because of these linkages, the loss of family land creates a deep emotional wound, almost like the loss of one's own family member. To mitigate this loss, those who have experienced it often attempt to retain symbols of that land as one might retain locks of hair of a deceased family member. Through time, myths and legends of that lost landscape arise, preserving a sense of mystery and wonder about those lost places. In turn, these legends and symbols serve as lessons for those fortunate enough to have retained control of their family land today.

Merging Family and Land

One of the consequences of the complex networks of kin using, owning, and occupying family land for multiple generations is that one's geographical location and personal identity become linked with general character traits associated with one's kin. Students of the South in general have long recognized this association. In his fieldwork, anthropologist Allen Batteau discovered that one's identity "begins with being 'raised up' in a particular locale and lasts even after death, when one is buried in a family cemetery on a hillside overlooking the homeplace." Anthropologist Karen Blu, researching in the North Carolina Low Country, admitted that it took her awhile to discover that "'being placed' in the landscape communicated much about social identity and social life, about assumptions concerning local 'character,' about likely political clout, about stories commonly told of events in a locality, and about a number of other things to listeners better attuned than I." During her fieldwork, Blu discovered that connections "between family name, kinship group, and geographic locale are commonly accepted ones. They are generally considered to be important pieces of information about someone with whom one has dealings."[1]

For the mountain folk of southwestern Virginia, anthropologist Melinda Wagner found that culture and nature are bound together "by the residents' emphasis on their perceptions of the environment's beauty; the residents' orienting themselves by the geological markers in their environment; the part nature plays in the history, folklore, and stories of the culture; the uses the culture has made of nature; the cultural knowledge of nature that the people carry; and the land-based connections between people. These elements, together with the long genealogical history on the same land that many of the culture-bearers carry, help create the residents' identities."[2]

The physical and social connection between people and land becomes even more firmly cemented as family churches, often associated with family cemeteries, bring scattered kin home for homecomings, events designed to remember deceased family, absent family, and family memories typically reinforced by food and faith. In these ceremonies, religious scholar Larry McGehee explained, "'flesh and blood' homefolks become transubstantiated emblems of a divinity which hangs upon the mountains in its mists, beckoning the homeless home, the godforsaken to God." At Holly Springs, a "thriving little country church" in Pickens County (figure 15), writer Lilly Smith described her community's homecoming as "the banner day of the whole year. . . . Many responded, drawn by some large or small mound in the cemetery where they had once stood in deep mourning, feeling as if the keystone of life had been taken away."[3]

Beyond social and spiritual identity, land and people merge metaphorically into a common physical identity. As an African American woman walked her family's Kentucky land (owned by the family "since the time of slavery"), she felt that "country is as much a part of me as my full lips, my wide hips, my dreadlocks, my high cheekbones."[4] At the same time, locals display a tremendous degree of detailed knowledge of the physical features of their immediate landscapes—the locations of specific trees, wildflower or berry patches, rock outcroppings, springs, curves in roads—and, of course, stories associated with these places.

Deliberately, anthropologist Melinda Wagner used a specific verb to describe the ties to land felt by her southwestern Virginia informants. These locals, Wagner wrote,

> are rooted by their genealogical tie to their land that was owned by their ancestors. They are rooted by the work they have done to maintain the buildings these ancestors built. They are rooted by the cemetery at the top of the hill that contains their relatives' bones and where they know their own and their spouses' will one day be. They are rooted by the sight of the huge "sugar trees" that they planted as saplings when they first moved there and by the taste of the apples from the trees they began grafting fifty years ago. They are rooted by the past, present, and future on the land. They are living in a "genealogical landscape."[5]

Because of this synthesis, local historian Anne Hendricks noted that "love for the land and love for people, whether they be family or neighbors, is intermingled." Anthropologist Angele Smith declared that "our sense of who we are and where we come from is linked to our experiences and memories of living in a place and acting in a landscape." "Mountain people have a deep feeling of belonging and of loyalty," social worker Jack Weller observed. "They belong to a family, a valley, a county, a state. They know they belong, and others know it, too."[6]

Anthropologist Keith Basso argued that a group's sense of place "may reach sacramental proportions, especially when fused with prominent elements of personal and ethnic identity." Reminiscing about a return to her old Pickens County homeplace in the 1930s, Flora Keith Overman described "an awe of stillness and wonder [that] came over me as I stood spellbound looking into the fireplace. I could in imagination see the low chair in which my grandmother nursed my blessed father at her breast. I imagined the cradle in which he lay, with soft wool from the lamb's back. I realized the ground whereon I stood was holy."[7]

In a series of interviews about the Dark Corner summarized by local historian Anne Hendricks, the compiler discovered that "'one of the common themes that seems to be running through just about all of the interviews is [that] people . . . have a real love for the land. It's perhaps, if not the most important thing in their lives, surely one of the most important.'" The editors (unnamed) in Lilly Smith's fictional biography believed that the family returned to the Eastatoee Valley because, for Smith's brother, the "haunting beauty of the mountains had ever been with him, and the call of the Big East-atoee was too powerful to resist. *There* was the only place he could find peace and rest and a crowning benediction to set him free."[8]

According to anthropologist Keith Basso, a sense of place "is what has accrued—and never stops accruing—from lives spent sensing places. Vaguely realized most of the time, and rarely brought forth for conscious scrutiny, a sense of place surfaces in an attitude of enduring affinity with known localities and the ways of life they sponsor. As such, it is greeted as natural, normal, and, despite the ambivalent feelings it sometimes produces, entirely unremarkable. . . . Sense of place is accepted as a simple fact of life, as a regular aspect of how things are."[9]

Because the mountain inhabitants' sense of place is both "normal" (and thus expected) and "felt" (rather than consciously acknowledged), locals have tremendous difficulty in describing their sense of place, especially to residents and to inquisitive anthropologists. When I asked them to explain that concept, many informants responded as did James Edwards, who stared into space, hesitated, and finally said something like "It's hard to put into words." Author John Lane described the locals' connection to the Chattooga River as "primal, a part of them. 'Something you see every day, you take for granted,' one friend explained. 'But you'd sure as hell would miss it if it were gone.' To locals, the river is often beyond description. To them it's something akin to home, a place you feel your connection to very deeply but cannot articulate."[10]

Andrea Bowers tried to articulate her connection to the valley in upper Pickens County where she had been raised:

> When we come here [to visit] . . . it is the people, but it's also the area too. It's all of it that you get here. But it's like, to me it's like when you get here you get back to the basics of what it's all about. You know, life, love, you know, just the seasons, just everything. The simplicity of it is very peaceful, and it kind of points me in a better direction when I need it for the future. . . . I want to move back home now. . . . I mean, I like Columbia [South Carolina], but . . . I would like to come home. . . . When I come back here, I think I'm a better parent . . . because I get a little more, I get back to my roots. Get a little more solid.

"For me, this is home," Chris Jackson said of his Pickens County mountain valley. "I've been all over the country and it doesn't look right anywhere else. I mean, and it's hard to explain, but it just doesn't look right. You get down past Interstate 85 headed toward Columbia and it's not the same. . . .

Now we grew up here. Course there's a lot of family here. . . . And we can go to these little cemeteries around here and go back two hundred years. And you can't do that just everywhere." His neighbor, Shirley Patterson, directly tied her family's history to the sensory connection toward the land itself. "I've lived several places. I mean I was comfortable there, but you just didn't have the same feeling that you have when you live here. . . . This is my roots. This is where I grew up. To walk on this soil, to touch this dirt." "When I go up there [homeplace]," Claudia Alexander recalled, "I just have all kinds of vivid memories of walking behind my daddy and him plowing all those fields— just the feel of that rich dirt beneath my toes, just walking through those fields." Ryan Trask felt the same sensory connection. "One of my favorite memories and smells and feelings right now, is you know, I can close my eyes and know what it feels like to walk through fresh-plowed soil when it's hot outside but the dirt's cold between your toes and the way that it smells. . . . So you know, the smell and the feel of all of that." "And a lot of times, you know," Trask continued, "I'll try to describe it to somebody, and I'll notice they've got a funny look on their face. . . . 'You don't smell the hemlocks? You don't smell the white pines? You can't pick out all the different smells that are in this bouquet?'" Douglas Alexander also linked multiple sensory experiences about both land and kin in his recollections of ginseng hunting with his father in extreme northern Pickens County. "I distinctly remember the mountain smell as we traversed the steep hillside. The creek beckoned to us with its rushing song and the tall hemlocks and laurel and ivy offered a quite [sic, quiet] serenity where the world was kept at odds. . . . Even today, if I need to get away, I close my eyes and go ginseng hunting again."[11]

Spiritual Connection to the Land

Because of this intimate and multisensory connection to the land (and simultaneously to one's family), many inhabitants consciously expressed the overwhelming feeling of joy, contentment, and serenity they feel as they return to the mountains after being separated from them for a while. For example, on a high school service trip to Charleston, university undergraduate Jason Taylor explained that "it's really nice down there, and there's plenty to do, but . . . we were like driving back and we like got into view of the mountains, and we were like, felt like this is it. Like, it's like this draw and you just love to see the mountains like driving down the road. . . . I just felt—I felt like I was back home. I was like, thank God!" Coming from even one county eastward, the first view of the mountains "made me have butterflies," Marsha

Baird admitted. Driving from the opposite direction, Ryan Trask felt the same connection. "When we cross this certain hill, coming down the grade from Tennessee, I roll the window down, and it's just an overwhelming sense of, 'Okay, I'm getting whole again.' . . . I don't have words to describe it. . . . If I go to the beach for a couple of days— . . . okay, that was good; let me get home!" "My heart jumps when I see that first row of mountains in the distance," Elizabeth Nelson declared. "It's like, I'm home."

A very insightful informant, Ryan Trask tried to articulate the inhabitants' perspective about the land:

> I feel like I've described what's in me, inadequately, about the land. And I've tried to talk about sense of place for me, and it's this place in particular—why the people are important, and why relationships are important and so forth—and the land and this valley and the mountains. If it's about a relationship, first and foremost I feel like it's the place where I can see God's handiwork and maybe that relationship. And so it's something that's just hard to put a price on. So when you talk about, or when I try to think about these people that were uprooted from the Keowee River Valley, or the Jocassee Valley, it wasn't because it was good farmland, I'm guessing. It was because it was a part of them, and they couldn't unwind themselves from the land— you couldn't separate the two, and they couldn't separate the land and themselves, I believe, from probably what they felt like was a relationship with their Creator. It's all bundled up together. And then you throw their families and friends in there and it gets real complicated. It's not something that you can just say, "Well, here's a check. Go move and buy you a new house." And that's what I feel when I'm here. . . . And that's what I was trying to describe—that sense of place. . . . I'm trying to describe and point out that the sense of place that I have is not dependent on amenities, house, people, or relationships. It's a relationship to I would say Creation; you may say Nature. It's a relationship to my Creator. . . . And I think that's what a lot of people [feel] that have this attachment to the mountains, the Blue Ridge Mountains, the Appalachian Mountains in particular.[12]

Anthropomorphizing of Land

In the quote above, Ryan Trask tried his best to articulate the interconnected elements that constitute the emotional meaning of family land to inhabitants. Not only is the land "home," but it also connects people to land in a (Christian) spiritual sense. For mountaineers, historian John Opie wrote, "the land . . . is not an idea or abstraction but a sacred mystery with enormous power and durability." In her study of southwestern Virginia, anthropologist Melinda Wagner found that residents described land with two types of metaphors: "one likened the land to a family member; the other gave the land a religious or spiritual essence."[13] The same is true of the inhabitants of the southern mountains.

Through this merging of land and people and spirit, the land itself seems to animate. "When I'm in a valley like this or in a holler [hollow] like you described," Ryan Trask explained, "I can walk up this holler behind my house, and I've done it a lot of times, and just, I like to just lie down. Just lie down. . . . I mean, I feel like God's just cupping me in His hand and I got everything I need right in that valley or in the holler." With this quote, Trask equated his physiological envelopment by a hollow in the hills with the metaphysical sense of being encased in the hands of his creator. The land surrounding Trask not only *feels* like hands but has also actually *become* the hands of God.

In the introduction to their book, journalists Mike Hembree and Dot Jackson compared the sense of the landscape between visitors and inhabitants. "Thousands who travel upcountry roads through the Keowee-Jocassee region know the area only as it exists today, a deep-water wonderland on the edge of the Southern Appalachians. For them, the Keowee River runs silent. For others, though, *it lives.*"[14]

A living landscape thus interacts with those insightful enough to feel that connection. With a home on family land overlooking the Blue Ridge Mountains, Shirley Patterson felt that "the beautiful rocks and the trees . . . peep out at you. . . . They have a different message for you every day. . . . Sometime[s] you can look at the mountains. They pull the shade down. They actually close you right off. Like today I'm not going to let you look in. And then the next day . . . they open the shades up, and you look and you say, 'Wow!' . . . Then some days they just give you a little small peep."

Like a resident in an apartment across an inner courtyard, Patterson personified the mountains as an actual human neighbor, raising or lowering curtains and peering around them. Like good southern neighbors, though, mountains may do more than peep. Upon returning to the Upstate, local author Gerald Orr described his feelings as he neared the Blue Ridge. "Finally, and best of all, a curtain of purple and blue hangs in the distance—the serrated tops of the Blue Ridge Mountains, dividing the Carolinas. I never tire of the sight of this range that wraps its arms around the land I love best in all the world." Shirley Patterson, too, used the common southern welcome of a hug to animate the Blue Ridge Mountains as she described her feelings about her mountain home. "There's something about . . . the serenity and the peace. It's just overpowering. You can't explain it; you have to feel it. And it's there and it's real. It's very real. And when you break around . . . that little curve right there [near her home], I take a moment and just apply my brakes. That whole area just opens up its arms and just hugs me." Like a friend or a lover, the animated landscape embraces those who care to experience the caress. "*You know, Jocassee wasn't just a house — or a piece of land,*" Debbie Fletcher's uncle told her one time. "*We had a love affair with that place.*"[15]

Anthropologist Keith Basso, writing about the Apaches, believed that scholars needed to recognize "a thematized concern with the ways in which citizens of the earth constitute their landscapes and take themselves to be connected to them. Missing is a desire to fathom the various and variable perspectives from which people *know* their landscapes, the self-invested viewpoints from which (to borrow Isak Dineson's [1979] felicitous image) they embrace the countryside and find the embrace returned."[16] Inhabitants of the southern mountains feel precisely the same way.

Land Incorporating People

Once intimately bound with inhabitants in complex ways and therefore animated, land symbolically incorporates, or enters people. "The 'feel' of a place," geographer Yi-Fu Tuan wrote, takes a long time to acquire, because "it is made up of experiences, mostly fleeting and undramatic, repeated day after day and over the span of years. It is a unique blend of sights, sounds, and smells, a unique harmony of natural and artificial rhythms such as times of sunrise and sunset, of work and play. The feel of a place is registered in one's muscles and bones."[17]

As Tuan had proposed, this process represents perhaps the deepest layer of the symbolic meaning of land for inhabitants. For example, describing her family's ancestral land in the mountains, Pamela Williams acknowledged that "to me it's beautiful. It's a beautiful place, a restful place; it's a retreat. . . . I could walk out on the deck and see the sun rise. . . . But just sitting out on there, listening to the birds, and listening to the ripple of the water. To me that's — you can't buy that, you know, you can't give that away. You just — that's in your bones." Elizabeth Nelson directly linked her mountain valley residence to her own body. "Well, it's my heart, it's my home. It feels like home because like [a neighbor] said to me one time, I love being down in the valley and looking up to the mountains for my inspiration, but you're surrounded by the warmth of all of this community and family. It's home. . . . There's so much that holds me and my heart here, the history, the family history, my family's still living here, the wonderful community, the beauty of it all." In a later interview she added, "If you just go out and sit and look at it [the landscape] you can't help but be touched by it in some fashion. It's a spiritual thing for me. I just feel like I'm very blessed that I and my family could have been allowed to live in this incredible place."

Other anthropologists have recognized this same connection made by Appalachian inhabitants. Working in southwestern Virginia, Melinda Wagner's team discovered that when land has been owned by generations of family for so long, "it ceases to be simply property; it moves from commodity to family member." In western North Carolina, anthropologist George Hicks quoted a man who acknowledged that "'they's just something about being here all your life that gets in your blood, I guess. They's no way in this world you don't miss it, and I mean hard, too.'"[18]

Because land symbolically has morphed into a family member and symbolically has entered into the bodies of inhabitants,[19] the physical loss of a family member logically, then, would negatively affect the physical landscape. For example, Elizabeth Nelson described her feelings upon her father's death. "There's a spirit about this place [her valley]. The day of my dad's funeral, my mom and I were in the car with my brother and sister-in-law and we started up the road out of the valley, and it had the most empty, spiritless feeling. I'm sure because my dad was gone. When we came back, the spirit was back, but it's a feeling you can never really explain in words." On the other hand, the emplacement of a body in family land would reenergize and reanimate the land. Pamela Williams described her husband's burial on family land in the family cemetery on the flanks of the Blue Ridge Mountains "in May, and I think the place just came alive. . . . You know how the dogwood trees was blooming. . . . When we buried him everything just seemed to say, 'Welcome home!'"

Death/Loss of Land

If land is symbolically personified and animated by naming, by using, by owning, by occupying, by remembering, and by interring and if land and home and family merge, what happens when that land or that home is lost?

As discussed in chapter 1, some family lands in the study area have been lost for a variety of reasons, but the one most commonly remembered is the removal of landowners from the Jocassee and upper Keowee Valleys for the Duke Power lakes; these removals also created the most anguish and resentment. As anthropologist Angele Smith argued, "clearance of landscapes is about rupturing the sense of belonging, home, identity, and meaning; it is about the politics of remembering and the politics of forgetting."[20] Almost everyone has an opinion about the removals.

On the one hand, some southern Appalachian residents accepted the inevitable march of progress and even recognized the benefits of the loss of their insularity. Norman Cleveland, then a current inhabitant of Eastatoee Valley, understood that "a lot of people had to move [when the lakes were built], but they was all happy because they got enough money out of it where they . . . could get what they wanted. . . . Nobody complained because they got enough money to have something so much better than what they had." Mike Davidson, a teenager at the time of the lakes' flooding, offered a more nuanced range of feelings about the loss:

> There really wasn't that many families that actually, you know, lived in the [Jocassee] Valley up there. And most of the people that owned land up there didn't stay up there year-round. So, you know, it didn't—my personal opinion is, . . . nobody didn't really get hurt. Like I said, Duke paid them a thousand dollars a[n] acre for that land.[21] And that, back then, that land wasn't worth a hundred. . . . On Keowee, you know, it was—yeah, there were people that had to move out that'd been farming that for years, and families moved. . . . It [land] had been in the family for two or three hundred years. But that wasn't the case at—Jocassee was completely different than Keowee.

Other residents recognized that while many left the inundating valleys because of better economic opportunities or because they had no other choice, it was still a difficult decision. As one former Jocassee Valley inhabitant observed,

> and then, after World War II, it appears to me, that because we had sent so many people overseas, and they'd traveled and seen the world, . . . that people started traveling more. Automobiles became more accessible, people had a little more money, they had better jobs and that kind of thing. . . . So, when I think about losing my home, yes I did, but I also think that . . . my brothers and sisters had to leave

to find work, to find employment. . . . Yes, we lost the valley, but I gained a whole new way of life. My cousin said it real well: . . . "It's amazing what can happen if you . . . get in that river and swim downstream!" . . . So, yes, we lost our homeland, but you know it's a very mixed bag for me. And not many people would appreciate me saying that.

"'Although we know it means advancement,'" Claudia Whitmire Hembree (born and raised in Jocassee Valley) quoted a relative as saying, the relative added, "'I think the flooding of Jocassee is a great tragedy. So many of us who love the mountains have had all of our old trails, rivers, and all erased by the covering of the area. I think a lot of us regret the building of the dams.'"[22] Residents who were young adults or children when their family land was sold had no control over the sale and now reflect fondly and wistfully on what had once been. Brenda Kendrick admitted that Jocassee Lake is a "beautiful area, but . . . you still think about everything that's covered by water. . . . [pause] I think too about, you know, a lot of places that I have seen that are now covered with water that children now don't even, can't even fathom what it looked like—the beauty that they've missed."

Using an anthropomorphic metaphor, Cash Godbold lamented that "I left a part of my heart in that splendid valley" as he reminisced about the closing of his aunts' girls' camp in Jocassee Valley. "When the valley was flooded it was hard for me to come to grips with the fact that some of my fondest memories are 300 feet underwater." "On a personal basis," Claudia Whitmire Hembree wrote, "the hardest time that I had with the [Jocassee] Valley being flooded was when I heard that the lake waters had covered the bridge at the Girl's Camp. In my mind and heart, that signaled the final blow to a lovely valley that had been home to the Whitmires and others for some 150 years. Occasionally it seems strange not to have a homeland to visit and share with my son Cliff." Many years later Godbold and his family returned to Lower Whitewater Falls (figure 7), a former destination for all-day hikes above the (now-submerged) girls' camp. Godbold reflected, "I gazed down the valley where the river runs into the present lake and knew that my children would never know the pristine life I had lived in the Jocassee Valley."[23]

During her interview, Brenda Kendrick remembered and reflected on the above-cited passage from Claudia Hembree's book about the author's inability to show her grandchildren where she had grown up:

I thought that's sad. . . . I know it [the lakes] brought a lot of industry and a lot of new people and—to the county that probably never would've come here otherwise without the lakes. But it'd be, kind of be sad not to be able to go back and show your children where you used to play and what you used to do. . . . I mean, even though my grandparents' house is gone and that makes it kind of sad but I think it's—I like it because some of the family still owns the property. It's still there and I could go if I wanted to. Remember where the house was, and what we used to do. . . . I think it's good to be able to do that.

As evidence that losing one's homeland is extremely traumatic for many inhabitants, anthropologist Angele Smith wrote that "this is also witnessed by acts of resistance against the forces that are clearing the lands and by attempts to revitalize the 'emptied' landscapes."[24] "But I've also met countless families and individuals that were pretty bitter about having to leave," Ryan Trask commented, "that [Jocassee Valley] was their little piece of heaven, and I can relate to that. If they flooded this valley [Eastatoe, figure 6] and there were a lake and I had to leave I'd probably be lying down in front of a bulldozer somewhere."

As described in chapter 2, many local residents believe that Duke Power began to buy up mountain land for decades prior to the flooding of the valleys. They argue that the company purchased the land under the guise of timber companies such as Crescent Land and Timber, wholly owned by Duke Power but not openly revealed to the landowners. Thus, many locals assumed they were getting fair market value for their timberlands, while Duke purchased cheap land that the company knew would later be developed as lakefront property and sold at a much higher price. One Dark Corner inhabitant recalled his great-aunts showing him where they used to live, "'and the bitterness they have for the day when the land was sold.'"[25] Patrick O'Connell, whose family had been displaced by upper Lake Keowee, explained. "Yeah, they [Crescent Land and Timber] come in here and lied to people in here about it, big time. People started a-getting kind of wised up a little bit, so they started having to pay for it."

Some held out; others (with hindsight) sincerely regretted their economic decisions. Joan Randall's father owned land deep in Jocassee Valley, and she remembered her father postponed selling his land as long as possible:

I don't know why Daddy didn't—wasn't selling. . . . Well, we went to court after he died. They give us a pretty good price for it—I mean, no fortune. I had heard that (now I can't tell it to the truth) that when they first went in there to buying it . . . people just sold their land pretty cheap—what they thought they was getting a good price, too. After they found out what they was going to do they worried about it because they sold it so cheap; thought they'd held onto it they could've got more—and they worried theirself to death about it. . . . Why he didn't [sell] I have no idea— . . . just didn't want to give up.

"What is the impact of clearance and removal of people from their homes and lands?" anthropologist Angele Smith wondered. "If the meaning of landscapes in terms of a sense of place and identity is so great, then what must be the terrible impact on people who have had to leave, for whatever reason?"[26] In his interview, Ralph Glenn answered Smith's questions:

The old people that lived on the Keowee River, when they were displaced, . . . a very, very substantial number of them didn't live more than a year after they left the river. It was the only home they'd ever known; it was their life. Everything they had was wrapped up in that, and they were uprooted from it. . . . They got a nice new brick house over in Salem [Oconee County] on Main Street, and they'd go over there and sit there, 'cause they didn't have a garden in the backyard. They couldn't go collect ginseng out of the mountain behind the house. They didn't have a spring to go get cool water out of in the summertime. They didn't have their neighbors. They didn't have the river. . . . They were given all these material things, and the spiritual things weren't there anymore. . . . And, I'm quick when I talk to people that are new here. The first thing everybody's got to blurt out of their mouth is, "Oh, these lakes are so wonderful!" And I look at them and just kind of shake my head and say, "Yeah, but at a terrible cost."

"A lot of people didn't want to move at all," Robert Davidson remembered,

and a lot of them people moved and died. They moved out of there and *died*. They didn't none of them live; I don't believe it was nare [nary] one of them that lived five years that come out of that Jocassee [Valley]. They—all them people died. Why, I don't know. . . . They didn't want to move. No, they didn't want to move at all, [softly] let me tell you. They forced them out, you know. They paid them well for the land and all that kind of stuff, but they still didn't want to move. . . . And there's some of them never did. Some of them never did move out of there till they died. It was several of them stayed right in there till they died.

"Oh, it killed them all" to move out of the valley, another former resident emphasized. Her father, for example, contracted Alzheimer's disease shortly after the family was forced to sell their lands to Crescent Land and Timber, and she blamed the loss of family land for her father's loss of mental acuity. "They done away with nature," she concluded.

Legends even told of others who took their own life after losing their family land.[27] Robert Davidson told a story about an old man returning from getting "a drink of liquor" at a friend's house. When

> this old man come along and picked [him] up, commenced asking him questions. . . . And he asked him who owned that land right there. . . . He told him he was buying land for Crescent, Carolina Crescent Timber Company. . . . The old man paid him a down payment on it and then so he bought it right out from under them before they knowed what was going on. . . . And old man [Smith] got to trying to buy land back and trying to buy a place and he couldn't buy none and he got on a big gun; he was just killed because he sold his [land] . . . too cheap.

Patrick O'Connell knew of a neighbor who had "moved on up the road up there in a trailer. I reckon he got to thinking about it [having sold his land] so bad, he just killed hisself. Broke his heart out. . . . See, he give it away."

As Patrick O'Connell indicated, the loss of family land metaphorically and (perhaps) even literally might break one's heart like the occurrence of a family death, because land merges with family and memory and symbolically morphs into another family member. As geographer Donald Davis recognized, "for rural Appalachians, to be separated from their natural surroundings is to be removed from the very thing that makes them who they are as individuals." From their study of Tennessee Valley Authority (TVA) dam construction in east Tennessee decades earlier, historians Michael McDonald and John Muldowny discovered that "what was to vanish beneath the reservoir was not so much a way of life as the living social organisms of community, kinfolk, and neighbor—the end products of generations whose visible remnants, the tombstones in family plots, served as mute reminders of the continuity of existence." Local author Jerry Vickery described his feelings about the death of his father, which he linked to the death of his former home, now under Lake Keowee: "I had a hard time dealing with Daddy's death. . . . I was still having a hard time adjusting to life off the river. As long as Daddy was alive, our family's river lifestyle was alive, even though we were no longer living there. Daddy was a river rat and never changed. . . . To this day I still miss him and the river life experience that surrounded us while he was alive. . . . Leaving the river had been harsh."[28]

Inhabitants recalled vividly their feelings about the loss of their family lands almost as if they were viewing a corpse at a wake. Upstate naturalist Dennis Chastain remembered as a teenager riding into the Horsepasture area right before the valley flooded. "'They were telling people that this is your last opportunity to go up there. . . . We piled in the car after church that Sunday and drove up there. It was kind of sad. I remember very well the experience of riding up there and knowing that within a matter of days or weeks all that would be under water." Elizabeth Nelson recalled her final view of the Thompson River Valley. "The river was so wide and had huge rocks, and it was just beautiful back in there. . . . And then we rode back in there the last time we came up before they started flooding . . . and you think, 'We'll never see this again. We'll never, ever see this.'" Reconciled to the loss, Deborah Mitchell chose not to watch the actual flooding "because at that time, that day, I just said, 'Okay, it's gone.' [pause] And that was sort of it." "My world was there" in lower Eastatoe Valley, Ralph Glenn admitted. "That was the epicenter of everything. And so it was clearly the worst day of my life [upon moving out as a teenager]. I cried and cried and cried." As local writer Pearl McFall prophesized, "the children who grew up there . . . will feel like a loved one has passed from them when Jocassee is submerged forever under a great lake."[29]

Because of their deep emotional distress over the loss of their land and because a loved one did pass, inhabitants often used metaphors of burial to describe the lakes covering their former homes.[30] When Debbie Fletcher as a little girl heard the news of the future Lake Jocassee, "I remember walking out onto the [Attakulla] Lodge's huge front porch . . . and seeing . . . the power company man, bringing morbid news of plans to build a huge dam which eventually would envelop our valley under the shroud of a huge lake . . . and leave a huge hole in our souls." "I have tried to accept the lake for its obvious beauty," Fletcher reflected further into her book, "but I don't believe I'll return there for a while. . . . I've watched boats swiftly slicing through the water 300 feet above Attakulla Lodge's resting place, knowing that the passengers were not aware of—and perhaps did not care about—the paradise buried deep below." Several years later Fletcher recalled a boat trip to a quiet cove on Lake Jocassee, where her party anchored and she jumped into the lake, expecting the rush of cool mountain water; instead, "the water was warm. It felt unnatural. I surfaced (crying a bit) and pleaded for help to get me out quick. *'I feel like I just jumped into someone's grave!'*" In

1993 Claudia Hembree interviewed Frank Finley about his Jocassee Valley recollections, and Finley used the same metaphor. "'But so many of us who have loved that country will never forgive them of robbing us of it. I've been up on Lake Jocassee one time since they covered it. It reminded me so much of a canopy over a grave that I have never wanted to go back.'"[31]

As with a death in the family, the symbolic death and burial of treasured homelands must be reconciled in some way. Deborah Mitchell explained her grieving process. "And people say, 'Well, do you ever think about Jocassee,' I said, 'Yeah, a *lot*.' . . . But as far as dwelling on it—if I've learned anything about losing homeplace it's this: that you cannot live in the past. . . . They call it the Serenity Prayer, about knowing the things you can change, and the wisdom to know the difference, and everything. And, you know, this is ancient history. This is history, and I can't do a thing about it. So, life goes on, you know. And yes, I think about it a lot."

Later, Mitchell elaborated:

> I ran into this man who's a counselor in Oconee County, and he has counseled . . . people who are still having trouble dealing with this [land loss]. . . . No, I don't think I ever cried over it, you know? . . . It's just like accepting a death. Some people do it real well, and some people mourn forever and never get over it. . . . I made a decision after the valley was gone: if you can't beat 'em, join 'em. So we went up there and bought a piece of property. . . . But I thought, you know, that's the wisdom to know the difference of what you can and can't change.

Even buildings become animated by the spirit of the place, and the loss of those buildings also penetrates mountain souls. The log cabin home of J. D. Chappell, a well-known and beloved inhabitant of Eastatoee Valley, was animated by Dot Robertson in her essay obituary of Chappell: "In the dusk of this burial day," Robertson eulogized, "the roof of that now-empty cabin seems to sag a little, in its sadness." Debbie Fletcher described the destruction of her revered childhood summer vacation spot, the Attakulla Lodge. "It had been raped, pillaged by looters who helped themselves to whatever was of any use. . . . It was like saying goodbye to a dying friend, but without hope of Heaven's reunion."[32]

Debbie Fletcher's quest to reconnect with the inundated Attakulla Lodge brought her national attention. As documented in videos and in essays, Fletcher recruited diving companies to discover the submerged building, determine its structural integrity, and then dive on the structure to recover a piece of the building as a memento. Later, Fletcher herself trained to dive so she could follow a tether partway down to the structure and feel that connection. Fletcher described her feelings as she dove with a friend above the Jocassee Girls' Camp site. "To have lost something very special in your life, then suddenly have a reconnection, produces unspeakable, joyous emotions. I delighted in laughing with her [the friend], completely understanding how she felt. I feel the same way when we dive on Attakulla Lodge. . . . Holding the line and knowing I'm connected to my family home—although still 220 feet away—makes me happy. I feel like I'm home again."[33]

In the Appalachians in general and in the southern mountains in particular, "many individuals speak of the old homeplace with tears in their eyes," folklorist Michael Ann Williams documented.[34] While interviewing Harry Edison in Eastatoee Valley, I noticed that he had preserved his grandparents' homeplace (as had many informants) even though it was empty and dilapidated. When asked why it had not yet been torn down, Edison replied that he knew he had to do it but hesitated. "It's family; I hate to do it." While Edison may have meant that the house "is family property," in his statement he actually anthropomorphized the building: *it* is family. Edison also confessed that he had an equally difficult time tearing down his parents' country store, but at least he had salvaged some tin from the roof for his modern garage.

Local writers Mike Hembree and Dot Jackson told several stories of former Keowee Valley residents who lost their homeplaces to the lake. The former home of Dena and Charlie Steele, both buried at Keowee Baptist Church nearby, now lies underwater, but "the hilltop site of their house is still discernible at a campsite in Mile Creek Park [Pickens County]. One of two hemlock trees that used to shade the porch is still standing guard over the old stone steps, which now descend toward a broad expanse of clear, blue-green water." Another valley family held a picnic on the porch of the old homeplace before it was inundated, linking food, family, and place together for a final tribute. "'If I ever dream, I dream I'm there, in that old place,'" a woman remarked about her former family home.[35]

Perhaps the most poignant homeplace death, literally a sacrifice, was that of the old Johnson Chapman place. Journalist Mike Hembree interviewed Cleo Chapman about her husband's two-century-old homeplace. When they were first married, Hembree wrote, Mrs. Chapman and her husband Johnson lived with his parents in a big three-story house along the upper Keowee River. "The Chapman house was one that would know much love. In the end, its love did not run out. Its life did." "'My husband had never lived anywhere else,' [Cleo Chapman stated]. . . . 'One night it was raining and I looked outside and saw that the old house was on fire. I looked around for my husband and he was gone. Then he came back through the house and I knew he had something to do with it. He pulled his shoes off and said, "That's the hardest thing I've ever done in my life except burying my mother and father."''" Rather than see his old homeplace buried underwater, Johnson Chapman burned it down himself.[36] From an inhabitant's perspective, Chapman's act was not arson but rather cremation.

If land and people merge because people are buried in family land and if land then becomes animated and sacred because of those burials, then the loss of that land becomes even more painful if the burials in that land are also lost to deep lakes. Whether due to this cultural acknowledgment, ethical sensitivity, or simply legal requirement, Duke Power recognized the critical importance of moving graves before the valleys were flooded; the company (or its subsidiaries) did their best to locate all cemeteries (even small family ones surrounded by private property) and move as many graves as they could before the lakes went in. As the TVA discovered with the construction of the Norris Dam in Tennessee, "what to TVA were but bodies were to the Appalachians a collective soul."[37]

In the movie *Deliverance*, with footage shot during the flooding of the Jocassee Valley, Ed (played by Jon Voight) peers through some underbrush at a macabre scene of workers excavating graves and moving caskets around as another man sits on a bulldozer. The cemetery was that of the old Mt. Carmel Baptist Church (Oconee County) during actual grave removal for the Jocassee Dam construction, with both the church and graves moved to higher ground. Families had the right to keep their loved ones in their original graves or to have them moved, at Duke's expense, to the cemetery of their choice with a new grave marker provided by Duke Power if requested. Many local cemeteries (such as the one at Old Pickens Presbyterian Church) contain newer markers for nineteenth-century burials, indicating graves that had been moved due to the construction of the dams. A woman raised near the contemporary Cliffs at Vineyards marina remembered moving her maternal family's graves and hearing her mother sobbing "they moved Pa and Ma today."

As might be expected, the removal of deceased human beings from culturally and religiously sacred ground generated some supernatural tales. For example, when someone drowns in the lake today, locals describe them as "swimming in somebody's living room" because a lot of houses are still there, under the water. Claudia Hembree reported a curious tale linking the present to the past in a supernatural, sympathetic manner. In an interview

Hembree conducted with Lucille Whitmire Elrod, Ms. Elrod told of the loss of a hand in a hunting accident by John Cash. The hand was buried in the old Mt. Carmel Church Cemetery, and "'when Mr. Cash started having phantom pains, someone dug up the hand and discovered that the fingers were drawn up. The fingers were straightened, reburied, and the pain never bothered him again. Mr. Cash's hand was moved to Hillcrest [Memorial Park, Pickens] in the cemetery removals'" after the lakes were constructed.[38]

Retaining Ties to Lost Lands

One of the ways Americans mourn the loss of a loved one is to retain a part of the person's body (such as a lock of hair or the cremated remains), a personal object once owned by the deceased (such as items of clothing or jewelry), or an image of the departed, placed in a prominent location. Likewise, mourners over the submergence of homeplaces and family lands retain parts of those places, those symbolic bodies. Sometimes houses or parts of houses were salvaged. As Lake Jocassee's waters began to rise, David Nelson recalled, he bought an abandoned home and moved it into the Eastatoee Valley, where he lived until his passing. Deborah Mitchell and her husband returned to Jocassee Valley after her family home had been destroyed but before the valley had flooded:

> We had a spring in the backyard, a real pretty, wonderful mountain spring, and my dad had hand-split these rocks, to go in the drainage . . . , and some of them were like three or four feet long by a couple of feet wide. . . . So as it turned out, we took three of those big rocks out to my cousin's house, put them down in the woods at the edge of the driveway, and we brought . . . [some] to Greenville, . . . and then when we built our lake house, they became the foundation, you know, cornerstones for our house.

Many types of stones were salvaged. Beth Lepre acknowledged that "I have a stone from the stepping area that was in, at one of the old houses . . . in Jocassee. It's out there in my yard. . . . I made a bench out of it. It's a big stone that my dad got before it flooded; . . . I'm sure he had memories of it. . . . His mother and father . . . grew up there so he had memories of the stepping-stone. I don't have particular memories of the stone—just that he gave it to me." "I have a few Jocassee [Valley] souvenirs, and that's okay. It's what I need," Deborah Mitchell confessed.[39] John Summers, living on family land near the former Holcombe home where the Devil's Fork State Park

Visitor Center now sits, pointed out "that white rock right yonder, that come out of Whitewater River [Jocassee Valley]. . . . Right in front of an old house right up there on the river." Gerald Holcombe, who grew up in the old Holcombe home, took stones from the Jocassee Valley, and he and his children embedded them into a concrete sidewalk behind his new home,[40] creating a cobbled walk that re-creates the sensation of rounded cobbles on bare or shorn feet, so that walking into Holcombe's present home feels like walking along the river's bed near his former home.

Both wild and garden plants were also uprooted and moved. Besides the large river rock, John Summers also acknowledged taking "all kind of stuff" from Jocassee Valley. "That hollyhock bush [*Alcea* sp.] right there with the flowers on it?" Summers noted. "That come out of Ms. [Deborah Mitchell's] yard up there right on the riverbank."[41] Deborah Mitchell admitted that her family also "got some plants and things, you know. . . . We brought some *Shortia* [Oconee Bell, figure 3] home, but that doesn't like to be interrupted, and that didn't live, but I brought some of that home. And I brought some [*Camelia*] *sasanqua*, or Yellowbells, and I have a yard full of those back here now." Elizabeth Nelson proudly stated:

> In my backyard up here is a red honeysuckle [*Lonicera* sp.], which is native; my mother brought that out of Jocassee Valley and put it here, and it has grown and multiplied. And also she brought Oconee Bell. There was a whole mountainside just across the river from my grandparents' home, and she brought Oconee Bell and planted it in two places. . . . There's some still across the creek at my brother's house at the little branch bank. . . . And there are old roses here that she [her mother] brought from the valley, from Jocassee, and lilies. . . . You know, when you moved from an old place you always took some of your flowers with you. That was common. . . . Well, for the females anyway, the flowers have always been near and dear to their hearts. I have roses here that were my Grandmother [Smith]'s, and I have plants that were my mother's. You know it's just—I can't think of the right word—part of their legacy, I guess—handed down.

Even though her family land was not inundated, Claudia Alexander has lost her old homeplace because it had decayed into an uninhabitable shell, but she approved of her (female) cousin's attempt to re-create nearby a flower garden "like Momma would have done." Alexander also reinforced the association between generations of women, memories, and flowers from family land:

My momma had that whole hillside in flowers. . . . It was covered up with flowers—every kind of wildflower, every kind of rose, every kind of bush. Since she's passed away, though, like I said, some of my family wanted some of the flowers so we've given them out. For me I got a couple of rose bushes I planted out here [at her new home] in her memory. . . . I say, "This is Momma's garden." And that's very important because when [my daughter] was little I said, "Come help me in the flowers." I want her to have memories of helping Momma plant roses or flowers.

In the homes of many former valley inhabitants hang photographs or paintings of important local places, often photographed or painted by family members. For example, within his wall of relatives' photos, Robert Davidson also had a framed photo of Chapman Bridge, the traditional gateway to Jocassee Valley; his adult son Mike had the same photo in his own home. Norman Cleveland, Davidson's friend, owned two photos of the bridge, both framed and on his living room wall. Cynthia Niles possessed multiple photos and paintings of both Chapman Bridge and McKinney Chapel, and her mantelpiece consisted of a twenty-foot-long pine log retrieved from her husband's parent's house before it flooded. Harry Edison had a photo of Eastatoee Baptist Church on the wall, and Charles Watson had hung a photograph of his old one-room school with his former classmates lined up outside. In his living room, Jeffrey Donnelly prominently displayed two oil paintings of his former homes, while Theodore Franklin had a painting of the house he currently occupied. Joan Randall owned a painting (done by a grandchild) of her father's Jocassee Valley country store hung on the wall along with dozens of framed photographs of relatives.

Places Live in Legends

As with the death of well-known people, legends about places now buried under Lake Jocassee also have surfaced. One well-known legend, that of the open Bible on the pulpit of the drowned Mt. Carmel Baptist Church, links memory, land, and faith together. Deborah Mitchell provided details. "Some of the divers went in there [Lake Jocassee] one time and told some of the locals, 'Oh, we found this old cemetery out here, dived down to it and walked through the church and stood at the pulpit.' And this local boy looked at them and said, 'I can show you that pulpit.' Said, 'It's out here on the hill.'" In an interview for this book, the same "local boy" quoted by Mitchell added,

We have divers come in up there. They say, "Oh, they go in the church [Mt. Carmel Baptist, underwater] and the Bible's still out on the pulpit." Anybody could go in that church that wants to; they don't even have to have [scuba] tanks on. It's sitting over there on the other side of the [Keowee-Toxaway] State Park. I was superintendent of Sunday School when it was all moved. I was in on the moving of it. . . . They moved the cemetery and everything right out there past Devil's Fork State Park. The same—it's the same church building and everything that set down there in the valley.

Undoubtedly, the best-known legend from the Jocassee area is the eventual outcome of the Attakulla Lodge. One of the privately owned hotels in Jocassee Valley by the 1960s, the lodge (named after a historical Cherokee leader) was the vacation spot for Debbie Fletcher, who spent summers there with her family in the 1960s, documented in her book *Whippoorwill Farewell*. On numerous websites, divers claim that they have explored the submerged building, still on its foundations, under three hundred feet of murky lake water. Despite divers' claims to Fletcher that the building still stands, the most recent video, although with poor water visibility, appears to show a wooden building frame, perhaps with a roof but no walls or interior. Whether that constitutes "still standing" (as Fletcher stated on her website) is left to the reader to decide.[42]

However, one of the men who helped clear the land for Lake Jocassee (and appeared in the film *Deliverance*, driving a bulldozer in an earthmoving scene) insisted that the Attakulla Lodge no longer stands. "Now, there's a lot of this stuff they're showing, or that're coming up that really ain't true," he mentioned. "I bought five houses and two of the barns [before the flooding]. We couldn't leave nothing with a roof on it. . . . It'd have to be dozed down. . . . Now, . . . the old Attakulla Lodge. Now, we tore that thing down. . . . And part of that old Attakulla Lodge, old man [Jones's] house was built out of it. He moved when he moved out of the valley. . . . Now, [a neighbor] has still got some of the old doors out of the old Attakulla Lodge."

Conclusion

The story of the Attakulla Lodge, perhaps still living under the waters of Lake Jocassee like a comatose Elvis Presley surviving secretively on Graceland's second story, reflects more than another urban (actually rural) legend. The survival or loss of buildings and of land reflects in a larger sense the inhabitant's deep emotional connection to familial and thus familiar physical places, whether lost or preserved. Like Victorian hair jewelry, mementos of rocks and flowers maintain a connection to ancestors, both human and geographical. Photographs and paintings of important places hang alongside those of children and grandchildren. Since land and people symbolically and actually merge through burials and since family and kin are extremely important, for inhabitants land symbolically becomes another member of an extended, intricate family network. Such a transformation thus might explain the deeply emotional sense of loss or the equally powerful attempts to retain ties to family land. To an inhabitant, family land becomes symbolically another member of one's family, a connection unrecognized by visitors and residents. To inhabitants, however, the tie is visceral, deep—in one's bones. This cultural transformation of dirt and rock into animated kin is discussed further in chapter 8.

CHAPTER SEVEN

These Special Places
The Ambiguous, Anthropomorphic Mountains

While both Joe Sherman and James York would agree that "there's some-thing" in the Blue Ridge foothills of upper South Carolina, both have come to completely opposite conclusions about what that substance might be, Sherman's "something" being a recognition of the beauty and majesty of the hills, while York (and his wife) acknowledging the dangers of illegal ac-tivities hidden in the coves of those same geographical features. While men-ace and majesty define the area, there is something else in the hills too, an almost indescribable essence that inhabitants can sense on a deep emotional level. By linking these perspectives together, residents and visitors gain a bet-ter understanding of the meaning of land to inhabitants: why they struggle so much to hold onto it and why they suffer so much when they lose it.

Residents recognize the dangers inherent in the land to which they have "recently" moved (measured from last week to decades earlier). Dangers may stem from the remoteness of the area to the animals that roam those remote spaces. Dangers might also include the eccentric or reclusive locals and their discordant cultural attitudes. From a resident's point of view, Confederate battle flags flying in front of run-down mobile homes, with old cars or old dogs lounging in the overgrown front yards, summarize the region outside of the confines of the well-manicured private lakeside or valley developments.

Simultaneously, residents certainly recognize the beauty of the area, one of the principal reasons why they moved there in the first place. Living in their somewhat self-isolated lakeside or mountain neighborhoods, they have established a sense of community focused around a range of leisure activi-ties mostly conducted within their landscaped developments, along smoothly paved roads, across luxuriant lawns, and within comfortable homes. Fre-quently very well educated and curious about their surroundings, residents engage with neighboring local communities to explore in more detail the area's regional history and culture, especially that of the more distant and romanticized Native American past. As residents learn more about the his-torical places submerged beneath the lakes or protected in state parks, they recognize the melancholy assumed to be felt by locals who may have lost family land to the same developments in which residents now live. Most often, this loss is measured by a general American yardstick, the economic or aesthetic value of lost land, since this is the primary resident measurement of land's value.

Residents are in an ambiguous position in this "borderland" place. Those living in the protected lakeside or mountain settlements see themselves as "pioneers in the middle of nowhere," surrounded by wilderness occupied by sometimes friendly and most often useful rednecks, untamed denizens of this frontier territory. Typically much better educated than most of their local neighbors and typically of much higher socioeconomic status, residents frequently eat, sleep, and recreate within their bounded enclosures, occasionally venturing out to explore the natural beauty and historic heritage of their frontier surroundings. At the same time, by participating in local activities such as community organizations and charities and by spending income at local grocery stores and for service providers, residents see themselves as being at home in their mountain or lakeside retreats. In fact, it might be the longest they have occupied a place, having moved multiple times in their lives during their quest for the American dream. To inhabitants, however, these in-migrants can never be inhabitants, since like most Americans they view the land as valuable only from an economic, recreational, or aesthetic perspective and have no genealogical connection to the land. From an inhabitant's perspective, residents may possess land, but the land does not possess them.

Inhabitants, though, view the same landscape differently. While certainly recognizing the beauty of the area with all five of their physical senses, often in the same intimate detail reserved for lovers, inhabitants also recognize the dangers of the area: the natural ones from the physical environment, the faunal ones from venomous snakes and dangerous predators, and even the human ones from their eccentric or cantankerous neighbors and relatives. Even supernatural forces, both benign and malevolent, occasionally haunt abandoned homes and familiar places. When asked about this apparent contradiction between a majestic and menacing landscape, Ryan Trask explained:

> The "place" and the interconnectedness that I attempt to describe would not be complete without the unmatched fear of hearing an unseen timber rattler alerting somewhere just below your feet. It would not have the same power and command the same respect without the "fear" and adrenaline that surges as you plunge over a Class V rapid on the Chat[t]ooga. One's insignificance is not

understood or appreciated until you are "lost" in the woods overnight, or until you are charged by a 400-plus-pound black bear. One's appreciation of and relationship to the mountains (or perhaps other wild places) are not complete without the dangers, fears, and challenges that are inseparable components of these special places.[1]

The ambiguity of the same place as both menacing and majestic and even the same people as "dangerous" or merely "eccentric" enhances the region's liminality, an amorphousness this region has had for centuries. Whether perceived as America's southern frontier, the colonial backcountry, or a reconstituted Scots, Irish, and English borderland, the mountains acquired a liminal or contested sense from early in U.S. history. Moreover, this liminality continued through the perceived antislavery sentiments of American Civil War–era southern mountaineers, the search for authentic English and Highland folklore from "our contemporary ancestors," and the apparent social isolation of "yesterday's people." Today, the ambiguous area is contested between inhabitants and residents, between developers and preservers, and between independent entrepreneurs and the forces of globalized capitalism.

Perhaps this label of liminality or "outlaw territory" is deliberate. Just as Southeast Asian hill tribes have manipulated various aspects of their cultures in order to maintain the optimal relationship between themselves and lowland state-level societies, perhaps the inhabitants in the Appalachian Mountains have utilized the same strategies for the same reasons. By using multiple resource strategies, inhabitants maintain as much independence as possible from exploitative capitalism while preserving the freedom to pursue their own livelihoods on their own terms.

Another way to perceive this liminality is through a postmodern lens. From this perspective, multiple voices (inhabitant and resident) blend with multiple values (emotional versus utility) to explain the ambiguous position of those in the mountains. Contrasts abound. "Pure" Americans contrast with "ignorant hillbillies," and the psychologically depressed "yesterday's people" cannot possibly be the same folk as the noble mountaineers serving as "our contemporary ancestors." Even the same traits may be viewed in opposition: is cultural "isolation" a demonstration of political and economic independence, a sign of uninformed backwardness, or a consequence of geography? Is the contestation over land due to economic exploitation, inevitable modernization, or a misunderstanding of meaning? Which perspective prevails in both contemporary media and history? And which group's perspective dominates over the others and why?

Current theorists deftly combine a materialist focus on the control and manipulation of capital with a multifaceted understanding of the flow of that capital across a globalized world system. Consequently, it is possible to understand the heartache to inhabitants of lands lost to real estate development because of economic decisions made by lawyers in corporate board rooms in New York utilizing monies gained by profits generated from factories in Guatemala or Vietnam. Deterritorialized decisions in far distant places that generate land loss in the Appalachians thus might create the emotional and nostalgic connection to land characteristic of the region. For some theorists, then, the bitterness of Ralph Glenn over the gating of the road to McKinney Chapel or the refusal by Peter Abney of a promotion and transfer in order to continue to live on family land may be seen as end results of a chain of decisions stretching around the world.

While local responses to the forces of globalized neoliberal capitalism might explain the visceral tie to family land felt by inhabitants, I believe that the ethnographic evidence demonstrates that this tie had existed already in Appalachian inhabitant culture and is manifested primarily during times of potential land loss. At other times the value remains unexpressed, unquestioned, and assumed, and thus it is difficult for inhabitants to articulate when asked about it, since there is nothing to which to compare the value. In other words, without family land under direct threat, it is very difficult for inhabitants to explain how they feel about family land. As researchers respect similar cultural values toward land in other groups, I prefer to privilege the voices of inhabitants of the southern mountains and respect their recognition of the pervasive and profound ties to family land that they feel and have felt, independent of the forces of neoliberal globalized capitalism.

How, then, can we discover the "something in these hills" that inhabitants feel? Very different from the love of place perceived by most Americans, the love of a dangerous and wonderful place felt by inhabitants may be traced through a series of interconnected steps. Inhabitants develop a close connection to their family lands because (in both the past and the present), family names are placed on the land, living spaces are often made of materials from those lands, and those lands are used to extract resources (often in the Kentucky way). Family land continues to be owned by descendants and continues to be occupied by relatives, often in close physical and social contact, and descendants tell family stories about family events on family lands. Frequently, family members are entombed in family land as well.

Through this process, family land symbolically morphs into something animated. Family land merges with family members so that family land takes on a symbolic human essence, becoming a part of a family's kinship system. Animated and anthropomorphized, land gains in essence a soul, generating in its human owners and occupiers a spiritual sense of connection that many inhabitants interpret through a Christian lens of a greater closeness to God (figure 15). To inhabitants, land metaphorically touches them as they physically touch the land. The coolness of a grandmother's garden soil crumbling in a granddaughter's hands and the fragrance of her favorite roses wafting in the humid summer air invigorate inhabitants; to them, it is the equivalent of a grandmother's warm caress and the smell of her skin. Ultimately, the essence of land symbolically enters the bodies of inhabitants; it gets into their bones and into their hearts. Because of this spiritual connection and this synthesis between land and person, the loss of family land due to development or sale generates deep emotional senses of loss, almost equivalent to the death of a family member. In fact, metaphorically it *is* the death of a family member. Thus, myths arise about lost lands like stories about lost ancestors, and inhabitants retain parts or images of those lost landscapes as if they were mementos of lost loved ones.

There is a further ambiguity or contrast in the images of the southern mountains that has parallels with the process by which inhabitants connect to family land. Stereotypes of "our contemporary ancestors" or "yesterday's people" generally examine the mountaineers and their strategies for survival in a more materialistic direction, just as the relationship between inhabitants and their family lands may be viewed as tangibly encountered: place-names, natural resources, medicinal plants, property deeds, fertile soil, family stories, and weathered tombstones. On the other hand, the postmodern focus on alternative perspectives and more symbolic interpretations parallels the cultural process by which land merges with, enters into, and metaphorically becomes a member of one's family. In other words, the ambiguity of theoretical interpretation parallels the cultural process by which dirt and rock animate and incorporate.

Furthermore, combining these two themes of liminality and anthropomorphism reinforces the idea of an animated landscape even more. If inhabitants view land in an ambiguous way and if land is like a member of one's kinship network, then land is like a relative whom one must accept unconditionally. Just as families have good and bad individuals and even as "good" and "bad" are relative terms depending on context, so too are the mountains both majestic and menacing, sometimes both simultaneously and sometimes depending on one's perspective. And as families accept and love their kin regardless of moral goodness or badness, so do mountaineers accept and love their family land and region regardless of the degree of danger they may feel there.

Conclusion

One December afternoon I walked with Ryan Trask through a publicly owned nature preserve on a trail paralleling Reedy Cove Creek, a small rocky tributary of the Big Eastatoee River. Along the trail Trask pointed out two interesting natural objects just off the trail but clearly visible to anyone who might bother to look: a large hemlock tree with a small persimmon tree almost growing out of the same trunk and a foot-thick beech tree atop a table-sized rock where the tree's roots had followed cracks in the rock and the rock's surface down to the earth (figure 16). The former, he explained, could have been caused by a hunter treeing a raccoon in that hemlock tree sometime in the past, and the frightened raccoon defecated, releasing feces with a persimmon seed inside. The seed eventually sprouted and grew alongside the hemlock. The beech tree through the rock captured for Trask the power of life over inanimate objects.

As Trask pointed out these two trees, it was obvious that anyone walking through the woods would have noticed these same trees (as long as they were not facedown in a smartphone). On the other hand, it would be difficult to have noticed them with the same detail and the same hyperintimate understanding as Trask had done. His detailed observations reflected the more profound understanding that Trask and most other inhabitants had of his mountain surroundings. As Trask reflected on the contrast between inhabitant and resident knowledge that afternoon, he noted that we (residents or tourists) visit the woods, while he lives in the woods. The same could be said for Trask's neighbor Elizabeth Nelson, who described in loving detail the seasonally changing plants in her favorite cove along her favorite turn in the road leading into her favorite valley and home. While both recognize and respect the dangers of their land, just as they recognize and respect the "dangers" of family members, they and their inhabitant neighbors also accept and love their majestic mountains as they accept and love their kinfolk because those mountains *are* their kinfolk.

This intimate awareness of natural surroundings, especially of family lands, establishes for inhabitants the spiritual connection to their lands and the metaphorical incorporation of those lands into the essence of a relative. At the same time, inhabitants also know and recall who lives in which houses, who those people are related to, who used to live in those houses (or on that property), and to whom those ancestors were related. By combining both the intimate knowledge of local topography and an equally detailed awareness of social relations through time, inhabitants construct a four-dimensional matrix of place consisting of an intimate knowledge of natural and human-modified land features as well as the social connections of the humans who occupy or have occupied those landforms through multiple generations. For example, while visitors may view a cluster of trailers, a cow pasture with a creek, and a green road sign, inhabitants can tell any audience with the ample spare time to listen who lives in those trailers, what their personal and familial histories are, the moral standing of that family, the family's connection to the name on the street sign, where that creek begins and how it got its name, locations of interesting rock formations along that creek bed, and stories about events that have happened along that creek bed or in that cow pasture. Like any family member, land has a physical, social, temporal, and spiritual essence that inhabitants know intimately.

In the same way that lovers know the physical details of each other's bodies, and in the same way that lovers care deeply for each other, inhabitants know and love their family lands. Just as fingers trace smile lines or scars on an aged body, family stories reanimate overgrown garden patches and decaying barns. Embracing a lover after a long separation equates for inhabitants with the emotions of seeing the Blue Ridge on the horizon after a vacation to the coast. Old lovers holding each other's wrinkled hands, remembering their complicated past, and demonstrating their bond with each other only with their eyes match the emotions of intimacy and association an inhabitant receives from digging her hands into her grandmother's former garden space, smelling the scent of "her" flowers, imagining her face, and hearing her voice. And in a sense, the consummation of an amorous relationship reflects the metaphorical transformation of family bodies into family land. Land embraces inhabitants as inhabitants embrace land.

By understanding the powerful spiritual connection that inhabitants feel to their ambiguous land as equivalent to the deeply emotional connection inhabitants feel toward their ambiguous relatives and by comprehending inhabitants' symbolic transformation of land into an animate being directly tied to themselves, residents and visitors can better understand why most inhabitants are so reluctant to see their land "die" to development. "It's hard to put into words," Trask said that cold December day on the trail, but he and his neighbors have done so by means of their words in this book. Now when residents or visitors read Joe Sherman's poem about "something in these hills," they can better understand exactly what that "something" is and why inhabitants try so hard to preserve, protect, and remember that "something." More than beauty and more than utility, the "something in these hills" is the memory of a host of generations of relatives passing through that landscape and merging with that landscape like the roots of that Reedy Cove beech tree flowing over and through that rock. This is a synthesis between animate and inanimate entities that is very difficult for inhabitants to articulate, since it is not as much consciously acknowledged as it is unconsciously experienced by them. But it is an experiential feeling that others can now better understand.

APPENDIX

Informant Biographies

Informants are listed alphabetically by pseudonym. Most biographical details were current at the time of interviews, but I have updated known death notices to indicate the passing of my contributors.

Peter Abney, born and raised in upper Pickens County and in his seventies. Mr. Abney lived on family land surrounded by his in-laws. He worked for the state as a career but had retired. Active in his local church, he knew the family of Shirley Patterson, and they were friends. Mr. Abney was of European descent and has passed away.

Claudia and Brian Alexander, a married couple from upper Pickens County. Mr. Alexander is in his fifties, is a friend of James York, and works as a laborer. Claudia Bradshaw Alexander (sister of Garvin Bradshaw) was born and raised in upper Oconee County in the early 1960s, and she worked as an administrative assistant for a local governmental agency. Both are of European descent.

Bruce Anderson, born and raised in upper Oconee County. Mr. Anderson owns an agriculturally based family business in upper Oconee County. He is in his sixties and had graduated with a college education. He is of European descent.

Marsha and Dennis Baird, a married couple in their seventies living in upper Pickens County. Mr. Baird was born and raised in mill towns in Greenville County, but his ancestors were from the mountains. Mrs. Baird had been raised on farms in Pickens County. Both had graduated from college, and Mr. Baird had worked for a regional company until his retirement. Both are of European descent.

Carol and Jack Benson, a retired couple in their fifties. The Bensons moved to their upper Pickens County gated community from a southwestern state. Both are college educated. Mr. Benson had worked for a major U.S. corporation for his career, and they had lived in many places in the United States. Both are of European descent.

Andrea Bowers, daughter of Joseph and Beth Yeats. Mrs. Bowers was born and raised in upper Pickens County but now lives downstate. She is in her late forties and married and is of European descent.

Garvin and Cheryl Bradshaw, a married couple living in upper Oconee County. Mr. Bradshaw was a lifelong resident of Oconee County and was interviewed when he was in his seventies. He was the brother of Claudia Bradshaw Alexander and lived on family land in the county. A laborer all his life, he had no more than a high school education. He was of European descent and has passed away.

Pamela Charles, neighbor of Shirley Patterson. Ms. Charles has spent her life in upper Pickens County and manages a small business. She is in her late fifties and is of European descent.

Josephine Chavis, born and raised in upper Oconee County. Mrs. Chavis was college educated and taught school. In her younger years she traveled extensively to other continents. Her husband had a successful family business and had recently passed away. Mrs. Chavis, in her late eighties, still lived in her own home near her birthplace. She was of European descent and has passed away.

Gregory Clayton, born and raised in the mountains between North and South Carolina. Mr. Clayton's family eventually settled in upper Pickens County. He was in his seventies and had been a laborer. He lived on his late wife's property in upper Pickens County. Of European descent, Mr. Clayton has passed away.

Norman Cleveland, in his seventies, from upper Pickens County. During his life he had done many things, including moonshining (sometimes with Robert Davidson). Mr. Cleveland was of European descent and has passed away.

Denise and Benjamin Craig, a retired married couple in their late sixties. The Craigs live in upper Pickens County on Mrs. Craig's family land. Mrs. Craig, with a college education, is from the middle part of the state, but her family is from upper Pickens County; she is related to the Davidson, Edison, and Flowers families. The Craigs are both of European descent.

Nancy Abney Daniels and Edward Daniels, mother and son. Nancy Daniels is the married daughter of Peter Abney, and Edward Daniels is her college-aged resident son. Mrs. Daniels is a college-educated school teacher in her fifties, born and raised in upper Pickens County and living on family land. She is of European descent, as is her son.

Mike Davidson, born in the early 1950s and raised in upper Pickens County. Mr. Davidson is the son of Robert Davidson and still lives near his extended family in upper Oconee County. A master of many trades with a high school education, Mike Davidson has traveled overseas several times and has worked for several Upstate companies. He is of European descent.

Robert Davidson, born and raised in the upper valleys of Pickens County. Mr. Davidson was in his late eighties. He worked at many trades, including moonshining, and probably had not graduated from grade school. He was good friends with Douglas Edison, nephew of Anne Flowers, and the father of Mike Davidson. Of European descent, Robert Davidson has passed away.

Jeff and Carol Donnelly, a married couple in their seventies. The Donnellys live in a valley in upper Pickens County. Mr. Donnelly was born and raised in that valley, but after high school he enlisted in the military and worked on the West Coast for decades, only to return to his upper Pickens County valley in the 1990s. Mr. and Mrs. Donnelly are both of European descent.

Amy Driver, a whitewater guide living in upper Oconee County. Ms. Driver is in her early forties. Originally from the Northeast, she and her family moved to Oconee County in the early 1970s to develop a river rafting company, and she has been here ever since. She is of European descent.

Rachel and James Edwards, both born and raised in upper Pickens County. The Edwards are in their late sixties. Mr. Edwards operated a small store, and Mrs. Edwards had been a professional gospel singer in her youth and still enjoyed playing music and singing. Both are of European descent; Mr. Edwards has passed away.

Douglas Edison, born and raised in upper Pickens County. Mr. Edison's family grew up in the upper Keowee Valley. Mr. Edison was in his seventies for the interviews. He had worked for a state agency for much of his life and was a good friend of Robert Davidson. Of European descent, Mr. Edison has passed away.

Harry Edison, cousin to Douglas Edison. Harry Edison was born and raised in and still lives in upper Pickens County. Married to his high school sweetheart, Mr. Edison is in his early sixties and works at a textile plant in the same county. He is of European descent.

David and Marie Ellison, born and raised in upper Oconee County. Mr. Ellison was a retired farmer. He and his wife own her family's land in the county, and they lived near their children. Mr. Ellison was probably in his seventies at the time of the interview. Of European descent, Mr. Ellison has passed away. Mrs. Ellison is also of European descent.

Alice Flowers, youngest daughter of Anne and Joshua Flowers. Alice Flowers was born and raised in upper Pickens County and is now in her seventies. She is of European descent.

Anne and Joshua Flowers, married for over seventy-five years, both were in their nineties at the time of the interview. Neither had graduated from high school, but they had spent almost all their lives in upper Pickens County. Anne Flowers is the aunt of Robert Davidson. Mr. and Mrs. Flowers were of European descent, and both have passed away.

Theodore Franklin, born and raised in upper Pickens County. He currently lives there on his wife's family land. Retired and perhaps in his seventies, he is friends with Rachel and James Edwards and is of European descent.

Ralph Glenn spent his childhood and some retirement years in upper Pickens County. Mr. Glenn also had a long military career. He was in his fifties at the time of the interviews and was married with children. He is of European descent.

Chris Jackson, born in upper Pickens County. Mr. Jackson graduated from Pickens High School. He spent part of his life working in the Southwest, only to move back to his family land. He is in his late sixties. He is a brother to Julie Jackson, and both are of European descent.

Julie Jackson, born in upper Pickens County. Ms. Jackson graduated from Pickens High School. She spent part of her life working in the Southwest, only to move back to the family land. She is in her sixties. Sister of Chris Jackson, she is of European descent.

Stephanie Jamison, niece of Alice Flowers and granddaughter of Anne and Joshua Flowers. Ms. Jamison is in her forties. She was born and raised in Pickens County and is of European descent.

Brenda Kendrick, born and raised in Oconee County. Mrs. Kendrick was in her seventies at the time of the interview and was married. While she does not live on family land, members of her extended family still own the homeplace. Mrs. Kendrick is of European descent.

Pam and Gary Lee, a married couple living in a gated community in upper Pickens County. The Lees were probably in their late sixties at the time of the interview and were retired from positions in the Midwest. Both are very well educated and had been high school teachers. Both are of European descent.

Beth Lepre, born and raised in upper Pickens County. Ms. Lepre and her family vacationed frequently in Jocassee Valley before it was flooded. In her late forties, she worked for the county until she retired to care for her aging parents. She lives in her family's homeplace in upper Pickens County. Cousin to Elizabeth Nelson, Ms. Lepre is of European descent.

Sally and Doug Massey, a married couple in their late fifties and early sixties at the time of the interview. The Masseys live in a gated community in upper Pickens County. Retired from the Midwest, Mr. Massey still works part-time from a North Carolina community. Mr. and Mrs. Massey are both of European descent.

Deborah Mitchell, born and raised in upper Pickens County. Mrs. Mitchell is in her seventies and is widowed. She has an advanced college education and has taught school for a career. Having lost her family home to the flooding of the lakes, Mrs. Mitchell now lives in Greenville County. She is related to Elizabeth Nelson and is of European descent.

David Nelson, born and raised in upper Pickens County. Mr. Nelson was in his nineties during the interviews. He is Elizabeth Nelson's father's brother; their family has been in their valley for centuries. Of European descent, Mr. Nelson has passed away.

Elizabeth Nelson, college educated and in her late fifties. Ms. Nelson lived in the same upper Pickens County valley where she has spent most of her life. She is the niece of David Nelson and at the time of the interview lived in her family's homeplace. She is a cousin to Beth Lepre and is also related to Deborah Mitchell. Ms. Nelson is of European descent.

Cynthia Niles, born in upper Oconee County. After marriage Mrs. Niles moved into upper Pickens County, where she still lives. Members of her family worked for the federal government. Now in her late sixties, she married as a teenager and may not have finished high school. She is related by marriage to Robert Davidson and directly to Douglas Edison, although distantly. She is of European descent.

Patrick O'Connell, former neighbor and longtime friend to Cynthia Niles and her late husband. Mr. O'Connell is in his sixties and was born and raised in upper Pickens County. His family home is now under the lakes. Mr. O'Connell is of European descent.

Shirley Valentine Patterson, born and raised in upper Pickens County. Mrs. Patterson (in her sixties) had spent several decades in the North before moving back to her family land. She worked at various jobs, and her husband was a professional in a nearby city. Mrs. Patterson is the sister of Michael Valentine and is friends with Peter Abney. The Valentine extended family still own and occupy family land obtained in 1865 by their formerly enslaved ancestors. Mrs. Valentine is of African American descent.

Bernard Quinn, about eighty years old, was recruited for the project by his friend, Shirley Patterson. Born in the lower part of the state, Mr. Quinn and his family own a business in a large Upstate city. Earlier in his career, he had worked for the state and had gotten to know the rural areas of upper Pickens County. Of African American descent, Mr. Quinn has passed away.

Kayla Radcliffe, born and raised in upper Pickens County. Ms. Radcliffe was about twenty and a college student during the interviews. She is a graduate of Pickens County High School. For an update on her life, see chapter 5, note 33. She is of European descent.

Joan Randall, born in the upper parts of Oconee County. Mrs. Randall's family moved to a larger village in the county so she could attend high school regularly. Her father ran a business in Jocassee Valley for years. In her eighties at the time of the interview, she lived in a comfortable home in a town in Pickens County. Mrs. Randall has passed away.

Forrest Sanders, a friend of Kayla Radcliffe. Mr. Sanders was a college student about twenty years old and was a graduate of Pickens High School. He was born and raised in Pickens County and is of European descent.

John Summers, born and raised in upper Oconee County and in his seventies. Mr. Summers lives on his family land surrounded by his extended family. He had a high school education and had worked for a regional company but was now retired. He is of European descent.

Jason Taylor, a friend of Kayla Radcliffe. Mr. Taylor was a college student about twenty years old and a graduate of Pickens High School. He was born and raised in Pickens County and is of European descent.

Donna and Ryan Trask, a married couple in their forties and both college educated. Mrs. Trask was raised in upper Pickens County and teaches school. Mr. Trask, born and raised in Pickens County, was an administrator for a higher education institution in the area. They lived on land they purchased in upper Pickens County near Mrs. Trask's parents. For an update on their lives, see chapter 5, note 36. Both are of European descent.

Michael Valentine, born and raised on a farm in upper Pickens County. Mr. Valentine married and left the area for the Northeast, only to divorce and return. He was an older brother to Shirley Patterson. Mr. Valentine lived in his family homeplace and was in his eighties at the time of the interviews. Of African American descent, Mr. Valentine has passed away.

Charles Watson, born and raised in upper Pickens County. Mr. Watson had worked for a state agency and is now retired and living on family land in upper Pickens County. He is related directly to Douglas Edison and Robert Davidson and by marriage to Peter Abney. Mr. Watson is in his sixties and is of European descent.

Pamela Williams, in-law to Shirley Patterson. Mrs. Williams was born in the middle part of the state but has spent most of her life in the Upstate after she married into a well-established local family. She lives in a large city in the Upstate, but her daughter still lives on upper Greenville County ancestral family land acquired by a formerly enslaved ancestor in 1865. She is of African American descent.

Joseph and Beth Yeats, a married couple in their eighties and friends and neighbors to Colleen Zimmerman. Mr. Yeats was born in a Pickens County mill village and married into the Arnold family, who lived in upper Pickens County; the couple spent their married life farming Arnold family land. Mr. Yeats served in the military, and the couple was friends to Shirley Patterson's family. Of European descent, Mr. and Mrs. Yeats have both passed away.

Margaret and James York, born and raised in upper Pickens County. The couple (late sixties and early seventies) had met originally in grade school. Mr. York had been a laborer all his life, moving throughout the county, and his wife worked for the county; in retirement, Mr. York collected and sold all sorts of materials. Of European descent, Mr. York has passed away.

Colleen Zimmerman, friend and neighbor to Joseph and Beth Yeats. Mrs. Zimmerman had married into a family in upper Pickens County in the mid-1950s and has lived there ever since. She is in her seventies and originally came from the northeastern United States. Mrs. Zimmerman is of European descent.

Notes

Chapter One

1. See Joe Sherman, "Something in These Hills." According to retired University Historian Dr. Jerry Reel (personal communication, February 27, 2019), there is an "apocryphal story" about the phrase existing earlier, and Sherman borrowed the phrase for his essay. Reel has been unable to locate an original source.

2. The "outsider/insider" dichotomy is critiqued later in the chapter.

3. The concept is explained in Turner, *Forest of Symbols*, 93–111.

4. Smith, *Myth, Media, and the Southern Mind*, 117. See also Reed, *Enduring South*, 33; Jones, *Appalachian Values*.

5. For an explanation, see Coggeshall, *Liberia, South Carolina*, 201–8.

6. Tilley, *Phenomenology of Landscape*, 23.

7. For a review of the literature, see Coggeshall, *Liberia, South Carolina*, 202–3.

8. See the review in Barcus and Brunn, "Towards a Typology of Mobility and Place Attachment," 29.

9. The quotes come from Cash, *Mind of the South*, 4 ("frontier upon frontier") and 9; Caudill, *Night Comes to the Cumberlands*, 5 ("raggle-taggle") and 12 (other traits); Giemza, "Introduction," 6.

10. Cash, *Mind of the South*, 9 (first sentence quotes), 10 ("frontier stage"), new southern frontier, 107. See also Reed, *Enduring South*, 46; Whisnant, *All That Is Native and Fine*, 6; Beaver, "Appalachian Families," 149; Weller, *Yesterday's People*, 10. The perspectives of historians Odum and Vance are summarized in Cobb, *Away Down South*, 169.

11. Fischer, *Albion's Seed*, 629–30, 642.

12. Fischer, *Albion's Seed*, 639.

13. Griffin, "Irish Migration to the Colonial South," 55.

14. For a summary of the scholarship on African Americans in Appalachia including their erasure, see Coggeshall, *Liberia, South Carolina*, 13–15. See also Anglin, "Lessons from Appalachia."

15. Campbell, *Southern Highlander*, 72 ("true Americans") and 91 ("blood"); Whisnant, *All That Is Native and Fine*, 57 (for the "purity" quote) and 81 (for the external forces comment); Raine, *Land of Saddle-Bags*, 62; Shapiro, "Introduction," to *Southern Highlander*, xxvi; Campbell, *Southern Highlander*, 94.

16. Frost, "Our Contemporary Ancestors," 70; Raine, *Land of Saddle-Bags*, 5; Wilson, "Elizabethan America," 206 and 208 (the Scots-Irish comment).

17. Wilson, "Elizabethan America," 208; Frost, "Our Contemporary Ancestors," 71; see also Weller, *Yesterday's People*, 13–14; Cash, *Mind of the South*, 213 and 214 ("mured up"); see also Raine, *Land of Saddle-Bags*, x.

18. Opie, "Sense of Place," 117. The "harmonious relationship" comment is from Bingham, "Impact of Recreational Development," 65.

19. Weller, *Yesterday's People*, 14; McDonald and Muldowny, *TVA and the Dispossessed*, 7.

20. Caudill, *Night Comes to the Cumberlands*, 31.

21. Hsiung, "Stereotypes," 103–4. The "discrete region" quote is from Shapiro, "Introduction," xxvii. For the lengthier discussion of the benefits of separation, see Shapiro, *Appalachia on Our Mind*; see also Caudill, *Night Comes to the Cumberlands*, 13; Campbell, *Southern Highlander*, 20–21; Caudill, *Night Comes to the Cumberlands*, 77; Eller, "Place and the Recovery of Community," ix; Higgs, "Versions of 'Natural Man' in Appalachia," 161; Dickey, "Last Wild River."

22. Whisnant, *All That Is Native and Fine*, 110. See also Shapiro, "Introduction," xxviii; Turner, "South Unbound," 141.

23. Ledford, "Landscape and a People Set Apart," 64. See also Olson, *Blue Ridge Folklife*, 64; Hsiung, "Stereotypes," 107, citing A. R. Harkins, "The Hillbilly in Twentieth-Century American Culture" (PhD diss., University of Wisconsin, Madison, 1999), 2–3.

24. Hartigan, *Odd Tribes*, 155–58; see also Wray, *Not Quite White*, 68 on subcategories of "whiteness"; Williamson, *Hillbillyland*, 2. Williamson (*Hillbillyland*, 16) defines "hillbilly" as "rough, rural, poor but fruitful, blatantly antiurban, and often dangerous, but not necessarily hailing from the Southern Appalachians or even from any mountains." I disagree, preferring to limit the term to describe only residents of the Appalachians and the Ozarks. I believe that Williamson conflates "redneck" with "hillbilly," and I think the terms distinguish two different (but overlapping) categories of people. Hartigan, *Odd Tribes*, has a more nuanced description of the various subcategories of "whiteness."

25. Williamson, *Hillbillyland*, 16 ("necessary frontier rudeness"); Olson, *Blue Ridge Folklife*, 62 ("strongly ambivalent"). On the stereotype countering self-images of the middle class, see Williamson, *Hillbillyland*, 20; Smith, "Transforming Places," 54; Hartigan, *Odd Tribes*. About innocent naïveté, see Olson, *Blue Ridge Folklife*, 66–67 and Ballard, "Where Did Hillbillies Come From?," 139. While the hillbillies who moved to Beverly Hills were from a fictional town in Arkansas, the character of Granny (and presumably her ancestors) hailed from the fictional town of "Bug Tussle," Tennessee. The fictional "Dogpatch" was said to be in the Kentucky mountains, and the fictional "Mayberry" was based on Andy Griffith's hometown of Mt. Airy, North Carolina.

26. Reed, *Enduring South*, 45–46 (quote from 46); Frost, "Our Contemporary Ancestors," 76; Fischer, *Albion's Seed*, 687; Dickey, "Last Wild River."

27. Williamson, *Hillbillyland*, 157; Lane, *Chattooga*, 98; McDonald and Muldowny, *TVA and the Dispossessed*, 133.

28. Weller, *Yesterday's People*, 10–11. On Scots-Irish ancestry, see also Caudill, *Night Comes to the Cumberlands*; Fischer, *Albion's Seed*.

29. Caudill, *Night Comes to the Cumberlands*, 325.

30. Caudill, *Night Comes to the Cumberlands*, 326.

31. Weller, *Yesterday's People*, 21–22. See also Campbell, *Southern Highlander*, 73; Caudill, *Night Comes to the Cumberlands*, 326.

32. Weller, *Yesterday's People*, 155 ("debilitating dependence" quote) and 83 for the next four sentences.

33. Caudill, *Night Comes to the Cumberlands*, 326; Weller, *Yesterday's People*, 11; Caudill, *Night Comes to the Cumberlands*, 392 and 85 ("inbreeding").

34. Vance, *Hillbilly Elegy*, 4 (for "hub of misery"), 7 ("lack of agency"), 163 ("learned helplessness"), 145 ("culture and faith"), and 231 ("inheritance of our culture").

35. Olson, *Blue Ridge Folklife*, 65 (both sentences); Cooke-Jackson and Hansen, "Appalachian Culture and Reality TV," 184. See also Eller, "Foreword," x; Hartigan, *Odd Tribes*.

36. Frost, "Our Contemporary Ancestors," 80 (all information).

37. Blee and Billings, "Where 'Bloodshed Is a Pastime,'" 133–34; Olson, *Blue Ridge Folklife*, 64. For the "backward" stereotype leading to exploitation, see also Ledford, "Landscape and a People Set Apart," 64; Batteau, *Invention of Appalachia*, 15.

38. Waller, "Feuding in Appalachia," 367, 370 (separate quotes on individual pages); Whisnant, *All That Is Native and Fine*, 13; Stephenson, "There's a Place Somewhere," 172.

39. Caudill, *Night Comes to the Cumberlands*, 325; Lewis, "Introduction," 1 ("internal colony"), 2 (for remaining quotes); see also Fisher and Smith, "Internal Colony," 45–50. For the colonizing effect of land development, see Gregg and Gamble, "This Land Is Your Land."

40. For the resource extraction idea, see Lewis and Knipe, "Colonialism Model," 17; see also Billings, Pudup, and Waller, "Taking Exception with Exceptionalism," 5–6. Walls, "Internal Colony or Internal Periphery?" 331; Lewis and Knipe, "Colonialism Model," 25.

41. McDonald and Muldowny, *TVA and the Dispossessed*, 9; Scott, *Art of Not Being Governed*, 128 ("our living ancestors"), 133 ("outlaw corridor"), and 329 ("barrier to tyranny"). For alternate forms of resistance to capitalism, see Plaut, "Extending the Internal Periphery Model," 361.

42. Halperin, *Livelihood of Kin*. The shallow and deep rural discussion is from 17–18, the summary is from 146, "multiple livelihood strategies" is from 4, and examples are from 67–68. See also Batteau, "Mosbys and Broomsedge," 446.

43. Williams, *Homeplace*, 36. The sense of place summary can be found in Reeves and Kenkel, "Agricultural Involution"; Batteau, "Mosbys and Broomsedge," 463; see also Smith, *Myth, Media, and the Southern Mind*, 131–32. For the consequences of negative mountain stereotypes, see Olson, *Blue Ridge Folklife*, 64; Weller, *Yesterday's People*, 14–17.

44. For the idea of the South in opposition to the North, see, for example, Reed, *Enduring South*, 88–89 and Cash, *Mind of the South*, 65–66. For Appalachian oppositions, see Olson, *Blue Ridge Folklife*, 65.

45. Billings, "Introduction," 12–13. The "oppositional images" quote is from Gupta and Ferguson, "Beyond 'Culture,'" 41. The "iconic landmarks" comment is from Kaika, "Dams as Symbols of Modernization," 277, and the "inseparable dialectic of creation and destruction" quote is from 297. The "more refined analysis" comment is from Whisnant, *All That Is Native and Fine*, 262.

46. Low and Lawrence-Zuniga, "Locating Culture," 18.

47. Gabbert and Jordan-Smith, "Introduction," 222.

48. Tuan, *Space and Place*, 6.

49. Smith, "Landscapes of Clearance," 15.

50. Tuan, *Space and Place*, 73.

51. Tuan, *Space and Place*, 6–7.

52. Richardson, "Introduction," 1; Richardson, "Place and Culture," 64; Tilley, *Phenomenology of Landscape*, 10–11; Stewart, "An Occupied Place," 151–52.

53. Smith, "Landscapes of Clearance," 14, 16; see also Tilley, *Phenomenology of Landscape*, 15. Kahn, "Your Place and Mine," 188. The existential space comment is from Tilley, *Phenomenology of Landscape*, 17. For the social construction of place, see Harvey, *Justice, Nature and the Geography of Difference*, 310, 316.

54. Tuan, *Space and Place*, 157–58, 178. Tuan cites T. G. H. Strehlow, *Aranda Traditions* (Carleton, Victoria, Australia: Melbourne University Press, 1947), 30–31.

55. Ashworth and Graham, *Senses of Place*, 3; see also Tilley, *Phenomenology of Landscape*, 18. Harvey, *Justice, Nature and the Geography of Difference*, 309. For the "polyphony of voices" comment, see Rodman, "Empowering Place," 641; subsequent quotes are from 652.

56. Gupta and Ferguson, "Beyond 'Culture,'" 39; Steele, *Sense of Place*, 9; Davis, "Politics of Wilderness," 50; Basso, "Wisdom Sits in Places," 84, 89.

57. Williamson, *Hillbillyland*, 18, 19. The book's notes cite Marjorie Hope Nicholson, *Mountain Gloom and Mountain Glory* (New York: Norton, 1963); no pages cited.

58. Gupta and Ferguson, "Beyond 'Culture,'" 40; Rodman, "Empowering Place," 641 on alternate meanings and power dimensions.

59. Gupta and Ferguson, "Beyond 'Culture,'" 47; see also Rodman, "Empowering Place," 647. The final quote is from Smith, "Landscapes of Clearance," 14.

60. For example, see the discussions by sociologist Dwight Billings (2018) and anthropologists Ann Kingsolver (2018) and Mary Anglin (2016).

61. Billings and Kingsolver, "Introduction: Place Matters," 6; see also Anglin, "Toward a New Politics of Outrage and Transformation." The comment about the history of Appalachia's global position is from Kingsolver, "'Placing' Futures," 18; the second quote is from 41; see also Schumann, "Introduction," 18; Anglin, "Toward a New Politics of Outrage." Harvey, *Justice, Nature and the Geography of Difference*, 316; Satterwhite, "New Critical Regionalism," 124.

62. Kingsolver, "'Placing' Futures," 17; see also Batteau, *Invention of Appalachia*, 33; "image of Appalachia" quote from 15. Piser, "Participation and Transformation," 262.

63. The idea of land redefined as a commodity is from Plaut, "Extending the Internal Periphery Model," 360. Smith, "Transforming Places," 51–52; see also Schumann, "Introduction," 11; Fisher and Smith, "Introduction," 1.

64. Smith and Fisher, "Conclusion," 271, citing Doreen Massey, *Space, Place, and Gender* (Minneapolis: University of Minnesota Press, 1994).

65. Smith and Fisher, "Conclusion," 267, replicated in Smith, "Transforming Places," 49; Billings and Kingsolver, "Introduction," 7; Kingsolver, "'Placing' Futures," 30; Smith, "Transforming Places," 52; see also Harvey, *Justice, Nature and the Geography of Difference*, 302.

66. Smith and Fisher, "Conclusion," 272; Harvey, *Justice, Nature and the Geography of Difference*, 326; Smith and Fisher, "Conclusion," 275.

67. Smith, "Transforming Places," 50; see also Fisher and Smith, "Introduction," 6. This is also the process in southern Louisiana described by sociologist Arlie Russell in *Strangers in Their Own Land*. For the relationship between globalized capital and social exclusion, see Harvey, *Justice, Nature and the Geography of Difference*, 323–24.

68. Anglin, "Toward a New Politics of Outrage," 53. Smith and Fisher, "Conclusion," 269; see also Billings and Kingsolver, "Introduction," 8. Fisher and Smith, "Internal Colony," 47, 48.

69. Smith, "Landscapes of Clearance," 14–15; see also Rodman, "Empowering Place," 644. Gupta and Ferguson, "Beyond 'Culture,'" 48; the Bombay and London comparison is from 50. Fisher and Smith, "Internal Colony," 48; Hirsch, "Landscape," 13.

70. Kingfisher and Maskovsky, "Introduction," 118, 120.

71. Harvey, *Seventeen Contradictions*, 50.

72. Gershon, "Neoliberal Agency," with the distinction between imaginations from 543 and the subsequent ideas from 544; Harvey, *Seventeen Contradictions*, 263; Gershon, "Neoliberal Agency," 546.

73. Smith, "Transforming Places," 57; House and Howard, *Something's Rising*, 133 (Bonds quote) and 217 (Shelby and Keltner quote).

74. House and Howard, *Something's Rising*, 227, 231.

75. Wagner, "Space and Place"; Gregg and Gamble, "This Land Is Your Land," 56. See also the comment by Batteau (*Invention of Appalachia*, 190) about Professor Bill Best from Berea College, who observed in a 1979 essay that the Appalachian value of "attachment to community" interfered with developers' plans, implying that the trait was already present before development had been planned.

76. For this perspective from the Apaches, see Basso, "Wisdom Sits in Places," 83–84.

77. Kingsolver, "'Placing' One Another." See also Shapiro, *Appalachia on Our Mind*, 265; Harvey, *Justice, Nature and the Geography of Difference*, 265; Billings, Pudup, and Waller, "Taking Exception with Exceptionalism," 2–3; Terman, "Intersections of Appalachian Identity"; Kingsolver, "'Placing' Futures," 23–25; Smith, "Transforming Places," 60; Fisher and Smith, "Internal Colony," 47; Smith and Fisher, "Conclusion," 269; Gupta and Ferguson, "Beyond 'Culture,'" 35. An external reviewer of the manuscript brought this distinction to my attention.

78. For the perspective on deterritorialization, see Gupta and Ferguson, "Beyond 'Culture,'" 50. For the differentiation between place attachment and place identity, see Hernandez, Hidalgo, Salazar-Laplace, and Hess, "Place Attachment and Place Identity." Local naturalist Wes Cooler (personal communication, March 19, 2019) clarified the spelling of "Eastatoee." According to Cooler, "while this Cherokee name can be found with a variety of spellings since the 1700s it, like all most [*sic*] place names in the Lower Cherokee dialect, ends in a 'long E' sound, as in Keowee, Jocassee, Oconee, and (until the last century) Chaugee and Chatoogee. Sometime in the early 1900s residents of the Eastatoee Valley began spelling it with 2 Es at the end to ensure it was pronounced properly. This spelling is one of the ways we now differentiate insiders from outsiders."

79. Schumann, "Introduction." For this idea, Schumann cites Margaret Farrar, "Nostalgia and the Politics of Place Memory," *Political Research Quarterly* 64 (2011). The "marking difference" comment is from Schumann, "Introduction," 9.

80. Harvey, *Justice, Nature and the Geography of Difference*, 150.

81. Wagner, "Space and Place," 124–25, quote from 125.

82. Hirsch, "Landscape," 1.

83. Basso, "Wisdom Sits in Places," 84.

Chapter Two

1. Clay, *Chattooga River Sourcebook*, 7.

2. Murphy, *Carolina Rocks!*, 20–21 and 30–31. For a more detailed geological history, see Weidensaul, *Mountains of the Heart*, 12–15.

3. Clay, *Chattooga River Sourcebook*, 7.

4. Rainfall information comes from Frick-Ruppert, *Mountain Nature*, 5–6, quote on 6.

5. For biodiversity, see Frick-Ruppert, *Mountain Nature*, 7. For cove forests, see Weidensaul, *Mountains of the Heart*, 53. For hardwood species, see Benson, *Cultural Resources Overview*, 17–18. For subcanopy species, see Frick-Ruppert, *Mountain Nature*, 78–79; for ground species, see 75–76.

6. On kudzu, see Coggeshall, *Carolina Piedmont Country*, 4, 25.

7. For fish species, see Weidensaul, *Mountains of the Heart*, 71–73. For a more complete ecological and biological inventory, see Frick-Ruppert, *Mountain Nature*; Weidensaul, *Mountains of the Heart*. Genus and species names are given only for flora and fauna described in later chapters.

8. For background information, see Mooney, *Myths of the Cherokee*.

9. For colonial settlement, see Clay, *Chattooga River Sourcebook*, 22–23; although cf. Hembree, *Jocassee Valley*, 20. Batteau, "Contradictions of a Kinship Community," 26. Olson, *Blue Ridge Folklife*, 30.

10. Davis, "Living on the Land," 153; Fischer, *Albion's Seed*, 638. For the general way of life, see "Early Days," by Pauline Nicholson in Duncan, Nicholson, Queen, and Wallace, eds., *An Informal History of Mountain Rest*, 4. For the source of the moonshining process, see Fischer, *Albion's Seed*, 730; Olson, *Blue Ridge Folklife*, 167–69. On mountain speech, see Montgomery, "Voices of My Ancestors."

11. On the region's dangerous reputation, see Kephart, *Our Southern Highlanders*, 266. Lederer's comment is from Ledford, "Landscape and a People Set Apart," 53; the negative perceptions comments are from 55.

12. Coggeshall, *Liberia, South Carolina*.

13. Kephart, *Our Southern Highlanders*, 11–12; McDonald and Muldowny, *TVA and the Dispossessed*, 29–68; Hembree, *Jocassee Valley*, 93–98.

14. The retaliation rule is from Fischer, *Albion's Seed*, 765; blood feuds from 767. Hembree and Jackson, *Keowee*, 65. See also Caudill, *Night Comes to the Cumberlands*, 46–51; Campbell, *Southern Highlander*, 104, on feuding.

15. The name "Dark Corner" "came from an episode after the Civil War, where a speaker in a cart so displeased his listeners that they picked up the shafts of the cart

and started running. The speaker fell out, brushed himself off, and said, 'You people up here are in the dark; you don't understand what is going on.'" The story is from Howard, *Dark Corner Heritage*, 2; the quote is from 41. Batson, *History of the Upper Part of Greenville County*, 489. On moonshining, see also Helsley, *Hidden History*, 102; Kephart, *Our Southern Highlanders*, 126–44; Batson, *History of the Upper Part of Greenville County*, 489; Williams, *Great Smoky Mountains Folklife*, 103. For a good description of the moonshining process, see Olson, *Blue Ridge Folklife*, 167–69. Helsley, *Hidden History*, 99; concluding statement from 106.

16. On the local impact of cotton mills, see Coggeshall, *Carolina Piedmont Country*; Gauzens, *Salem*, 164; McFall, *It Happened in Pickens County*, 146; Clay, *Chattooga River Sourcebook*, 24–25.

17. Bingham, "Impact of Recreational Development," 59–60, for the summary of development; "perpetual subordination" quote from 60.

18. On the Jocassee Camp for Girls, see Hembree, *Jocassee Valley*, 89. Lucille Godbold (1900–1981) was herself a very interesting character in the Jocassee Valley. Local residents described her as very androgynous, and one can see and hear her later in life in a South Carolina Hall of Fame program (South Carolina ETV, "Lucille Godboldt.") Godbold, "Camp Jocassee for Girls," 6. For outsiders with new ideas, see Gauzens, *Salem*, 28. For the Attakulla Lodge, see Hembree, *Jocassee Valley*, 101–2; paradise quote from 105, broadened horizons idea from 110.

19. Virtually every local and regional history mentions moonshining in the area. See, for example, Hembree and Jackson, *Keowee*, 44; Howard, *Dark Corner Heritage*, 41. For a description of the process, see Olson, *Blue Ridge Folklife*, 167–69. Hembree, *Jocassee Valley*, 104; Sassafras Mountain comments are from Robertson, "Life on Sassafras Mountain," 70. Veal, "Revenuer Days."

20. On chestnuts, see Davis, "Historical Significance of American Chestnut," 1; Frick-Ruppert, *Mountain Nature*, 136. For the uses of chestnut wood, see Davis, "Historical Significance of American Chestnut," 3–4.

21. Frick-Ruppert, *Mountain Nature*, 136. Davis, "Historical Significance of American Chestnut," 5–6; concluding quote from 6.

22. On the local timbering economy, see Hembree, *Jocassee Valley*, 113 and 120; see also Nicholson, "Early Days," in Duncan, Nicholson, Queen, and Wallace, eds., *Informal History of Mountain Rest*, 4–5 and 13; Caudill, *Night Comes to the Cumberlands*, 61–69. On the impact of logging roads, see Hembree, *Jocassee Valley*, 120.

23. Badenoch, *Keowee Key*, 17; see also Lane, *Chattooga*, 31.

24. For the relocation of graves and churches, see Hembree, *Jocassee Valley*, 127; Lane, *Chattooga*, 31. For a similar program with the TVA in the 1930s, see McDonald and Muldowny, *TVA and the Dispossessed*, 5. For the comment about the lake construction, see Lane, *Chattooga*, 31. On the yellow poplars, see Hembree, *Jocassee Valley*, 123.

25. Hembree and Jackson, *Keowee*, 75. Robertson, "Memories of Another Time," 13. For similar results with the TVA in the 1930s, see McDonald and Muldowny, *TVA and the Dispossessed*, 26.

26. Chastain is quoted in Hembree and Jackson, *Keowee*, 102. Economic advantages are discussed in Hembree, *Jocassee Valley*, 7.

27. Dickey, *Summer of Deliverance*, 14. For the resentment of the federal control idea, see Duncan, Nicholson, Queen, and Wallace, eds., *History of Mountain Rest*, 30. The roughnecks quote and the lack of access idea are from Dickey, "Last Wild River."

28. Williamson, *Hillbillyland*, 162–63.

29. For backlash from the film, see Lane, *Chattooga*, 97; Dickey, "Last Wild River." For the county politician's comment, see Duncan, Nicholson, Queen, and Wallace, eds., *Informal History of Mountain Rest*, 32; for the subsequent comments, see Dickey, "Last Wild River."

30. Williamson, *Hillbillyland*, 291.

31. On development, see Bingham, "Impact of Recreational Development," "unsuspecting natives," 61; other quotes from 62. Dickey, "Last Wild River"; Bingham, "Impact of Recreational Development," 62; see also Lane, *Chattooga*, 32. For the impact of new settlements, see Blackwell, *"Used to Be a Rough Place,"* 98.

32. Davis, "Jim Anthony Helping His Son."

33. For the impact of newcomers, see Badenoch, *Keowee Key*; the "communities" comment is from 37, and the contrast comment is from 62.

34. McCuen, *Including a Pile of Rocks*, 485.

35. Lane, *Chattooga*, 32.

Chapter Three

1. Kephart, *Our Southern Highlanders*, 379.

2. Kephart, *Our Southern Highlanders*, 266 and 296.

3. Kephart, *Our Southern Highlanders*, 466; the "dark corners" comment is from 267–68. Blackwell, *"Used to Be a Rough Place,"* xxiii.

4. Heilbrun, "Masculine Wilderness," 41. The other quote is from an anonymous newspaper article, no provenance, titled "They Gathered at the River for 'Deliverance.'" Georgiana Vertical Files Collection, Hargrett Rare Book and Manuscript Library, University of Georgia Libraries.

5. Dickey, "Last Wild River."

6. See, for example, Mayo, "How to Be Safe While Visiting Waterfalls."

7. Reynolds, *My Life*; quotes are from 151, 154, and 155 (for the stunt).

8. The statistics are from Duncan, Nicholson, Queen, and Wallace, eds., *Informal History of Mountain Rest*, 31. Buzz Williams is quoted in Dickey, "Last Wild River."

9. Sparks, "Can We Keep the Chattooga Wild?"; Cullen, "They Come by the Thousands"; Harrell, "The Chattooga." All three articles are from the Georgiana Vertical Files Collection, Hargrett Rare Book and Manuscript Library, University of Georgia Libraries.

10. Dickey, "Last Wild River."

11. Duncan, Nicholson, Queen, and Wallace, eds., *Informal History of Mountain Rest*, 31; Lane, *Chattooga*, 5.

12. Dickey, *Deliverance*, 55.

13. Dickey, *Deliverance*, 65–66.

14. Dickey, *Summer of Deliverance*, quotes from 170, 171, and 181.

15. Reynolds, *My Life*, with the comments about Coward and McKinney from 157; filming of the scene and the overall feeling comments from 158. The warning is from Dickey, *Deliverance*, 270, and is repeated by James Dickey himself in the film.

16. For the cultural impact of the film, see Williamson, *Hillbillyland*, 291.

17. Sparks, "Can We Keep the Chattooga Wild?," 18. Georgiana Vertical Files Collection, Hargrett Rare Book and Manuscript Library, University of Georgia Libraries.

18. Lopez, "Campaign Diary." This story also appears in Hartigan, *Odd Tribes*, 157. For the destruction of Bob's Place, see Silvarole, "Bob's Place Remembered."

19. Lanham, *Home Place*, posthumous degree comment from 156, "scraggly haired hillbilly" from 154.

20. Lanham, *Home Place*, 155–56.

21. Sloan is cited in Smith, *Call of the Big Eastatoe*, ix. Wilkes is quoted from "Methodism in the Mountains," *Pickens Sentinel*, September 28, 1893, in a private manuscript by Will Gravely titled "McKinney Chapel" (n.d.). The manuscript is in the Faith Clayton Genealogy Room, Rickman Library, Southern Wesleyan University, Central, South Carolina.

22. Thralls, "Splash: Caution." Georgiana Vertical Files Collection, Hargrett Rare Book and Manuscript Library, University of Georgia Libraries. The other quote is from Dickey, "Last Wild River."

23. Tuan, *Space and Place*, 156; Opie, "Sense of Place," 113–19.

24. Weller, *Yesterday's People*, 46.

25. Tuan, *Space and Place*, 185.

26. Tilley, *Phenomenology of Landscape*, 21 for the quote and 20–21 for the Western view of the land; see also Harvey, *Seventeen Contradictions*, 22. Rodman, "Empowering Place," 647.

27. Harvey, *Seventeen Contradictions*, 60 for the "under the sun" comment, "use values" quote from 250, "functionalist aesthetic values" from 262, home treatment 191, wasted land comment 40, "vulture capitalism" 162, "dispossession" 276, and "anachronisms" 277.

Chapter Four

1. Wagner, "Space and Place," 127.

2. Fletcher, *Whippoorwill Farewell*, 9–10.

3. Orr and Tankersley, *Don't Kiss Your Turtle Goodbye*, 135.

4. Kayte Lessor is quoted in Hembree, "Horsepasture River," 164.

5. Vickery, *Forgotten Society*, 191–92.

6. Dickey, "Last Wild River."

7. Orr and Tankersley, *Don't Kiss Your Turtle Goodbye*, 63.

8. Chastain is quoted in Hembree and Jackson, *Keowee*, 100.

9. Ledford, "Landscape and a People Set Apart," 62.

10. Hembree, "Horsepasture River," 161.

11. Porter, *Wildflowers among the Cotton Seeds*, 122.

12. Vickery, *Forgotten Society*, 192.

13. Garner, "Deliverance Syndrome"; Hicks is quoted in the anonymous article "Tourists Attracted to Dangers." Both clippings were found in the Georgiana Vertical Files Collection, Hargrett Rare Book and Manuscript Library, University of Georgia Libraries.

14. There are videos online that show the running of these rapids. See, for example, Begley, "First Run on Five Falls."

15. For the story of the recovery of Rachel Trois's remains, see Williams, "Accident Database."

16. "Be Waterfall Wise" website.

17. Water moccasins are not native to the Upstate.

18. For stories about venomous snakes killing fruit trees, see item 7949 in Hand, *Popular Beliefs and Superstitions*, 7:497–99.

19. Although this sounds like a traditional belief, I was unable to locate it in Hand, *Popular Beliefs and Superstitions*.

20. Alexander, "Reedy Cove Recollections," 22–23.

21. About bear sightings near school playgrounds, see also the interview with Ambler School teacher Julie Cheek (Hardin, "Ambler School History"). The document is in the Faith Clayton Genealogy Room, Rickman Library, Southern Wesleyan University, Central, South Carolina.

22. Despite the infrequent stories about them, most likely mountain lions are extinct in the southern Appalachians.

23. Alexander, "Reedy Cove Recollections," 27–28, and second-day outcome, 29.

24. Porter, *Wildflowers among the Cotton Seeds*, 124–25.

25. Alexander, "Reedy Cove Recollections," 69–74. The "mad dog" quote is from 70, and the "sight of the mad dog" quote is from 73.

26. McKinney, "Industrialization and Violence in Appalachia," 141; Lane, *Chattooga*, 8.

27. Kephart, *Our Southern Highlanders*, 296.

28. While I was unable to find the popular belief that Christ was crucified on a dogwood in Hand, *Popular Beliefs and Superstitions*, I did locate it in Randolph, *Ozark Magic and Folklore*, 262.

29. "Plumb" as an intensifier dates back to the late sixteenth century, according to the *Oxford English Dictionary*.

30. While this sounds like a popular belief, I was unable to locate it in Hand, *Popular Beliefs and Superstitions*.

31. "Right" as an intensifier dates back to the twelfth century, according to the *Oxford English Dictionary*.

32. For the presidential campaign story, see Lopez, "Campaign Diary." For the story of the arson, see Silvarole, "Bob's Place Remembered." Bob's Place both before and after the fire can be viewed in a YouTube video: "Last of Bob's Place."

33. Vince Aiken is quoted in Robertson, "Life on Sassafras Mountain," 70.

34. Muller, "Chasing Bootleggers."

35. Blackwell, *"Used to Be a Rough Place,"* 97.

36. The *Oxford English Dictionary* traces "suck eggs" back to seventeenth-century England. The term refers to a dog or weasel that steals but also to a person.

37. Hembree and Jackson, *Keowee*, 65; the Few interview is from 72.

38. Connelly, "The Train That Ran from Pickens to Eastatoe."

39. Coulbourn, "Filming of 'Deliverance.'" Georgiana Vertical Files Collection, Hargrett Rare Book and Manuscript Library, University of Georgia Libraries.

40. "Snipe hunting" is discussed in Bronner, *American Children's Folklore*, 170–71.

41. Discussion of the "Vanishing Hitchhiker" tale can be found in Brunvand, *Vanishing Hitchhiker*, 24–46.

42. The popular belief of a bird in the house predicting death is item 5280 in Hand, *Popular Beliefs and Superstitions*, 7:61.

43. According to the *Oxford English Dictionary*, the U.S. regional term "booger" most likely descends from a corruption of the sixteenth-century English word "boggard," meaning a local goblin or sprite.

Chapter Five

1. Geertz, "Afterword," 262. The "thick description" discussion is from Geertz, "Thick Description," 6–10.

2. James Weiner, *Empty Place* (Bloomington: Indiana University Press, 1991), 32, cited by Casey, "How to Get from Space to Place," 14; Tilley, *Phenomenology of Landscape*, 18; Frake, "Pleasant Places," 235, and then the elaboration on 238; Basso, "Wisdom Sits in Places," 66; Wagner, "Space and Place," 126; Tilley, *Phenomenology of Landscape*, 19.

3. Hembree, *Jocassee Valley*, 23.

4. Blue, "Heritage of Oconee County," 6–7. Holder, "Notes Relating to Pickens County, SC," 7.

5. Helsley, *Hidden History*, 99; Batson, *History of the Upper Part of Greenville County*, 457–58.

6. McFall, *Keowee River*, 7; Chastain, "Whose Horses."

7. The Abner Creek place-name story is from Robertson, "Life on Sassafras Mountain," 69; the Lewis place-name story is from Alexander, "Reedy Cove Recollections," 36.

8. Note how the speaker differentiates between a "load" and a "mess" of fish. The *Oxford English Dictionary* defines a "mess" as a haul of fish sufficient for a meal. The term dates back to 1577.

9. For basketry in the Upstate, see Coggeshall, *Carolina Piedmont Country*, 215–16.

10. Newton, *Close-Close Close Kin*, 31–32.

11. Coggeshall, *Liberia, South Carolina*, 243n25.

12. Raine, *Land of Saddle-Bags*, 211; Williams, *Great Smoky Mountains Folklife*, 103; Fischer, *Albion's Seed*, 763.

13. "Spring lizard" is South or South Midlands for "salamander." The term has been documented as far back as 1848. See Hall, *Dictionary of American Regional English*, 5:211.

14. Davis, "Homeplace Geography," 15.

15. For the emotional ties to the homeplace, see Hicks, *Appalachian Valley*, 58–60.

16. Davis, "Epilogue," 215; Williams, *Homeplace*, 118; Blu, "'Where Do You Stay At?,'" 220.

17. Williams, *Homeplace*, 135.

18. Blu, "'Where Do You Stay At?,'" 220.

19. Williams, *Homeplace*, 126–28; Batteau, "Mosbys and Broomsedge," 462.

20. Williams, *Homeplace*, 130.

21. Williams, *Homeplace*, 125–26.

22. For the importance of controlling family land through generations, see Blackwell, "*Used to Be a Rough Place*," 77; Opie, "Sense of Place," 113; Hall and Stack, "Introduction," 3; Beaver, "Appalachian Families," 150. The comment about family identity is from Beaver, "Appalachian Families," 146; see also Wagner, "Space and Place," 123. The "central axis" quote is from Opie, "Sense of Place," 115.

23. For the preference for children to inherit family land, see Bryant, *We're All Kin*, 67–74. For the ties between family, land, and faith, see Hall and Stack, "Introduction," 3.

24. Beaver, "Appalachian Families," 150.

25. The *Oxford English Dictionary* offers an obsolete meaning of "barely" for the adverb "scarcely."

26. Batteau, "Contradictions of a Kinship Community," 33; see also Batteau, "Mosbys and Broomsedge," 445; Williams, *Homeplace*, 36. For the close settling of kin, see Weller, *Yesterday's People*, 60. For the mixing of bloodlines, see Caudill, *Night Comes to the Cumberlands*, 84–85. For similar ideas, see Bryant, *We're All Kin*, 84.

27. Bryant, *We're All Kin*, 68. Williams, *Homeplace*, 36. Blu, "'Where Do You Stay At?,'" 206; see also Halperin, *Livelihood of Kin*, 2. Bryant, *We're All Kin*, 74.

28. For the idea of morality being tied to place, see Batteau, "Mosbys and Broomsedge," 448; Eller, "Place and the Recovery of Community," 4; Reed, *Enduring South*, 35. Fischer, *Albion's Seed*, 662–68.

29. Eller, "Place and the Recovery of Community," 4.

30. For the challenges to college students, see Vance, *Hillbilly Elegy*, 147.

31. For a similar situation from Tennessee, see McDonald and Muldowny, *TVA and the Dispossessed*, 67.

32. McDonald and Muldowny, *TVA and the Dispossessed*, 67; Frost, "Our Contemporary Ancestors," 75; Cooke-Jackson and Hansen, "Appalachian Culture and Reality TV," 198; see also Vance, *Hillbilly Elegy*. For the general discussion, see Barcus and Brunn, "Towards a Typology of Mobility and Place Attachment."

33. After graduating from college, marrying, and moving out of state for several years, Radcliffe has divorced, moved back into a mobile home behind her parents' home, remarried, and acquired a job and is socially active and very happy.

34. Hicks, *Appalachian Valley*, 55.

35. See also Hicks, *Appalachian Valley*, 55.

36. Reluctantly, Trask and his family have left the state for a significant professional promotion. However, the family maintains their property in their South Carolina home valley, and Trask and his family visit whenever they can.

37. Eller, "Place and the Recovery of Community," 4; Smith, "Landscapes of Clearance," 14. Native views are from Basso, "Wisdom Sits in Places," 57.

38. Steele, *Sense of Place*, 131; see also Casey, "How to Get from Space to Place," 25. The narrative comment is from Williams, *Homeplace*, 20, and the quote is from 135–36.

39. Basso, "Wisdom Sits in Places," 85, and then 56.

40. Tilley, *Phenomenology of Landscape*, 27; see also Davis, "Living on the Land," 153. Tilley, *Phenomenology of Landscape*, 27 and 33.

41. Alexander, "Reedy Cove Recollections," 39.

42. Hembree and Jackson, *Keowee*, 41; see also Davis, "Homeplace Geography," 15.

43. See also Williams, *Homeplace*, 133; Davis, "Homeplace Geography," 15.

44. Lane, *Chattooga*, 173–74.

45. McDonald and Muldowny, *TVA and the Dispossessed*, 195; Falk, *Rooted in Place*, 133.

46. Vickery, *Forgotten Society*, 243.

47. This is a theme briefly explored in Coggeshall, *Liberia, South Carolina*, 201–8.

48. Leonhardt is quoted in Robertson, "Warm Glow of the Country Church," 77. The Soapstone Church quote is from Coggeshall, *Liberia, South Carolina*, 206.

Chapter Six

1. The quote about identity is from Batteau, "Mosbys and Broomsedge," 450. The other quotes are from Blu, "'Where Do You Stay At?,'" 201 and 205. See also Kingsolver, "'Placing' One Another."

2. Wagner, "Space and Place," 127.

3. On the cultural meaning of homecomings, see Coggeshall, *Carolina Piedmont Country*, 154–57. The "flesh and blood" quote is from McGehee, "Religion in the 'Sense of Place in Appalachia,'" 127–28. Smith, *Call of the Big Eastatoe*, 402.

4. Wilkinson, "On Being 'Country,'" 186.

5. Wagner, "Space and Place," 123. For the "genealogical landscape" concept, Wagner cites Barbara Allen, "The Genealogical Landscape and the Southern Sense of Place," in *Sense of Place: American Regional Cultures*, ed. Barbara Allen and Thomas J. Schlereth (Lexington: University Press of Kentucky, 1990), 160–63.

6. Hendricks, "Dark Corner," 97; Smith, "Landscapes of Clearance," 16; Weller, *Yesterday's People*, 158.

7. Basso, "Wisdom Sits in Places," 87; Overman, "Keith Family," 5.

8. Hendricks, "Dark Corner," 96; Smith, *Call of the Big Eastatoe*, viii.

9. Basso, "Wisdom Sits in Places," 83–84.

10. Lane, *Chattooga*, 18.

11. Alexander, "Reedy Cove Recollections," 79–80. For the sensory connection to land and the merging of people and land, see the Judy Bonds interview in House and Howard, *Something's Rising*, 131–50.

12. See also Smith, *Call of the Big Eastatoe*, vii; Smith, *Myth, Media, and the Southern Mind*, 116, and the Shelby and Keltner interview in House and Howard, *Something's Rising*, 217.

13. The "sacred mystery" quote is from Opie, "Sense of Place," 113–14; Wagner, "Space and Place," 130.

14. Hembree and Jackson, *Keowee*, 7 (my emphasis).

15. Orr and Tankersley, *Don't Kiss Your Turtle Goodbye*, 27; Fletcher, "'Painful Reminder,'" 11.

16. Basso, "Wisdom Sits in Places," 54.

17. Tuan, *Space and Place*, 183–84.

18. Wagner, "Space and Place," 124, citing a 1994 student paper by Lin Usack, "Cultural Attachment to Land Study," Radford University, Radford, Virginia, 8; Hicks, *Appalachian Valley*, 5.

19. See also Wagner, "Space and Place," 130; the Shelby and Keltner interview is in House and Howard, *Something's Rising*, 217.

20. Smith, "Landscapes of Clearance," 23.

21. A local reader of a preliminary draft of this manuscript doubted the initial high price for land mentioned by Mike Davidson.

22. Hembree, *Jocassee Valley*, 161. For similar feelings about a TVA dam in upper east Tennessee, see McDonald and Muldowny, *TVA and the Dispossessed*, 67.

23. Godbold, "Camp Jocassee," 7; Hembree, *Jocassee Valley*, 7; Godbold, "Camp Jocassee," 7.

24. Smith, "Landscapes of Clearance," 14.

25. The Dark Corner inhabitant is quoted in Hendricks, "Dark Corner," 97.

26. Smith, "Landscapes of Clearance," 17.

27. See also McDonald and Muldowny, *TVA and the Dispossessed*, 61, for suicides caused by TVA dam dispossession in east Tennessee.

28. Davis, "Epilogue," 215; McDonald and Muldowny, *TVA and the Dispossessed*, 88; Vickery, *Forgotten Society*, 237.

29. Chastain is quoted in Hembree and Jackson, *Keowee*, 90; McFall, *Keowee River*, 5.

30. Although a nonlocal state resident, author James Dickey (*Deliverance*, 136) also used the metaphor of burial to describe the evidence of horrific crimes soon to be hidden by the lake in his novel: "'Well, did you ever look out over a lake?'" questioned Dickey's protagonist Lewis. "'There's plenty of water. Something buried under it—under it—is as buried as it can get.'"

31. Both quotes are from Fletcher, *Whippoorwill Farewell*, 5 and 147–48. The later recollection is from Fletcher, "'Painful Reminder,'" 11. The Finley interview is from Hembree, *Jocassee Valley*, 161.

32. Robertson, "Eastatoe Mourns Death"; Fletcher, *Whippoorwill Farewell*, 1.

33. Fletcher, "Deep-Water Dive," 7. Websites for information about Fletcher's search for the lodge include "A Lost World."

34. Williams, *Homeplace*, 116. On the preservation of the homeplace, see Williams, *Homeplace*, 130.

35. Hembree and Jackson, *Keowee*. The Steele story is from 73–74, and the picnic and dream stories are from 73.

36. Hembree, "Sunset, South Carolina," 90. See also Hembree and Jackson, *Keowee*, 64.

37. McGehee, "Religion in the 'Sense of Place in Appalachia,'" 127, citing McDonald and Muldowny, *TVA and the Dispossessed*, 195.

38. Hembree, *Jocassee Valley*, 107.

39. At one point early in our interview, Mrs. Mitchell showed me an ostrich egg-sized oval rock from the Whitewater River. She also had a slab of what looked like metamorphosed sandstone with little black club-like fossils; this, she explained, was

from the Jocassee Dam quarry site. When I mentioned that the site was closed to the public, Mrs. Mitchell winked and claimed that she had a "secret source."

40. Hembree and Jackson, *Keowee*, 53. I have seen this walkway.

41. See also Hembree and Jackson, *Keowee*, 53.

42. Debbie Fletcher and her friends support a website that maintains that the lodge is still standing. See "Jocassee Remembered," http://www.jocasseeremembered.com. See also Connor, "Here's What's at the Bottom of Lake Jocassee." Viewers may decide for themselves what remains by viewing "Lake Jocassee 300' Dive to Attakulla Lodge."

Chapter Seven

1. Email to author, August 13, 2009.

Sources Cited

Articles from the Georgiana Vertical Files Collection in the Hargrett Rare Book and Manuscript Library, University of Georgia Libraries (Athens, GA) may be difficult to locate. The collections were reorganized a year after my research, so I am only assuming that the articles may still be located in this collection.

Alexander, Douglas R. "Reedy Cove Recollections." The Mary Oates Gregorie Historical Collection, Captain Kimberly Hampton Memorial Library, Pickens County, SC, 2014.

Anglin, Mary. "Lessons from Appalachia in the 20th Century: Poverty, Power, and the 'Grassroots.'" *American Anthropologist* 104 (2002): 565–82.

———. "Toward a New Politics of Outrage and Transformation: Placing Appalachia within the Global Political Economy." *Journal of Appalachian Studies* 22 (2016): 51–56.

Ashworth, Gregory J., and Brian Graham, eds. *Senses of Place: Senses of Time*. London: Routledge, 2005.

Badenoch, Alice. *Keowee Key: The Origins of a Community*. Seneca, SC: Jay's Printing, 1989.

Ballard, Sandra. "Where Did Hillbillies Come From? Tracing Sources of the Comic Hillbilly Fool in Literature." In *Confronting Appalachian Stereotypes: Back Talk from an American Region*, ed. Dwight Billings, Gurney Norman, and Katherine Ledford, 138–49. Lexington: University Press of Kentucky, 1999.

Barcus, Holly, and Stanley Brunn. "Towards a Typology of Mobility and Place Attachment in Rural America." *Journal of Appalachian Studies* 15 (2009): 26–48.

Basso, Keith. "Wisdom Sits in Places: Notes on a Western Apache Landscape." In *Senses of Place*, ed. Steven Feld and Keith Basso, 53–90. Santa Fe, NM: School of American Research Press, 1996.

Batson, Mann. *A History of the Upper Part of Greenville County, South Carolina*. Taylors, SC: Faith Printing, 1993.

Batteau, Allen. "The Contradictions of a Kinship Community." In *Holding on to the Land and the Lord: Kinship, Ritual, Land Tenure, and Social Policy in the Rural South*, ed. Robert Hall and Carol Stack, 25–40. Southern Anthropological Society Proceedings, No. 15. Athens: University of Georgia Press, 1982.

———. *The Invention of Appalachia*. Tucson: University of Arizona Press, 1990.

———. "Mosbys and Broomsedge: The Semantics of Class in an Appalachian Kinship System." *American Ethnologist* 9 (1982): 445–66.

Beaver, Patricia. "Appalachian Families, Landownership, and Public Policy." In *Holding on to the Land and the Lord: Kinship, Ritual, Land Tenure, and Social Policy in the Rural South*, ed. Robert Hall and Carol Stack, 146–54. Southern

Anthropological Society Proceedings, No. 15. Athens: University of Georgia Press, 1982.

"Be Waterfall Wise," Explore Brevard, Transylvania County Tourism Development Authority, https://explorebrevard.com/waterfall-safety/.

Begley, Clinton. "First Run on Five Falls—Section IV—Chattooga River (GA/SC)," YouTube, July 6, 2012, https://www.youtube.com/watch?v=P5tjeCiRRnY.

Benson, Robert. *Cultural Resources Overview of the Sumter National Forest.* Athens, GA: Southeastern Archaeological Services, 2006.

Billings, Dwight. "Introduction." In *Confronting Appalachian Stereotypes: Back Talk from an American Region*, ed. Dwight Billings, Gurney Norman, and Katherine Ledford, 3–20. Lexington: University Press of Kentucky, 1999.

Billings, Dwight, and Ann Kingsolver. "Introduction: Place Matters." In *Appalachia in Regional Context: Place Matters*, ed. Dwight Billings and Ann Kingsolver, 3–15. Lexington: University Press of Kentucky, 2018.

Billings, Dwight, Mary Beth Pudup, and Altina Waller. "Taking Exception with Exceptionalism: The Emergence and Transformation of Historical Studies of Appalachia." In *Appalachia in the Making: The Mountain South in the Nineteenth Century*, ed. Mary Beth Pudup, Dwight Billings, and Altina Waller, 1–24. Chapel Hill: University of North Carolina Press, 1995.

Bingham, Edgar. "The Impact of Recreational Development on Pioneer Lifestyles in Southern Appalachia." In *Colonialism in Modern America: The Appalachian Case*, ed. Helen Lewis, Linda Johnson, and Donald Askins, 57–70. Boone, NC: Appalachian Consortium Press, 1978.

Blackwell, Joshua. *"Used to Be a Rough Place in Them Hills": Moonshine, the Dark Corner, and the New South.* Bloomington, IN: AuthorHouse, 2009.

Blee, Kathleen, and Dwight Billings. "Where 'Bloodshed Is a Pastime': Mountain Feuds and Appalachian Stereotyping." In *Confronting Appalachian Stereotypes: Back Talk from an American Region*, ed. Dwight Billings, Gurney Norman, and Katherine Ledford, 119–37. Lexington: University Press of Kentucky, 1999.

Blu, Karen. "'Where Do You Stay At?': Home Place and Community among the Lumbee." In *Senses of Place*, ed. Steven Feld and Keith Basso, 197–227. Santa Fe, NM: School of American Research Press, 1996.

Blue, Lillie. "Heritage of Oconee County, Volume 1 1868–1995." Marceline, MD: Blue Ridge Arts Council, in cooperation with Wadsworth Pub. Co., 1995. Duke Power's Keowee-Toxaway Project papers, Mary Oates Gregorie Historical Collection, Captain Kimberly Hampton Memorial Library, Pickens County, SC.

Bronner, Simon. *American Children's Folklore.* Little Rock, AR: August House, 1988.

Brunvand, Jan. *The Vanishing Hitchhiker: American Urban Legends and Their Meanings.* New York: Norton, 1981.

Bryant, F. Carlene. *We're All Kin: A Cultural Study of a Mountain Neighborhood.* Knoxville: University of Tennessee Press, 1981.

Campbell, John C. *The Southern Highlander and His Homeland.* Lexington: University Press of Kentucky, 1969. Originally published by New York: Russell Sage Foundation, 1921.

Casey, Edward. "How to Get from Space to Place in a Fairly Short Stretch of Time: Phenomenological Prolegomena." In *Senses of Place*, ed. Steven Feld and Keith Basso, 13–52. Santa Fe, NM: School of American Research Press, 1996.

Cash, Wilbur J. *The Mind of the South*. New York: Knopf, 1941.

Caudill, Harry. *Night Comes to the Cumberlands: A Biography of a Depressed Area*. Boston: Little, Brown, 1963.

Chastain, Dennis. "Whose Horses Really Were Hidden in the Old Historic Horsepasture?" *Jocassee Journal* 5 (2009): 2–3.

Clay, Butch. *Chattooga River Sourcebook: A Comprehensive Guide to the River and Its Natural and Human History*. Birmingham, AL: Chattooga River Publishing, 1995.

Cobb, James C. *Away Down South: A History of Southern Identity*. New York: Oxford University Press, 2005.

Coggeshall, John M. *Carolina Piedmont Country*. Jackson: University Press of Mississippi, 1996.

———. *Liberia, South Carolina: An African American Appalachian Community*. Chapel Hill: University of North Carolina Press, 2018.

Connelly, Herbert. "The Train That Ran from Pickens to Eastatoe, Part II," *Pickens Sentinel*, Wednesday, May 13, 1987. Appalachian Lumber Company Manuscript, Vertical File, South Caroliniana Library, University of South Carolina, Columbia.

Connor, Eric. "Here's What's at the Bottom of Lake Jocassee," *Anderson Independent Mail*, June 21, 2018, https://www.independentmail.com/story/news/local/south -carolina/2018/06/21/remembering-what-bottom-lake-jocassee/587431002/.

Cooke-Jackson, Angela, and Elizabeth K. Hansen. "Appalachian Culture and Reality TV: The Ethical Dilemma of Stereotyping Others." *Journal of Mass Media Ethics* 23 (2008): 183–200.

Coulbourn, Keith. "The Filming of 'Deliverance.'" *Atlanta Journal and Constitution*, July 25, 1971. Georgiana Vertical Files Collection, Hargrett Rare Book and Manuscript Library, University of Georgia Libraries.

Cullen, Robert. "They Come by the Thousands to Try the Wild Chattooga." *Augusta Chronicle-Herald*, July 24, 1977. Georgiana Vertical Files Collection, Hargrett Rare Book and Manuscript Library, University of Georgia Libraries.

Davis, Angelia. "Jim Anthony Helping His Son with a New Development Near Marietta in Pickens County." *Greenville News*, January 17, 2020.

Davis, Donald. "Epilogue." In *Homeplace Geography: Essays for Appalachia*, 215–16. Macon, GA: Mercer University Press, 2006.

———. "Historical Significance of American Chestnut to Appalachian Culture and Ecology." In *Restoration of American Chestnut to Forest Lands: Proceedings of a Conference and Workshop*, May 4–6, 2004, ed. Kim C. Steiner and John E. Carlson, 2005. The North Carolina Arboretum Natural Resources Report NPS/NCR/CUE/ NRR 2006/001, National Park Service, Washington, DC.

———. "Homeplace Geography." In *Homeplace Geography: Essays for Appalachia*, 7–16. Macon, GA: Mercer University Press, 2006.

———. "Living on the Land: Blue Ridge Life and Culture." In *Homeplace Geography: Essays for Appalachia*, 134–53. Macon, GA: Mercer University Press, 2006.

————. "The Politics of Wilderness in Appalachia." In *Homeplace Geography: Essays for Appalachia*, 33–51. Macon, GA: Mercer University Press, 2006.

Dickey, Bronwen. "The Last Wild River." *Oxford American* 61 (Summer 2008), https://main.oxfordamerican.org/magazine/item/1083-the-last-wild-river.

Dickey, Christopher. *Summer of Deliverance: A Memoir of Father and Son*. New York: Simon and Schuster, 1998.

Dickey, James. *Deliverance*. Boston: Houghton Mifflin, 1970.

Duncan, Dennis, Pauline Nicholson, Margaret Sue Queen, and Joe Wallace, eds. *An Informal History of Mountain Rest, South Carolina*. Taylors, SC: Faith Printing, 1984.

Eller, Ronald. "Foreword." In *Confronting Appalachian Stereotypes: Back Talk from an American Region*, ed. Dwight Billings, Gurney Norman, and Katherine Ledford, ix–xi. Lexington: University Press of Kentucky, 1999.

————. "Place and the Recovery of Community in Appalachia." In *Sense of Place in Appalachia*, ed. S. Mont Whitson, 3–19. Morehead, KY: Office of Regional Development Services, Morehead State University, 1988.

Falk, William. *Rooted in Place: Family and Belonging in a Southern Black Community*. New Brunswick, NJ: Rutgers University Press, 2004.

Fischer, David. *Albion's Seed: Four British Folkways in America*. New York: Oxford University Press, 1989.

Fisher, Steve, and Barbara Ellen Smith. "Internal Colony—Are You Sure? Defining, Theorizing, Organizing Appalachia." *Journal of Appalachian Studies* 22 (2016): 45–50.

Fisher, Steve, and Barbara Ellen Smith. "Introduction: Placing Appalachia." In *Transforming Places: Lessons from Appalachia*, ed. Stephen Fisher and Barbara Ellen Smith, 1–15. Urbana: University of Illinois Press, 2012.

Fletcher, Debbie. "Deep-Water Dive Brings Back Memories of Camp Jocassee for Girls." *Jocassee Journal* 12, no. 1 (2011): 6–7.

————. "'A Painful Reminder of What Once Was.'" *Jocassee Journal* 11, no. 1 (2010): 11.

————. *Whippoorwill Farewell: Jocassee Remembered*. Bloomington, IN: Trafford Publishing, 2003.

Frake, Charles O. "Pleasant Places, Past Times, and Sheltered Identity in Rural East Anglia." In *Senses of Place*, ed. Steven Feld and Keith Basso, 229–57. Santa Fe, NM: School of American Research Press, 1996.

Frick-Ruppert, Jennifer. *Mountain Nature: A Seasonal Natural History of the Southern Appalachians*. Chapel Hill: University of North Carolina Press, 2010.

Frost, William Goodell. "Our Contemporary Ancestors in the Southern Mountains." *Appalachian Heritage* 4 (1976): 70–80. Originally published in 1899.

Gabbert, Lisa, and Paul Jordan-Smith. "Introduction: Space, Place, Emergence." *Western Folklore* 66 (2007): 217–32.

Garner, Phil. "The Deliverance Syndrome." *Atlanta Journal and Constitution Magazine*, November 18, 1973. Georgiana Vertical Files Collection, Hargrett Rare Book and Manuscript Library, University of Georgia Libraries.

Gauzens, Joseph. *Salem: Twice a Town*. Pickens, SC: Hiott Printing, 1993.

Geertz, Clifford. "Afterword." In *Senses of Place*, ed. Steven Feld and Keith Basso, 259–62. Santa Fe, NM: School of American Research Press, 1996.

————. "Thick Description: Toward an Interpretive Theory of Culture." In *The Interpretation of Cultures*, 3–30. New York: Basic Books, 1973.

Gershon, Ilana. "Neoliberal Agency." *Current Anthropology* 54 (2011): 537–55.

Giemza, Bryan Albin. "Introduction." In *Rethinking the Irish in the American South: Beyond Rounders and Reelers*, ed. Bryan Giemza, 3–16. Jackson: University Press of Mississippi, 2013.

Godbold, Cash, Jr. "Camp Jocassee for Girls a Magical Place along Whitewater River." *Jocassee Journal* 12, no. 2 (2011): 6–7.

Gravely, Will. "McKinney Chapel." Manuscript, n.d. Faith Clayton Genealogy Room, Rickman Library, Southern Wesleyan University, Central, South Carolina.

Gregg, Nina, and Doug Gamble. "This Land Is Your Land: Local Organizing and the Hegemony of Growth." In *Transforming Places: Lessons from Appalachia*, ed. Stephen Fisher and Barbara Ellen Smith, 47–62. Urbana: University of Illinois Press, 2012.

Griffin, Patrick. "Irish Migration to the Colonial South: A Plea for a Forgotten Topic." In *Rethinking the Irish in the American South: Beyond Rounders and Reelers*, ed. Bryan Giemza, 51–74. Jackson: University Press of Mississippi, 2013.

Gupta, Akhil, and James Ferguson. "Beyond 'Culture': Space, Identity, and the Politics of Difference." In *Culture, Power, Place: Explorations in Critical Anthropology*, ed. Akhil Gupta and James Ferguson, 33–51. Durham, NC: Duke University Press, 1997.

Hall, Joan Houston, ed. *Dictionary of American Regional English*. Vol. 5. Cambridge, MA: Harvard University Press, 2012.

Hall, Robert, and Carol Stack. "Introduction." In *Holding on to the Land and the Lord: Kinship, Ritual, Land Tenure, and Social Policy in the Rural South*, ed. Robert Hall and Carol Stack, 3–7. Southern Anthropological Society Proceedings No. 15. Athens: University of Georgia Press, 1982.

Halperin, Rhoda H. *The Livelihood of Kin: Making Ends Meet "the Kentucky Way."* Austin: University of Texas Press, 1990.

Hand, Wayland. *Popular Beliefs and Superstitions from North Carolina*, Vol. 7 of the *Frank C. Brown Collection of North Carolina Folklore*, Newman White, gen. ed. Durham, NC: Duke University Press, 1952.

Hardin, Janet. "Ambler School History." Manuscript, 2000. Faith Clayton Genealogy Room, Rickman Library, Southern Wesleyan University, Central, South Carolina.

Harrell, Bob. "The Chattooga: A Risk of Death Each Ride." *Atlanta Constitution*, May 4, 1981. Georgiana Vertical Files Collection, Hargrett Rare Book and Manuscript Library, University of Georgia Libraries.

Hartigan, John, Jr. *Odd Tribes: Toward a Cultural Analysis of White People*. Durham, NC: Duke University Press, 2005.

Harvey, David. *Justice, Nature and the Geography of Difference*. Malden, MA: Blackwell, 1996.

————. *Seventeen Contradictions and the End of Capitalism*. New York: Oxford University Press, 2014.

Heilbrun, Carolyn. "The Masculine Wilderness of the American Novel." *Saturday Review*, January 29, 1972, 41.

Helsley, Alexia Jones. *Hidden History of Greenville County*. Charleston, SC: History Press, 2009.

Hembree, Claudia Whitmire. *Jocassee Valley*. Pickens, SC: Hiott Printing, 2003.

Hembree, Michael, and Dot Jackson. *Keowee: The Story of the Keowee River Valley in Upstate South Carolina*. Self-published, 1995.

Hembree, Mike. "Horsepasture River: Jewel in the Wild." In *Journey Home*, ed. Jimmy Cornelison, Reese Fant, Mike Hembree, and Dot Robertson, 161–65. Greenville, SC: Greenville News-Piedmont, 1988.

———. "Sunset, South Carolina: A Place and Its People." In *Journey Home*, ed. Jimmy Cornelison, Reese Fant, Mike Hembree, and Dot Robertson, 87–96. Greenville, SC: Greenville News-Piedmont, 1988.

Hendricks, Anne. "The Dark Corner of Greenville County." In *Proceedings and Papers of the Greenville County Historical Society, 1994–1998*, Vol. 11, ed. Jeffrey Willis, 80–100. Greenville, SC: Greenville County Historical Society, 1998.

Hernandez, Bernardo, M. Carmen Hidalgo, M. Esther Salazar-Laplace, and Stephany Hess. "Place Attachment and Place Identity in Natives and Non-Natives." *Journal of Environmental Psychology* 27 (2007): 310–19.

Hicks, George. *Appalachian Valley*. New York: Holt, Rinehart and Winston, 1976.

Higgs, Robert. "Versions of 'Natural Man' in Appalachia." In *An Appalachian Symposium: Essays Written in Honor of Cratis D. Williams*, ed. Jerry Williamson, 159–68. Boone, NC: Appalachian State University Press, 1977.

Hirsch, Eric. "Landscape: Between Place and Space." In *The Anthropology of Landscape: Perspectives on Place and Space*, ed. Eric Hirsch and Michael O'Hanlon, 1–30. Oxford, UK: Clarendon, 1995.

Holder, Frederick C. *Notes Relating to Pickens County, SC*. Oconee County Historical Society, 1987. The Mary Oates Gregorie Historical Collection, Captain Kimberly Hampton Memorial Library, Pickens County, SC.

House, Silas, and Jason Howard, eds. *Something's Rising: Appalachians Fighting Mountaintop Removal*. Lexington: University of Kentucky Press, 2009.

Howard, James. *Dark Corner Heritage*. Landrum, SC: n.p., 1980.

Hsiung, David. "Stereotypes." In *High Mountains Rising: Appalachia in Time and Place*, ed. Richard Straw and H. Tyler Blethen, 101–13. Urbana: University of Illinois Press, 2004.

Kahn, Miriam. "Your Place and Mine: Sharing Emotional Landscapes in Wamira, Papua New Guinea." In *Senses of Place*, ed. Steven Feld and Keith Basso, 167–96. Santa Fe, NM: School of American Research Press, 1996.

Kaika, Maria. "Dams as Symbols of Modernization: The Urbanization of Nature between Geographical Imagination and Materiality." *Annals of the Association of American Geographers* 96 (2006): 276–301.

Kephart, Horace. *Our Southern Highlanders: A Narrative of Adventure in the Southern Appalachians and a Study of Life among the Mountaineers*. New York: Macmillan, 1942.

Kingfisher, Catherine, and Jeff Maskovsky. "Introduction: The Limits of Neoliberalism." *Critique of Anthropology* 28 (2008): 115–26.

Kingsolver, Ann. "'Placing' Futures and Making Sense of Globalization on the Edge of Appalachia." In *Appalachia in Regional Context: Place Matters*, ed. Dwight

Billings and Ann Kingsolver, 17–47. Lexington: University Press of Kentucky, 2018.

———. "'Placing' One Another in 'Cedar,' Kentucky." *Anthropological Quarterly* 65 (1992): 128–36.

Lanham, J. Drew. *The Home Place: Memoirs of a Colored Man's Love Affair with Nature.* Minneapolis: Milkweed Editions, 2016.

Lane, John. *Chattooga: Descending into the Myth of Deliverance River.* Athens: University of Georgia Press, 2004.

"Lake Jocassee 300' Dive to Attakulla Lodge Diving into History South Carolina," YouTube, July 20, 2018, https://www.youtube.com/watch?v=H1_iENNHE6E.

"Last of Bob's Place aka Scatterbrains Sunset, South Carolina," YouTube, June 4, 2017, https://www.youtube.com/watch?v=UxfLdrVEcrY.

Ledford, Katherine. "A Landscape and a People Set Apart: Narratives of Exploration and Travel in Early Appalachia." In *Confronting Appalachian Stereotypes: Back Talk from an American Region*, ed. Dwight Billings, Gurney Norman, and Katherine Ledford, 47–66. Lexington: University Press of Kentucky, 1999.

Lewis, Helen. "Introduction: The Colony of Appalachia." In *Colonialism in Modern America: The Appalachian Case*, ed. Helen Lewis, Linda Johnson, and Donald Askins, 1–7. Boone, NC: Appalachian Consortium Press, 1978.

Lewis, Helen, and Edward Knipe. "The Colonialism Model: The Appalachian Case." In *Colonialism in Modern America: The Appalachian Case*, ed. Helen Lewis, Linda Johnson, and Donald Askins, 9–31. Boone, NC: Appalachian Consortium Press, 1978.

Lopez, Steve. "Campaign Diary: A Visit to Bush Country." *Time*, February 28, 2000, 36.

"A Lost World," YouTube, October 19, 2014, https://www.youtube.com/watch?v=LvwXePqujWw.

Low, Setha, and Denise Lawrence-Zuniga. "Locating Culture." In *The Anthropology of Space and Place: Locating Culture*, ed. Setha Low and Denise Lawrence-Zuniga, 1–47. Malden, MA: Blackwell, 2003.

Mayo, Nikie. "How to Be Safe While Visiting Waterfalls," *Anderson Independent Mail*, July 6, 2018.

McCuen, Anne. *Including a Pile of Rocks.* Greenville, SC: Southern Historical Press, 2005.

McDonald, Michael, and John Muldowny. *TVA and the Dispossessed: The Resettlement of Population in the Norris Dam Area.* Knoxville: University of Tennessee Press, 1982.

McFall, Pearl Smith. *It Happened in Pickens County.* Pickens, SC: Sentinel, 1959.

———. *The Keowee River and Cherokee Background.* Pickens, SC: n.p., 1966.

McGehee, Larry. "Religion in the 'Sense of Place in Appalachia': World without End." In *Sense of Place in Appalachia*, ed. S. Mont Whitson, 120–37. Morehead, KY: Office of Regional Development Services, Morehead State University, 1988.

McKinney, Gordon. "Industrialization and Violence in Appalachia in the 1890s." In *An Appalachian Symposium: Essays Written in Honor of Cratis D. Williams*, ed. Jerry Williamson, 131–44. Boone, NC: Appalachian State University Press, 1977.

Montgomery, Michael. "Voices of My Ancestors: A Personal Search for the Language of the Scotch-Irish." *American Speech* 80 (2005): 341–65.

Mooney, James. *Myths of the Cherokee and Sacred Formulas of the Cherokees*. Nashville: Charles and Randy Elder, Publishers, 1982.

Muller, Anna. "Chasing Bootleggers — Deputies Still Find Stills." *Pickens Sentinel*, August 26, 1987. Vertical Files of the South Caroliniana Library, University of South Carolina, Columbia.

Murphy, Carolyn Hanna. *Carolina Rocks! The Geology of South Carolina*. Orangeburg, SC: Sandlapper, 1995.

Newton, Buck Robinson. *Close-Close Close Kin*. Liberty, SC: The Monitor, 1987.

Nicholson, Pauline. "Early Days Along the Chattooga." In *An Informal History of Mountain Rest, South Carolina*, ed. Dennis Duncan, Pauline Nicholson, Margaret Sue Queen, and Joe Wallace, 3–5. Taylors, SC: Faith Printing, 1984.

Olson, Ted. *Blue Ridge Folklife*. Jackson: University Press of Mississippi, 1998.

Opie, John. "A Sense of Place: The World We Have Lost." In *An Appalachian Symposium: Essays Written in Honor of Cratis D. Williams*, ed. Jerry Williamson, 113–19. Boone, NC: Appalachian State University Press, 1977.

Orr, Gerald, and Ann Tankersley. *Don't Kiss Your Turtle Goodbye: True Tales of a Hill Country Vet*. Asheboro, NC: Down Home, 1995.

Overman, Flora Keith. "The Keith Family in South Carolina." Manuscripts Division, South Caroliniana Library, University of South Carolina, Columbia, 1930.

Piser, Gabriel. "Participation and Transformation in Twenty-First-Century Appalachian Scholarship." In *Appalachia Revisited: New Perspectives on Place, Tradition, and Progress*, ed. William Schumann, Rebecca Fletcher, Yunina Barbour-Payne, Jessica Blackburn, Jaclyn Daugherty, and Kelly Dorgan, 259–74. Lexington: University Press of Kentucky, 2016.

Plaut, Thomas. "Extending the Internal Periphery Model: The Impact of Culture and Consequent Strategy." In *Colonialism in Modern America: The Appalachian Case*, ed. Helen Lewis, Linda Johnson, and Donald Askins, 351–64. Boone, NC: Appalachian Consortium Press, 1978.

Porter, Doyle. *Wildflowers among the Cotton Seeds: Childhood Memories of Growing Up on Farms and in Cotton Mill Villages in Greenville and Pickens Counties, South Carolina 1941-1959*. Chapel Hill, NC: Chapel Hill Press, 2006.

Raine, James Watt. *The Land of Saddle-Bags: A Study of the Mountain People of Appalachia*. Richmond, VA: Presbyterian Committee of Publication, 1924.

Randolph, Vance. *Ozark Magic and Folklore*. New York: Dover, 1964.

Reed, John Shelton. *The Enduring South: Subcultural Persistence in Mass Society*. Lexington, MA: D. C. Heath, 1972.

Reeves, Edward, and Philip Kenkel. "Agricultural Involution and the Sense of Place in Eastern Kentucky." In *Sense of Place in Appalachia*, ed. S. Mont Whitson, 190–205. Morehead, KY: Office of Regional Development Services, Morehead State University, 1988.

Reynolds, Burt. *My Life*. New York: Hyperion, 1994.

Richardson, Miles. "Introduction." In *GeoScience and Man*, Vol. 24, *Place: Experience and Symbol*, ed. Miles Richardson, 1–2. Baton Rouge: Louisiana State University, 1984.

————. "Place and Culture: A Final Note." In *GeoScience and Man*, Vol. 24, *Place: Experience and Symbol*, ed. Miles Richardson, 63–67. Baton Rouge: Louisiana State University, 1984.

Robertson, Dot. "Eastatoe Mourns Death of 'Innocent' Friend, Neighbor." *Greenville News*, August 2, 1989.

————. "Life on Sassafras Mountain." In *Journey Home*, ed. Jimmy Cornelison, Reese Fant, Mike Hembree, and Dot Robertson, 66–71. Greenville, SC: Greenville News-Piedmont, 1988.

————. "Memories of Another Time." In *Journey Home*, ed. Jimmy Cornelison, Reese Fant, Mike Hembree, and Dot Robertson, 11–13. Greenville, SC: Greenville News-Piedmont, 1988.

————. "The Warm Glow of the Country Church." In *Journey Home*, ed. Jimmy Cornelison, Reese Fant, Mike Hembree, and Dot Robertson, 76–78. Greenville, SC: Greenville News-Piedmont, 1988.

Rodman, Margaret. "Empowering Place: Multilocality and Multivocality." *American Anthropologist* 94 (1992): 640–56.

Russell, Arlie. *Strangers in Their Own Land: Anger and Mourning in America's Right*. New York: New Press, 2016.

Satterwhite, Emily. "The New Critical Regionalism: Cross-Region Commonalities and Future Directions." In *Appalachia in Regional Context: Place Matters*, ed. Dwight Billings and Ann Kingsolver, 123–25. Lexington: University Press of Kentucky, 2018.

Schumann, William. "Introduction: Place and Place-Making in Appalachia." In *Appalachia Revisited: New Perspectives on Place, Tradition, and Progress*, ed. William Schumann, Rebecca Fletcher, Yunina Barbour-Payne, Jessica Blackburn, Jaclyn Daugherty, and Kelly Dorgan, 1–26. Lexington: University Press of Kentucky, 2016.

Scott, James. *The Art of Not Being Governed: An Anarchist History of Upland Southeast Asia*. New Haven, CT: Yale University Press, 2009.

Shapiro, Henry. *Appalachia on Our Mind: The Southern Mountains and Mountaineers in the American Consciousness, 1870–1920*. Chapel Hill: University of North Carolina Press, 1978.

————. "Introduction." In *The Southern Highlander and His Homeland*, by John C. Campbell. Lexington: University Press of Kentucky, 1969. Originally published New York: Russell Sage Foundation, 1921.

Sherman, Joe. "Something in These Hills," Clemson University Alumni Association, https://alumni.clemson.edu/something-in-these-hills/.

Silvarole, Georgie. "Bob's Place Remembered with Clean-Up, Plan to Rebuild." *Anderson Independent Mail*, May 28, 2017.

Smith, Angele. "Landscapes of Clearance: Archaeological and Anthropological Perspectives." In *Landscapes of Clearance: Archaeological and Anthropological Perspectives*, ed. Angele Smith and Amy Gazin-Swartz, 13–24. Walnut Creek, CA: Left Coast Press, 2008.

Smith, Barbara Ellen. "Transforming Places: Toward a Global Politics of Appalachia." In *Appalachia in Regional Context: Place Matters*, ed. Dwight Billings and Ann Kingsolver, 49–68. Lexington: University Press of Kentucky, 2018.

Smith, Barbara Ellen, and Stephen Fisher. "Conclusion: Transformations in Place." In *Transforming Places: Lessons from Appalachia*, ed. Stephen Fisher and Barbara Ellen Smith, 267–91. Urbana: University of Illinois Press, 2012.

Smith, Lilly. *Call of the Big Eastatoe*. Columbia, SC: State Printing Office, 1970.

Smith, Stephen. *Myth, Media, and the Southern Mind*. Fayetteville: University of Arkansas Press, 1985.

South Carolina ETV. "Lucille Godbold," South Carolina Hall of Fame interview, YouTube, November 20, 2012, https://www.youtube.com/watch?v=mMcjKGhF6Tw.

Sparks, Andrew. "Can We Keep the Chattooga Wild?" *Atlanta Journal and Constitution Magazine*, September 22, 1968. Georgiana Vertical Files Collection, Hargrett Rare Book and Manuscript Library, University of Georgia Libraries.

Steele, Fritz. *The Sense of Place*. Boston, MA: CBI Publishing, 1981.

Stephenson, John B. "There's a Place Somewhere." In *Sense of Place in Appalachia*, ed. S. Mont Whitson, 165–81. Morehead, KY: Office of Regional Development Services, Morehead State University, 1988.

Stewart, Kathleen. "An Occupied Place." In *Senses of Place*, ed. Steven Feld and Keith Basso, 137–65. Santa Fe, NM: School of American Research Press, 1996.

Terman, Anna Rachel. "Intersections of Appalachian Identity." In *Appalachia Revisited: New Perspectives on Place, Tradition, and Progress*, ed. William Schumann, Rebecca Fletcher, Yunina Barbour-Payne, Jessica Blackburn, Jaclyn Daugherty, and Kelly Dorgan, 73–88. Lexington: University Press of Kentucky, 2016.

"They Gathered at the River for 'Deliverance.'" N.d. Georgiana Vertical Files Collection, Hargrett Rare Book and Manuscript Library, University of Georgia Libraries.

Thralls, Leo A. "Splash: Caution: '*Deliverance* Country.'" 1975. Georgiana Vertical Files Collection, Hargrett Rare Book and Manuscript Library, University of Georgia Libraries.

Tilley, Christopher. *A Phenomenology of Landscape: Places, Paths and Monuments*. Oxford, UK: Berg, 1994.

"Tourists Attracted to Dangers of Famed 'Deliverance' River." *Athens Banner-Herald/ Daily News*, September 3, 1982. Georgiana Vertical Files Collection, Hargrett Rare Book and Manuscript Library, University of Georgia Libraries.

Tuan, Yi-Fu. *Space and Place: The Perspective of Experience*. Minneapolis: University of Minnesota Press, 1977.

Turner, Daniel. "South Unbound: A Case Study in Ron Rash's Appalachian Fiction." In *Navigating Souths: Transdisciplinary Explorations of a U.S. Region*, ed. Michelle Grigsby Coffey and Jodi Skipper, 135–50. Athens: University of Georgia Press, 2017.

Turner, Victor. *The Forest of Symbols*. Ithaca, NY: Cornell University Press, 1967.

Vance, James David. *Hillbilly Elegy: A Memoir of a Family and Culture in Crisis*. New York: HarperCollins, 2016.

Veal, Karen. "Revenuer Days Make Great Stories." *Athens Daily News*, November 8, 1988. Georgiana Vertical Files Collection, Hargrett Rare Book and Manuscript Library, University of Georgia Libraries.

Vickery, Jerry. *The Forgotten Society of the Keowee River Valley: A Biography of a Sharecropper, Johnny V. Hester*. Easley, SC: First Choice Printing, 2008.

Wagner, Melinda Bollar. "Space and Place, Land and Legacy." In *Culture, Environment, and Conservation in the Appalachian South*, ed. Benita Howell, 121–32. Urbana: University of Illinois Press, 2002.

Waller, Altina. "Feuding in Appalachia: Evolution of a Cultural Stereotype." In *Appalachia in the Making: The Mountain South in the Nineteenth Century*, ed. Mary Beth Pudup, Dwight Billings, and Altina Waller, 347–76. Chapel Hill: University of North Carolina Press, 1995.

Walls, David. "Internal Colony or Internal Periphery? A Critique of Current Models and an Alternative Formulation." In *Colonialism in Modern America: The Appalachian Case*, ed. Helen Lewis, Linda Johnson, and Donald Askins, 319–49. Boone, NC: Appalachian Consortium Press, 1978.

Weidensaul, Scott. *Mountains of the Heart: A Natural History of the Appalachians*. Golden, CO: Fulcrum Publishing, 1994.

Weller, Jack. *Yesterday's People: Life in Contemporary Appalachia*. Lexington: University Press of Kentucky, 1965.

Whisnant, David. *All That Is Native and Fine: The Politics of Culture in an American Region*. Chapel Hill: University of North Carolina Press, 1983.

Wilkinson, Crystal. "On Being 'Country': One Affrilachian Woman's Return Home." In *Confronting Appalachian Stereotypes: Back Talk from an American Region*, ed. Dwight Billings, Gurney Norman, and Katherine Ledford, 184–86. Lexington: University Press of Kentucky, 1999.

Williams, Buzz. "Accident Database, Report ID#3395," American Whitewater, May 31, 1999, https://www.americanwhitewater.org/content/Accident/detail /accidentid/3395/.

Williams, Michael Ann. *Great Smoky Mountains Folklife*. Jackson: University Press of Mississippi, 1995.

———. *Homeplace: The Social Use and Meaning of the Folk Dwelling in Southwestern North Carolina*. Athens: University of Georgia Press, 1991.

Williamson, Jerry Wayne. *Hillbillyland: What the Movies Did to the Mountains and What the Mountains Did to the Movies*. Chapel Hill: University of North Carolina Press, 1995.

Wilson, Charles M. "Elizabethan America." In *Appalachian Images in Folk and Popular Culture*, ed. William K. McNeil, 205–14. Ann Arbor, MI: UMI Research Press, 1989. Originally published in 1929.

Wray, Matt. *Not Quite White: White Trash and the Boundaries of Whiteness*. Durham, NC: Duke University Press, 2006.

Index

Printed in the USA
CPSIA information can be obtained
at www.ICGtesting.com
CBHW031542150624
10141CB00006B/615